THE DICTIONARY
OF THE WORK OF
W. R. BION

THE DICTIONARY
OF THE WORK OF
W. R. BION

Rafael E. López-Corvo

Routledge
Taylor & Francis Group

LONDON AND NEW YORK

First published 2003 by Karnac Books Ltd.

Published 2018 by Routledge
2 Park Square, Milton Park, Abington, Oxon OX14 4RN
711 Third Avenue, New York, NY 10017, USA

Routledge is an imprint of the Taylor & Francis Group, an informa business

Diccionario de la Obra de Wilfred R. Bion first published in 2002 by
Editorial Biblioteca Nueva, Madrid, 2002

British Library Cataloguing in Publication Data

A C.I.P. for this book is available from the British Library

ISBN 9781855753389 (pbk)

Designed and typeset by The Studio Publishing Services Ltd, Exeter EX4 8JN

To my wife, Ana Milagros, and my grandchildren,
Ashley Katalina and Adrian Rafael

CONTENTS

ACKNOWLEDGEMENTS

I would like to express my gratitude for the help and encouragement in the preparation of this work, I received from associates of the study group on Bion's work, integrated by members of the Venezuelan Psychoanalytical Association: Gonzalo González, Osea Lombardi de Gustuti, Marilucía Castellanos de Maestres, Ana Milagros Pérez Morazzani, Paolo Polito Di Sabato and Nancy Segarra. I am also extremely grateful to Lucía Morabito Gómez, for her laborious effort in translating, correcting and reviewing most of this work.

ABBREVIATIONS AND SIGNS

—.->	Advance of **no-breast*** through the horizontal axis of the **Grid***
ba	**basic assumption*** (See: text)
baD	**basic assumption of Dependence*** (See: text)
baA	**basic assumption of Pairing*** (See: text)
baF	**basic assumption of Flight-fight*** (See: text)
Cs*	Awareness. (See: text)
♀	Container
♂	Contained
♀♂	**Container–contained*** (See text)
D	Depressive position
=	Equivalent to. (See: Bion 1992, p. 54)
F	**Act of Faith*** (See: text)
H*	Hate
I*	**Idea*** (See: text)
>-)-=	Implies, means (See: Bion 1992, pp. 58–59)
K*	Knowledge (See: text)
K(ζ)	Formula representing a relation between constant K and a non-saturated element: ζ*
L*	Love

"↑   Envy, greed, murder, no respect for an object that does not exist.(See: **Cs* Withoutness***)

−"↑.   Place where the object that does not exist was (See: **Cs***)

−**K**   Minus knowledge.

O*   Origin.

PS   Paranoid–schizoid position.

ψ*   (Psi) The pre-conception or psychoanalytic function.

-.->−   Progression of **no-breast*** through both axes of the **Grid***

(.)   **Point*** (See: text)

R*   **Reason***: (See: text)

<-.—   Regression of **no-breast*** through the **horizontal axis*** of the **Grid***

<-.—↑   Regression of **no-breast*** through both axes of the **Grid***

s.d.s.   **Scientific deductive system***.

Σ*   (Sigma, Greek letter = S) >Totality of collective **consciousness*** (See: **Sigma***)

sm   **Proto-mental system*** (See: text)

T   **Transformation***, act of (See: text)

Tα   Transformation, process of

Tβ   Transformation, final product of

Tp   Transformation of the patient

Ta   Transformation of the analyst

Taα   Transformation, act of, in the analyst

Taβ   Transformation, final product in the analyst

TK   Transformation in **K***

TO   Transformation in **O***

TOp   Transformation in O of the patient

TOa   Transformation in O of the analyst

Tpα   Transformation, act of, in the patient

Tpβ   Transformation, final product of, in the patient

Txβ   Transformation, final product

W   **work group*** (See: text)

ζ*   (Xi, Greek letter = x) Meaning: >**psychoanalytic element*** non-**saturated***=, also distance.

(+ -) Y   **mental growth*** (See: text)

"But there is no solution once and for all;
each solution opens another universe"

"It takes a long time to find out who is
the biggest nuisance — the doubter or the
believer"

"Go on asking the same question as often
as you like and I will answer it if I can,
Although probably in a different way each time"

W. R. Bion

"Intuitions without concepts are blind,
Concepts without intuitions are empty"

E. Kant

FOREWORD

Eigen (1985)[1] has stated, with great exactness, that, "in order to read Bion fairly, one must read him closely and, in part, on his own terms. He is one of the most precise, if elusive, of psychoanalytic writers". A declaration that in simple terms labels the enormous task of attempting to understand and translate Bion's work, to render it more accessible to students and less sophisticated readers. This was my purpose, however, it would be pretentious if not misleading to believe that an endeavour of such a magnitude could be achieved without numberless downfalls, multitudes of complications and possibly, several blunders. Even researchers of the calibre of Grinberg and Bianchedi (1972) faced certain hurdles to follow Bion's proper intentions while attempting the earliest and only summary of his contributions. Take for instance the word *premotion*, mentioned in chapter 16 of Bion's book *Elements of Psycho-Analysis* (1963, pp. 75–76), where the reader is left with the doubt if dealing with a printing misspelling for 'premonition', or a neologism implying a condition previous to an emotional state.

---

[1] Eigen, M., (1985) Towards Bion's starting point: between catastrophe and death. *Int. J. Psychoanal. 66* 321–330.

I have a hypothesis: there is the feeling, when we follow his work sequentially, of a successive tendency towards a greater complication and a more elusive writing style. Starting with the clear contributions on groups—written as a psychiatrist—and later as a psychoanalyst, in his papers about psychosis, at one extreme; to the rambling and bemused prose present in *A Memoir of the Future*, at the other. His four books representing the main hardcore of his theory: *Learning from Experience, Elements of Psycho-Analysis, Transformations, Attention and Interpretation*, as well as *Cogitations*, could be placed right in the middle. However, if we read the compilation of his Brazilian conferences, which took place around the same time he was working on *A Memoir of the Future*, we are amazed at the transparency of his presentations and the efforts he made to communicate his theories. When we speak with Brazilians who met him and attended his conferences, we can intuitively gather the impression that they feel the rightful heirs to Bion's tradition.[2] As stated in the Introduction to this Dictionary, I think it is possible that the obscurity in his language might have been a consequence of Bion's sentiments about the rejection some of his ideas had produced within the British Psychoanalytical Society:[3] I feel that Bion was obscure with the British, sober with Americans and charming and understanding with Brazilians.

Another very important issue continuously present in Bion's contributions was his concern for the exactness of communication. We learned from Francesca and from many of Bion's own statements, that he enjoyed reading and often quoting poetry, however, the main body of his writing follows closely the precision of a scientific deductive system, and like Socrates through the mouth of Phaedo, he resisted the uncertainty of metaphors in order to protect himself from the fate of Palinurus. Expressions such as "in approximation to", for instance,—often used—mark his concern with precision. During the psychoanalytic session, says Bion, two

---

[2] See for instance Donald Meltzer's ambivalence in "The Kleinian Development, part III", in *The Clinical Significance of the Work of Bion* (1978).

[3] Perhaps we could now remember Bion's own words: "Individuals cannot reconcile themselves to a discrimination that means conscious separation of themselves from a belief in their Freud-like [or Bion-like] qualities and recognition that Freud [Bion], a genius (mystic), no longer exists. Another Freud [Bion] cannot be created no matter how essential he may be" (1970 p. 77).

individuals attempt a dialogue: one using a scientific deductive system similar to a 'geocentric' logic, 'obvious but not true'; while the other applies another deductive system based on a heliocentric reasoning: true, but not obvious; it is evident that reversion of perspective could be a frequent complication. Bion often in his theoretical dissertations also created neologisms in order to bring language within an area of comprehension.

I ask the reader for their munificence and understanding as they peruse the pages of this book; to bear in mind the difficult task, albeit in the whole picture, I feel very pleased with the effort and can assure you that it has been accomplished with great dedication and total candour. Finally I would like to confess, that although I was not so fortunate as to be touched by his physical presence, reading all about Bion's work throughout these years has induced a close affection toward his memory and an immense curiosity about his legacy.

Caracas, 2002

Introduction

The dictionary

A dictionary could be defined as "a reference book that enumerates in alphabetical order, terms or words that are important for an activity or a particular matter, together with a discussion of their meanings or applications"[1]. This is precisely the intention of the present dictionary, for it to be used as a "reference book", as an indispensable partner and a guide in the adventure of the fascinating discovery, although highly dense, complex and frequently frustrating, of Wilfred Ruprecht Bion's great legacy to psychoanalysis. Therefore, it should never replace the reading of his original texts. It is proper now to quote his words:

> Even in language itself a dictionary is not all that is needed; one has to understand the nature of language as well as the actual language in which one is attempting to speak. [1974, p. 202]

---

[1] Definition taken from *Webster's New Collegiate Dictionary*.

It is quite obvious that one of Bion's greatest concerns had to do with communication between two persons who do not know each other: the patient and the analyst. Such communication represents a struggle between two different deductive scientific systems: one entrenched within its ghosts, its resistances, its repetition compulsions, its old defences, the lies of the mind, the **inanimate** etc.; and the other stubborn in the search for incorruptible truth at all costs. However, truth has its consequences, its violence; in Bion's language: turbulence, catastrophic changes, caesuras, death of hopes, and painful achievements.

Bion was always suspicious of colloquial language, with its terms pawed by the passage of time, corrupted by meanings and saturated by antique desires impugning their origins. How different from mathematical elements, from numbers for instance, which remain unharmed as empty recipients always ready to be filled up by anything without ever losing their identity: two tigers, ten coins, five arrows, five computers. If only one could say "good evening" using mathematical elements, Bion once exclaimed.

The man

Just as it is important to know about the exceptional work of a great creator such as Bion, it is also important to try to understand those conscious or unconscious personal **factors** that could have induced or channelled his work. I believe, for instance, that the psychoanalytic methodology represented for Bion a **selected fact** which, to our benefit, gave sense to the accidents of his existence. Bion must be examined with an act of faith.

He was born of English parents on September 8, 1897 at Muttra, located in the United Provinces of Northwest India. He was a victim of Victorian imperialistic manners, which privileged austere education over the affective needs of the eight-year-old boy he was in 1906, when he was sent to a boarding school in England—the Bishop's Stortford College—from where he never returned to his paternal home. When, towards the end of his life, Bion finally hoped to return to Bombay, the sudden assault of death in the form of myeloid leukaemia, frustrated his plans. Meanwhile, the peaceful Los Angeles weather and the mysterious and exuberant

Brazilian jungle possibly served to lessen his search for the absent monsoon and the inchoate memories from India. In a letter dated March 23, 1951, he wrote to his girlfriend Francesca:

> I am rather lucky because I love weather—all sorts of weather. I think there is a lot to be said for being born, as I was, in India. To me, rain was of course the great event, the monsoon, and I can even now, though I left India when I was eight, recapture the thrill of the smell of parched land rain-soaked. [1985, pp. 73–74]

While his friend Frank Philips (1983) fondly remembers him:

> I think of his love ... of the wild flowers of England and France, and of his watching, enthralled, during a fierce thunderstorm the flashes of lightning and hearing the cracking and pounding of the thunder. [p. 38]

The burden of losing one's home at an early age has such determining effects, that it would certainly define the future character of an individual, something frequently confirmed by the transference of many patients. Therefore, it was not surprising that Bion became a specialist in the psychology of emptiness and the presence of absences. Bion's contributions became so relevant that they could be equated to the appearance of negative numbers in the history of mathematics. Thoughts are always set over the absence of things, always providing a binocular vision, which covers both its presence and the place where things used to be.

When he was only eighteen-years-old, he volunteered to enrol for World War I. Although initially rejected by the draft office, he managed to join the army with his parent's support. What could have motivated such a serious decision? The last vestiges of 1800s "machismo" kind of romanticism? A special form of reaction formation in order to deal with **castration anxiety** inspired perhaps by the ghost of "Arf Arfer"?,[2] or to threaten the physical integrity of "the loved-by-his-mother-Bion", as a revenge perpetuated by the "abandoned-Bion"? We will never know; what we do know is that war left injuries of the soul that constantly came back and perturbed him, as

[2] Term used to designate the irreverent fear that as a child he felt towards his father.

memories that became visible as terrible ghosts in associations relived by him every August 8th. Francesca Bion has summarized it as follows:

> The horror of that war inflicted on such young men did not contribute to their maturity; it destroyed their youth and made them "old" before their time. Bion's remarkable physical survival against heavy odds concealed the emotional injury which left scars for many years to come. (It was clear that that war continued to occupy a prominent position in his mind when, during the first occasion we dined together, he spoke movingly of it as if compelled to communicate haunting memories.) The nightmare to which he refers[3] still visited him occasionally throughout his life. He grew old and remembered. [1997a, p. 2]

Bion himself, exactly sixty years after Amiens, recalls the 8th of August 1918, as follows:

> "The faces of old ghosts look in upon the battle" [says Bion quoting Tennyson] . . . Once more the world has reached the same kind of place in its journey around the sun which it occupied in the battle of Amiens (8 August 1918) . . . The ghosts look in from the battle again; Asser, Cartwright, and Sergeant O'Toole, the poor fellow who complained that he was only an orphan, with his protuberant ears, his red flushed face, his feelings of depression and anxiety, and his confiding to me that this battle on which he was about to embark together with the rest of the tank crew (I was not one of the crew as I was now . . . second-in-command of the company) would be his last. He was, of course, quite correct; very soon after the battle started, Cartwright's tank received a direct hit, and the entire crew were killed. When I came across it, the bodies were charred and blackened, and poured out of the door of the tank as if they were the entrails of some mysterious beast of a primitive kind which had simply perished then and there in the conflagration . . . [1992, p. 368]

Grotstein (1993) has suggested the possibility of an association

---

[3] Bion described it in these terms: "It was almost impossible to distinguish dream from reality. The tat-tat-tat of the German machine-guns would chime in with your dream with uncanny effect, so that when you awoke you wondered whether you were dreaming" (1997a, p. 94).

between the circumstance of having been the sole survivor of his company and the later fabrication of terms such as **"thalamic terror"**, **"nameless terror"**, **"catastrophic change"**, etc. Bion appears to have just escaped death on various occasions, not only when he was the sole survivor of the physical disappearance of all his company, but also, as he himself recalls, when a sergeant pushed him aside preventing him from being shot in the head; or, when leaning on a trench embankment, he suddenly felt sprinkled by the brains of the officer in charge, who, talking beside him, had been hit by a sniper's bullet. Always menaced by the fear of being accused as a coward, Bion dealt with mechanisms of depersonalization: he felt that he was floating a metre or so above his body. However, regardless of his unfair superego demands, he was decorated for his courage, both by England and France. Francesca Bion refers to the chapter on the Cambrai battle that took place in November 1917 and which is referred to in *The History of the Royal Tank Regiment* :

> Some of the tankmen fought on when "dismounted." A striking example was that of Lt. W. R. Bion who, when his tank was knocked out, established an advanced post in a German trench with his crew and some stray infantry, and then climbed back on the roof of his tank with a Lewis gun to get better aim at an opposing machine-gun. When the Germans counter-attacked in strength he kept them at bay . . . until a company of Seaforths came up. Its commander was soon shot through the head, whereupon Bion temporarily took over the company. He was put in for the VC (Victoria Cross) and received the DSO. [F. Bion, 1995]

Bion grew up among groups, very large groups. From the age of eight at boarding school, and afterwards, at the age of eighteen when enlisted to fight in War World I, he was able to observe empirically and suffer existentially the social behaviour and the immediacy of anonymous multitudes. Therefore, it does not seem strange that after his psychiatric training he felt attracted by group psychotherapy. One of the great legacies Bion left corresponds to this period. It was not so much what he observed about group behaviour—which is already extremely significant by itself—but the very methodology with which he strenuously and courageously observed such groups. Jacques Lacan (1947), having interviewed Bion at that time, wrote:

... as if frozen in an immobile and moonlike mask, accentuated by the fine commas of a black moustache, which, no less than the large physique and the swimmer's chest that hold it up, contradict Kretschmer's formulae, when everything tells us that we are in the presence of one of those beings who are solitary in even their highest achievements, and as we find confirmed in this man's adventure in Flanders, where he followed his tank, switch in hand, into the breach, and paradoxically thus forced the iron gates of fate ... [Quoted by Bléandonu, 1994, p. 278]

It is surprising to note Bion's competence to guard himself against the coercing, repetitive, and continuous group pressure, from so many patients, to take over when in charge of the "leaderless groups" project, at a time when he had not yet undertaken his psychoanalytic training nor achieved, as did Ulysses, a productive deafness. For many of us who started psychiatric training with groups, it was much easier to react to the demand of a "therapeutic leading role", than to tolerate the uncertainty produced by the impatient expectation of latent emotional structures, which Bion has described as **basic assumptions**. Perhaps war left its marks on Bion's capacity for tolerance, in those critical moments of forced expectancy in the face of imminent danger, when boldness or imprudence could have signified a total loss. Possibly Bion's early separation from his parents, as well as having to coexist with the emotional anonymity of boarding schools, could have introduced **distance** and affective withdrawal as a defence against the pain produced by the loss, which he later might have transformed into a reparative mechanism for objective scientific observations. Francesca Bion (2000) recently questioned whether Bion's mother ever knew:

... how longingly he would think of "home" while suffering the miseries of prep school? [p. 11]

Julian, when asked about his father, said:

It was evident to me from an early age that my father was a man of tremendous courage and immense compassion. Because of his degree of self-control this was not always immediately apparent. [F. Bion, 1995, p. 9]

Borgogno and Merciai (2000), based on Bion's book *Cogitations*, have tried to prove an apparent coldness in Bion towards his patients, which they argued was expressed through attacks on them produced by virtue of his intelligent and brilliant perceptions, which at the same time were also "mentally narrow and generally unpredictable" (p. 68). Following these same lines, they have interpreted Bion's discourse with some of his patients:

> ... it thus seems that Bion renders null and void the patient's desperate appeal. How else to explain his deafness during analysis to a patient's account of a "pullover which is beautifully knitted by his wife but not suited for the baby's cold" or of "trains that did not behave as they should" [7 October 1959, p. 94] [p. 66]

It is interesting to note that these authors are at the same time co-editors, together with Parthenope Bion,[4] of a book that collects a series of works presented to celebrate her father's hundredth birth date. Bion (1985) has referred to a passage where the few-months-old Parthenope desperately cried and screamed calling for her father, while he remained impassive seated at some **distance** and at the same time prohibiting the nurse to lift her up. However, not being able to resist any longer, and ignoring the prohibition, the nurse took the baby in her arms. Finally, an ambivalent and regretful Bion concludes: "The baby had stopped weeping and was being comforted by maternal arms. But I, I had lost my child" (p. 70). Which could have been the determining **O** of such a drama? Did **envy**, from the "inner abandoned boy" in "pre analytic Bion", try to take revenge over the privileged (for having him) Parthenope? We do not know.

In his autobiography Bion recalls saying goodbye to his parents at a hotel room in London, at the time he was going away to war:

---

[4] Parthenope was the name chosen by Bion when reading Virgil's *Aeneid*, where it was used to christen a mermaid, half bird half woman, who was one of those mermaids whose singing enchanted sailors and brought boats to their destruction against the rocks. According to the myth, after failing with Odysseus, mermaids immolated themselves, including Parthenope, whose remains came ashore near Naples. Greeks then baptized the town with her name as "Parthenopolis", but being destroyed, it was rebuilt as "Neopolis", or "new town", that afterwards changed to Naples. By uncanny coincidence, Parthenope Bion and her daughter Patrizia also died in Italy, in a car accident on July 16, 1998.

I got there. In my parent's bedroom the electric light cast its livid warmth; they were glad to see me—that I knew. But I could feel that her boy's precocious departure for the war left my mother kissing a chitinous semblance of a boy from whom a person had escaped. But I was imprisoned, unable to break out of the shell which adhered to me. [1982, p. 104]

While Bléandonu (1994) expresses:

Later in the autobiography he often gives the impression that he had never had a father, a mother or, even less, a sister. Their obliteration might be a kind of "final solution" to the oedipal predicament. As a solution it resembles the psychotic's destruction of the thinking apparatus as a means of "undoing" the oedipal predicament. [p. 277)

Growing up among boys and men might have induced in Bion the need for unconsciously requesting affect from masculine figures, and thus producing confusion in his sexual identity. He gives an example of such confusion in his autobiography when referring to an event that took place during his adolescence, with Dudley, a close friend at boarding school:

One night when I was lying on my bed with pyjamas on waiting for Dudley to get into his bed, he suddenly discarded the towel he had round his waist and jumped astride me as if challenging me to wrestle. "*Now* how do you feel?" he said. I felt nothing physically; mentally a sense of boredom and anti-climax, which soon communicated itself to Dudley who, after a few futile attempts to provoke a struggle, got off. I was bitterly disappointed. I had no idea what I wanted, but I did know—and the realization grew with time— that I wanted it badly. I wished I had encouraged Dudley to go on and then I would have found out what he was going to do. But now I think Dudley did not know any more than I did. When I expressed this to my psycho-analyst years later he was convinced I knew. [1982, p. 74]

Before Klein, Bion had two analytic experiences. He never mentioned the name of his first analyst and contemptuously called him Dr FiP, a nickname taken from the initials of "feel–it–in–the–past", apparently parodying a common expression used by FiP during sessions. Bléandonu (1994) suggests that it could have been

J. A. Hadfield, a psychiatrist from the Tavistock Clinic. His second analysis, which lasted from 1937 to 1939 and was prematurely aborted due to World War II, was with John Rickman, who was in turn analysed by Freud and Ferenczi and later became Bion's good friend. It is quite possible that such experiences enabled Bion to solve his anxiety-provoking confusions and his fear of women. He first had a beautiful girlfriend, who ended up being unfaithful and then, in 1939 at the beginning of the war, he met Betty McKritick Jardine, a movie and theatre actress whom he finally wed. Three years later Betty died while giving birth to their daughter Parthenope, while Bion, selected by General Montgomery himself, was enrolled as an army psychiatrist and was making arrangements for Normandy's "D day". Unfortunately, he was not present at the time of her death. Thirty-five years later he still questions himself:

> What killed Betty and nearly killed her baby? Physical malformation? Incompetent obstetrics? Callous or indifferent authorities? Or the revelations of the hollow nature of the masculine drum that was being so loudly beaten by her husband's departure? [1985, p. 62]

And later on:

> I had begged Betty to agree to have a baby: her agreement to do so had cost her her life. [ibid., p. 70]

The Psychiatrist

After World War I, Bion studied History at Oxford (as well as French at Poitiers University), where he was noticed, not only for his encyclopaedic knowledge, but also for his outstanding skills in sports, such as rugby and swimming. Two determining events took place at this time: the tearing of a knee cartilage that destroyed his expected chance of being selected to play rugby for England. And his dismissal from Bishop's Stortford College, his own school, where he was teaching, after being accused by the mother of a young boy, of supposedly having seduced him, something Bion not only denied with acridness, but that also induced him to seek therapeutic help for the first time [1985, pp. 15-17].

He decided to study **medicine** at University College Hospital in London, graduating in 1930 after winning the gold medal for surgery. "He launched himself straight into psychiatric practice" (Bléandonu, 1994, p. 41). By 1932 he started his medical work at the Tavistock Clinic.

According to Bion, any **agglomeration** of individuals interacts according to predetermined links and constitutes a group, such as family, office, neighbourhood, school, a tourist tour, etc. Sutherland (1985), who worked with Bion during those years, stated that he used the word "group" to refer to both group therapy and society in general. "For him there was only one 'socio-dimension'" (p. 33).

Every group, Bion teaches us, gets together with a purpose, which represents its manifest reality, its reason to exist; it constitutes the "**work group**" **(W)**. However, hidden behind its shadows lies a virtual reality, an undefined and undetermined **space** that he labelled the "**proto-mental system**", a region where the so-called **basic assumptions** develop; these are predetermined conditions that at a given moment emerge and take over the work group, change its course and parasitize its purpose. Bion described three possibilities: (a) the creation of a couple that would produce a **messiah**, a **messianic idea** or a saving hope, and which he called "**pairing basic assumption**"; (b) the **fight or flight** group, conditioned by paranoid tactics similar to those observed during the war; and lastly (c) the **dependence** group, which reproduces the relationship between the baby's vulnerability and the adult omnipotence.[5]

Bion experimented with his methodology on "leaderless groups" during World War II, while he helped soldiers and officials who were victims of "entrenchment panic", then called "war neurosis". Later on he continued such experiments during his training at the Tavistock Clinic, which later became a world famous study group. However, regardless of his reason, it cannot be denied that the result of such deep insight on the fatalism of human social

---

[5] Bléandonu (1994) suggests that the classification of basic assumption was possibly inspired by a concept introduced by J. A. Hadfield, a psychiatrist from the Tavistock and possibly, as Bléandonu already mentioned, Bion's first therapist. Hadfield described the existence of three drives: "sexual libido, aggressive or self-preservative and the drive towards dependence" (p. 43).

behaviour was enough to declare Bion a "man of achievements", and of **"negative capability"**, using Keats' expressions.

In 1945 Bion started his analysis with Melanie Klein, as well as his psychoanalytic training.

The psychoanalyst

Bion recalls that during the years of his analytic training a small black cat who regularly defecated in front of the psychoanalytic institute was named "Melanie Klein": Melanie because it was black, Klein because it was small, and Melanie Klein for being so bold. During 1945 Bion started his analysis with this woman who possessed great clinical intuition and uncommon courage, and he continued until 1953.

> In the course of these eight years a number of important changes took place in his life. Once he was accepted by the British Psycho-Analytical Society as a member, he began to be identified, through his writing and his presentations, as a brilliant student of Klein. He found a new psychic equilibrium—he married for a second time, and flourished in the presence of a very understanding partner. He was able to find Parthenope again, and to father two more children. It was during this time that Bion prepared to publish his work on group dynamics, as well as his first articles on psychosis. Psychoanalysis had awakened in him a deep creativity which was to stay with him until the end of his life. [Bléandonu, 1994, p. 93]

According to Meltzer (1978), Bion's creativity increased greatly after Klein's death in 1960, suggesting that perhaps he had been subordinating his originality to the ideas of his analyst and teacher.

The old problem of the "double", already examined by Freud (1919) and others, especially in Latin America, served Bion under the epigraph of the "Imaginary twin", both to defend Klein's ideas about the existence of an early pregenital **Oedipus**, as well as to graduate from the British Psychoanalytical Society in 1950. It was his first psychoanalytic work, followed by exhaustive and paradigmatic research on psychoses and a phenomenological conceptualization of a thinking theory or, in his own words, of an "apparatus to think thoughts". Thus we have: "Notes on the theory of schizophrenia"

1953, "Development of schizophrenic thought" 1956, "Differentiation of the psychotic from the non-psychotic personalities" and "On arrogance" 1957, a year later "On hallucination", "Attacks on linking" 1959, and finally "A theory of thinking" 1962.[6]

It is quite obvious that, up to this moment, Bion is at great pains to maintain the clarity of his concepts. The four following books, however, which represent the fundamental pillars of his theoretical contributions, do not unravel as easily; instead they contrast for their hermetic opacity, where the concepts contained therein resist the possibility of an easy exegesis. Bion seems to have suddenly transformed into Oedipus' Sphinx itself and is a puzzling guardian of his secrets. Clarity would not return until the affectionate enthusiasm he received from the Brazilian and Argentinian Psychoanalytic Associations operated upon Bion's cryptic semantics, like the "kiss from the Prince that opened Snow White's eyes."[7]. Comparing the books *Transformations* and *Elements of Psycho-Analysis*, Meltzer (1978), somehow disturbed, complains about the difficulty encountered by the reader when faced with the mathematical signs used by Bion:

> In the present work no such hope sustains us in the face of the proliferation of mathematics-like notations, pseudo-equations, followed by arrows, dots, lines, arrows over (or should it be under?) words and not just Greek letters but Greek words. How are we to bear such an assault on our mentality? Is Bion Patient B in disguise? [p. 71]

Referring to the article "On arrogance", Meltzer (1978) ironically says:

> Certainly . . . the reading of the paper "On arrogance" at the Paris congress struck many people as a shocking display of the very hubris Bion was describing. [p. 31]

---

[6] All of these papers, plus the article on the "Imaginary twin", were compiled as a book together with a revision from Bion, under the title of (his) *Second Thoughts* (1967).

[7] It is always recommended that students who begin an enquiry into Bion's work, start with the *Brazilian Lectures* (1974), continue with *Second Thoughts* (1967) and finish with the four books included in *Seven Servants* (1977).

Could the heterodoxy present in Bion's contributions, specially his concepts of O and the **"act of faith"**—as can be seen in *Attention and Interpretation*—have generated an envious attack on behalf of the British psychoanalytic **establishment** of that time? In some editions of *Transformations* Bion quotes Shakespeare's *Macbeth* as an apothem that makes one wonder why he chose it:

Ay, in the catalogue ye go for men,
As hounds and greyhounds, mongrels, spaniels, curs,
Shoughs, water-rugs, and demi-wolves are clipt
All by the name of dogs.

On the other hand, if we follow the last chapters of *Attention and Interpretation*, we can perceive, with a rather slanted view, a complaint about the intolerance of psychoanalytic institutions. Regardless of the sophistication presented, as well as the hermetic generalization of their statements, the last chapters allow an opening towards a more mundane vision: the complaint submitted by someone against the intolerance awakened by a new, different, and exceptional contribution to psychoanalysis. In 1995 Francesca wrote, quoting Wilfred Trotter and the influence he had on her husband, in the following terms:

Trotter makes observations which remind one strongly of Bion's later views. He speaks of man's "resistiveness to new ideas, his submission to tradition and precedent"; of "governing power tending to pass into the hands of a class of members insensitive to experience, closed to the entry of new ideas and obsessed with the satisfactoriness of things as they are"; of "our willingness to take any risk rather than endure the horrid pains of thought." [pp. 3–4]

According to Symington and Symington (1966), when Bion introduced the concept of O, "some in the Klein group were quick to dissociate themselves from his thinking from that time onwards" (p. 10). Later on, after his trilogy *A Memoir of the Future* (1991) appeared, while he was in California, many British analysts considered Bion had mentally deteriorated after leaving England, to the point that "everything he wrote subsequent to his departure is to be dismissed as the rambling of a senile man" (Symington & Symington, 1966, p. 10).

At the beginning of 1968, Bion moved to Los Angeles in response to an invitation from a group of psychoanalyst innovators, who, searching for new directions, became interested in Klein and her followers. The children chose to continue their studying in Italy and England. The change provided new hopes of freedom, an outlet from the British atmosphere that, after a while, had become suffocating, allowing Bion to write his magnum opus in the form of a trilogy: *A Memoir of the Future*. "Had he remained in England", says Francesca, "he would certainly not have felt able to express himself in this frank and revelatory way" (*ibid.*, pp. 12–13). In the Epilogue to this book Bion wrote:

> All my life I have been imprisoned, frustrated, dogged by common-sense, reason, memories, desires and—greatest bug-bear of all—understanding and being understood. This is an attempt to express my rebellion, to say "Good-bye" to all that. It is my wish, I now realize doomed to failure, to write a book unspoiled by any tincture of common-sense, reason, etc. [1991, p. 578]

But not everything was smooth and easy. Bion, who by then was already just over 70 years old, had to face anti-Kleinian groups who were experiencing his presence as a threat to the status quo, to the old Freudian structures entrenched in "Ego-psychology" anachronism. Grotstein (1993) remembers:

> I remember an incident well where Albert Mason was able to obtain the auditorium of the Los Angeles Institute for Bion's presentation of his Grid. The audience included mostly Kleinian aficionados, but one classical member also attended out of curiosity. After Bion extemporaneously presented his conception of the Grid, the recording of which was later transcribed and published as one of his most important works, this classical analyst began criticizing Bion as to content and assumptions of his presentation and then even critiqued him on his "poor English". Bion's reply was, "Well then, there in nothing left to say that would not cause more heat than light!" [p. 61]

In 1971 Bion referred to his relationship with colleagues in California as a "total failure", although he had also said, with his characteristic dark humour, that "an analyst was welcomed only when his work was a failure". About Californians he said:

The relationship between myself and my colleagues here in Los Angeles could be accurately described as almost entirely unsuccessful. They are puzzled by, and cannot understand me. . . . There is, if I am not mistaken, more fear than understanding or sympathy for my thoughts, personality or ideas. There is no question of the situation—the emotional situation—being any better anywhere else. I could say much the same for England. [1992, p. 334]

Around this time, Bion was invited by the Argentinians and greeted by Léon Grinberg, who (together with Darío Sor and Elizabeth Tabak de Bianchedi) some time later published his well-known summary of his work. Grinberg (2000) remembered the verbal attack made by a senile analyst who had managed to make his way into the conference room. After a tense silence, Bion

. . . promptly said that he wished to pay tribute to someone, who "in working with something so terrible as the human mind" had become yet another victim within the psychoanalytic community. The outburst of prolonged applause that greeted Bion's words clearly reflected the admiration that those present felt for such an understanding, generous, and human response. [p. xx]

Obviously, at that moment, Bion had won the heart of the Argentinians. However, it was Brazil and Brazilians who, privileged by the exuberance of the "Amazonia", had managed perhaps to get closer to the childhood reminiscences of India, his native country. The justification of the hypothesis on the weight a tropical scenario might have had on Bion's preferences, could be inferred from comments he made about the uncanny feelings of familiarity the lecture on the *Mahabhrata* produced on him, which made him conjecture that the narrative of the Sanskrit text was read to him by his nanny as bedside stories. But if we try to be even–handed, we should not ignore the warm welcome that Brazil's psychoanalytical community provided to the *"mais grande psicanalista does mondo."* Francesca Bion (1995) recalled those feelings: "They are charming, affectionate, cultured people—a pleasure to know and to work with" (p. 13). Bion, on the other hand, compensated by providing them with a clarity and enthusiasm such as he had never expressed before to any public, it was a mutual affection of great productivity and immense benefit, and the echoes from those moments still vibrate in the pages that contain the transcriptions. Bion was obscure with the British, sober with Americans and charming and understanding with Brazilians. It could be rather paradoxical, however, that when Francesca complained about Bion postponing the final correction of the conferences: "It would have been easier to make a child take a dose of foul-tasting medicine",—Bion remarked: "I don't like examining my own vomit."[F. Bion, 1995}

A Memoir of the Future

Bion wrote two volumes of his autobiography, posthumously published by his wife Francesca: *The Long Week-End*, and, using an expression from Shakespeare, *All my Sins Remembered*. The latter was embossed with love letters to Francesca, which shared so much passion that it made sense of the fact that they were married two-and-a-half months after they met at the Tavistock. Both books could be considered a biography of Bion's "conscious history", whereas *A Memoir of the Future*, described by Bion as a "book of fiction", could perhaps represent a biography of his "unconscious".

A Memoir of the Future contains three parts published at different times, although, in 1991, it was finally bound in a full volume published by Karnac Books. The first book, *The Dream*, was originally published in 1975, followed two years later by *The Past Presented*, both originally printed by Imago Editora in Brazil. The last book, *The Dawn of Oblivion* (1979), and the addendum: *Key to A Memoir of the Future* (1981), were previously published by Clunie Press in Scotland. The size, as well as the intricacy and density of its contents, will make any evaluation of this book a very difficult task, particularly if we are limited by the brevity of an introduction. It requires an evaluation of its own.

The Grid

Bion has used a holistic and coherent "binocular vision" of the mind, covering a wide spectrum: from the ultraspiritual to the infraphysic; from the illumination by O to the reproduction of emotions measured inside the rigid squaring of the Grid. If his intention and dedication can be understood as a global conception of the mind, we should also, when understanding his work, conceive it from a holistic approach: one Bion for an act of faith, and at the same time, another for the "mathematization" of the mind, as a defender of contradictions who was able to palpate the certitude in the centre of uncertainty. After all, he often argued colloquially that the mouth should be observed from the anus, as a telescope, and *vice versa*. If we look only from the vertex of the Grid, we might accuse him of being guilty of "scientist positivism", trying to fulfil the ambition of building, without men, a science for men. But if we see him from the other extreme, from "**O**" or from an "**act of faith**", we could then accuse his work of "spiritualism" or "**omni-science**". However, in keeping with this view we might be committing the terrible sin of confusing the phenomenon itself with the instrument of observation: it is not Bion's mouth we should look at, but the mind's and its two faces, that glances like Janus: one inside towards the rigid structure of biology, the other outside towards the immeasurable becoming of timelessness. Attempting such an evasive perspective represents precisely Bion's absolute greatness. A comprehensive exposition of the Grid is provided in this dictionary.

A

Aberrant forms of change: Extraneous changes that take place within a group dominated by one of the three **basic assumptions**, when a new idea that demands development takes place but the active basic assumption is unable to tolerate it. Bion (1948b) states:

> If the dependent group is active, and is threatened by pressure of the **pairing-group** leader, particularly perhaps in the form of an idea which is suffused with Messianic hope, then if methods such as resorting to **bible-making** prove inadequate, the threat is countered by provoking influx of another group. If the **fight–flight group** is active, the tendency is to absorb another group. If the pairing-group is active the tendency is to **schism**. [p. 156]

Abstraction: From the Latin *abstrahere*, meaning to "take out", to "bring", to separate mentally from a particular object; or discretely to consider a specific property; in simpler words, to discriminate the universal from the individual (Foulquié, 1967). Bion (1962) summarizes abstraction as the capacity of **alpha-function** to change an emotional experience into an **alpha-element** [p. 56). **Psychotics** and philosophers of science, adds Bion, present a similar problem because they both try to change something abstract into something concrete. The former use what Segal (1957) described as "**symbolic equation**", while the philosopher in a similar fashion, attempts to concretize abstractions creating as Aristotle did, the "**mathematical objects**" or, as Bion did, the "**psychoanalytical objects**" (Bion, 1962, p. 68)

A theory could be abstracted from a model, similar to Bion's theory of **thinking**, which was based on the digestive model. Abstraction could reach such a level, that a simple word might condense, by means of a **constant conjunction**, a limitless number of emotions, to the point that Bion for instance, considers "daddy", "breast" or "penis", true **hypotheses** (1962, pp. 66–67; 1992, pp. 252–254). Abstraction, on the other hand, represents a mechanism by which the **Grid's vertical axis** progresses.

One of the reasons why psychoanalysis is not considered scientific, says Bion (1992), is because theories often used by psychoanalysts represent a combination of material from observation plus abstractions derived from them. In other words, empirical information is not satisfactory because it usually searches to create a theory instead of providing veridical information about what has been observed, while at the same time, the theory presented lacks the rigorous requirements of scientific investigation (pp. 152–154). Existing psychoanalytical theories would be similar to **ideographs**, representing an idea condensed in one word, or to abstractions with particularizations as opposite to **generalizations** (*ibid.*, pp. 256–257). It is essential, Bion concludes (1963), to formulate abstractions that allow generalizations similar to letters that when combined, could create thousands of words. "Similarly the elements I seek are to be such that relatively few are required to express, by changes in combination, nearly all the theories essential to the working psycho-analyst" (p. 2).

Accommodation: *see* **Assimilation**

Acting-out: Bion says little about this subject. He mentioned it in passing in relation to the theory of **container–contained** ($\female\male$), stating that when acting-out takes place during the analysis, the analysis is also part of acting-out because it is contained by it.

> When a patient can be said to be acting-out the analysis is "in" a situation of which the boundaries are unknown. If the behaviour

characterized as "acting-out" is brought to the analysis it can be accompanied by claustrophobic symptoms in the patient. [Bion, 1970, p. 110]

Although Bion gave no explanation about the relationship between acting-out and **claustrophobia**, it can be inferred according to the container–contained theory, that if analysis is contained by the acting-out, the patient could end up feeling trapped. He also referred to the attack made by **psychotic** patients on reality as a form of "anti-social acting-out", in order to get rid of the rest of **common sense** (reality) that still remains. "In analysis it contributes to the danger of murderous attacks on the analyst. The analyst's common-sense interpretations are attacked by being seen and felt [for instance] as sexual assaults" (Bion 1992, p. 31). "Anti-social" could be interpreted as a tendency towards narcissism, in the sense explained by Freud as "secondary narcissism", exactly opposite to **socialism** (social-ism).

Bion also states that failure to interpret patient's dreams, represents the greatest contribution an analyst could make towards production of acting-out, whereas the patient's greatest contribution would be the incapacity to dream (*ibid.*, p. 232).

Action: According to Freud (1911), it represents, together with **attention, notation, judgement**, and **thought**, one of the functions used by the ego to reach consciousness of reality.

> A new function was now allotted to motor discharge, which, under the dominance of the pleasure principle, had served as a means of unburdening the mental apparatus of accretions of stimuli, and which had carried out this task by sending innervations into the interior of the body (leading to expressive movements and the play of features and to manifestations of affect). Motor discharge was now employed in the appropriate alteration of reality; it was converted into *action*. [p. 221, original emphasis]

Bion has used this concept, together with those mentioned above, as part of the **horizontal axis** of the **Grid**, in order to structure particular qualities and functions of the mind. Attempting to explain the importance of **projective identification** in this function, Bion states:

Freud distinguishes between a stage where muscular action is taken to alter the environment and a stage when a capacity for thought exists. I propose to include in the category presented by the term "action" phantasies that the mind, acting as if it were a muscle and a muscle acting as a muscle, can disburden the psyche of accretions of stimuli. I include the Kleinian concept of the phantasy known as projective identification in the category of "action". [1965, p. 36]

See **Attention, Notation, Judgement, Thought, Horizontal axis, Grid.**

Act of faith (F): Represents the capacity to have faith in certain **ideas**, hunches or **intuitions** that suddenly spurt while **listening** during the analytical hour. It implies the capacity to accept the absolute **truth**, the existence of **O** as an ultimate reality, in order to structure the **interpretation**. Being able to reach such an attitude will depend on the analyst's discipline of listening while avoiding using any **memory** or **desire**. Bion (1970) states:

Through F [act of faith] one can 'see', 'hear', and 'feel' the mental **phenomena** of whose reality no practising psycho-analyst has any doubt though he cannot with any accuracy represent them by existing formulations. [pp. 57–58]

It is very important that Bion also considers F as an essential component of a rigorous scientific procedure, that has no relation with the ± **K** system, but belongs to the O system. Although F can not be represented in the **Grid**, it could be close to column 6 [*ibid.*, pp. 43–44).

Trying to explain the concept of F, Bion (1970) remembers what Freud once said in a letter to Andreas-Salomé, where he mentioned his method of achieving a state of mind that would provide clarity when the subject of investigation was particularly obscure. "He speaks [Freud] of blinding himself artificially. As a method of achieving this artificial blinding I have indicated the importance of eschewing memory and desire" (p. 43).

A **thought** has a **no-thing** as its **realization**, meaning that any thought is the consequence of the absence of the object. The act of faith, on the other hand, has as its background something that is unconscious and unknown because it has not happened yet, and it is associated with a state of **hallucinosis**, something more obvious in **psychotic** patients. The act of faith (F), says Bion, (1970) is

> essential to the operation of psycho-analysis and other scientific proceedings. It is essential for experiencing **hallucinations** or the state of hallucinosis. This state I do not regard as an exaggeration of a pathological or even natural condition: I consider it rather to be a state always present, but overlaid by other **phenomena**, which screen it. If these other **elements** can be moderated or suspended hallucinosis becomes demonstrable; its full depth and richness are accessible only to "acts of faith". [p. 36]

For Bion the act of faith represents a *scientific* state of mind only if it is free of any element of memory or desire; in other words, the act of faith allows a spontaneous thought, phantasy or hallucinosis to appear only if this procedure takes place without any memory or desire. He alerts us to the danger of connecting F with the supernatural or with undesirable aspects of the mind, and thus saturating it. He gave an example of a psychotic patient who during analysis felt that the analyst's words during the interpretation, flew over his head and could be detected by what Bion felt were the patterns on a cushion, and then travelled through his eyes back to him. In order for the patient to be able to experience things in this manner and in order for Bion to be able to grasp them, both the patient and analyst must have been, according to him, in a state of hallucinosis (*ibid.*, p. 36).

> The "meaning" of a statement in hallucinosis is not, however, the same as its meaning in the domain of rational thought ... In the domain of hallucinosis the mental event is transformed into a sense impression and sense impressions in this domain do not have meaning; they provide pleasure or pain. [*ibid.*, pp. 36–37]

A state of hallucinosis means that the analyst is trying to place him/herself in a condition of no saturation, without memory or desire, where any fantasy, idea or gut feeling that takes place should be approached with an act of faith, regardless of how absurd it might appear to be, and then be used to understand what is happening. The main difficulty for the analyst is in the domain of **countertransference**, in the capacity to "contain" painful memories or unresolved desires, or to abandon any narcissistic need. This is why Bion states that

> In the domain of hallucinosis the mental event is transformed into a sense impression and sense impressions in this domain do not have meaning; they provide *pleasure* or *pain*. [*ibid.*, p. 37, my italics]

It might have been possible that the concept of F was already in Bion's mind by the time of his experience with groups:

> There are times when I think that the group has an attitude to me, and that I can state in words what the attitude is; there are times when another individual acts as if he also thought the group had an attitude to him, and I believe I can deduce what his belief is; there are times when I think that the group has an attitude to an individual, and that I can say what it is. These occasions provide the raw material on which the interpretations are based . . . [1948b, pp. 142–143]

Later on, while referring to the treatment of schizophrenic patients, he states that countertransference must play an important part in the analysis of these patients, but he then proposes to leave the discussion for later on. (1967, p. 24). Bion only refers explicitly to this concept in his book *Attention and Interpretation*, and never mentions it again. We could argue, perhaps applying also his notion of F, that there could be a relationship between this concept and **Zen Buddhism**.

Agglomeration: Bion defines it in contrast to the concept of **articulation**, in so far as the latter means stability and integration to form a complex whole. Agglomeration implies a particular situation where the elements relate temporally and experimentally: "it is appropriate to a particular situation when that situation is viewed by the light of a particular hypothesis and during the time it is so viewed" (1992, p. 159). It could be considered as an antecedent of what Bion describes later as the **bizarre object**.

> What appears to be an articulated sentence is an agglomeration of objects, and is therefore not to be distinguished from the agglomeration manifest to the analyst as apparently inarticulate or incoherent speech. [*ibid.*, p. 161].

See **Articulation and Assimilation**.

Agoraphobia: *see*: **Claustrophobia**.

Algebraic calculus: *see*: **Calculus**.

Alpha-elements, or α-elements: The product of **alpha-function**, Bion describes them as "irreducibly simple objects" (1992, p. 181), representing sensual impressions (visual images, auditory patters, olfactory patterns, etc.), that could be stored as **memory** and eventually employed to create **dream thoughts, conscious thoughts**, unconscious waking **thinking, dream** formation, **contact-barrier**, memory and the capacity to **learn from experience** (1962, p. 26). Originally Bion referred to them as "real, live, existing and benevolent objects", capable of providing satisfaction to the baby, and as completely opposite to **beta(β)-elements**, which were in turn described as "dead and unreal objects" (1992, p. 133). He thought originally that α-elements might originate, beside the accumulation of sense data, from the transformation of β-elements by α-function, then named "dream-work-α" (*ibid.,* pp. 182–183).

The name of α first appeared in **Cogitations**, in a note without a date but believed to be from the beginning of 1960. There Bion conceived two levels in the organization of alpha-elements: one representing the impact of an external event, and the second one, the internal process of "digestion" of that event (1992, pp. 149–181):

1) Emotional experience → dream-work-α [α-function] → α-element → 'narrativization' → dream
2) Sensation of waking event in which personality is participating as in an unfolding narrative → dream-work-α [α-function]→ dream-thoughts.

There are two processes, one representing external emotional experiences that are dealt with by alpha-function, which converts them into α-elements and makes them undergo a process of narrativization (a historical sequence) (*see*: **Narrative**), so it can approximate to the emotional experience of waking life, and render it suitable for storage and waking conscious thoughts. During the second process, the **narrative** that has been stored is then changed into α-elements that lend themselves to be used in unconscious dream-thoughts, whether the personality is asleep or awake (1962, p. 8, 1992, pp. 149–150). A child, for instance, that is going through the emotional experience of learning how to walk, is able to do so because α-function stores the experience that will allow him to walk later without having to be conscious of it.

α-elements organize and cohere as they proliferate, to form a **contact-barrier**, an entity that marks the point of contact and separation between conscious and unconscious elements and originates the difference between them (1962, p. 17), or allows thoughts and dreams to take place as well as to discriminate between being asleep and being awake.

The process of elaboration of α and β-**elements** can be read in *Cogitations* pp. 62–63, written on August 10th, 1959. There Bion identifies alpha-function with **dream-work** and beta-elements with "indigested facts that have not being dreamed" (1992, p. 64). Such constructs could be understood as extensions of primary and secondary processes of classical theory.

Meltzer (1978) emphasizes the character of "empty concept" that, according to him, Bion had provided the alpha-elements with: "The 'emptiness' of this model was stressed over and over by Bion, along with the caution against over-hasty attempts to fill it with clinical meaning" (p. 119).

Alpha-function: Initially Bion referred to "**dream work** α", which he later tried to change when he felt it could bring confusion if it were to be used in a manner different from that which Freud had initially created it for (1992, p. 73); however, he continued using it in the same manner even after making such a remark. The term "α-function" was used for the first time in *Cogitations*, in a note possibly dated at the end of the sixties, which allowed Bion finally to discriminate between dream-work proper and α-function. To build this theory he used concepts from Freud's "The Interpretation of Dreams" (1900) and "Formulations on the Two Principles of Mental Functioning" (1911), as well as Klein's notion of guilt, super-ego and **paranoid–schizoid** and **depressive positions**.

α-function represents an **abstraction** used to describe the capacity to change sense information into α-**elements** (1992, p. 63), as well as providing the mind with material to create **dream thoughts** that could allow discrimination between being asleep or awake, conscious or unconscious and give a sense of identity and selfness (1967, p. 115). The brain never rests; what exists is a fluctuation between states of consciousness and unconsciousness, thanks to α-function and the permeability of the **contact barrier** that allows one side to remain awake while the other is asleep. Before he discriminated this function from dream-work, Bion stated that a series of steps were essential: (a) to pay attention to sensuous impressions; (b) to store this impression in the memory; (c) to change them into "**ideograms**"; and (d) depending on which principle dominates the mind, either to store them and to remember them if the **reality principle** dominates, or to expel them under the influence of the pleasure principle.

α-function is the product of an adequate relationship between the baby and the mother, which permits the existence of normal **projective identifications**. Usually the baby is not fit to use his sense information for himself, and this is why he needs to evacuate it into the mother and to depend on her capacity for **reverie**, to change it into α-elements that he will then be able to use. α-**function** works over sense experiences and **emotions**, and if successful, it will produce α-elements that could be stored as a **contact barrier** between unconscious and conscious, capable of producing **thoughts** (1962, pp. 17–18). If α-function becomes inoperative, sense impressions and emotions experienced by the person remain unaltered, creating what Bion named the **beta-elements**, or following Kant, the **thing-in-itself** or **noumenon**, different from α-function that represents the **phenomenon**. This function, besides been inseparable from thoughts, conscious reasoning and learning from experience, can also send conscious thoughts to the unconscious and thus alleviate consciousness from an exaggerated weight of thoughts, for instance when learning to create a habit. According to Bion, there is a paradox in **psychotic** patients of an unconscious that although "on the surface" cannot be made unconscious and used as material for mechanisms of **abstraction** and concretization (1992, p. 71).

Attacks on α-function induced by hate and envy towards the breast that is capable of producing love, understanding or wisdom, destroys the possibility in the patient to make contact with him/herself or with others as living persons (1962, p. 9, 119), a feeling possible to observe in mechanisms of "self-envy".[8] *See*: **Dream-work**.

Alpha-function, reversion of: *see:* **Reversion of α-function.**

Alpha-space (α-space): It consists of a space populated by objects that are real and possess their own reality and their own limits, infra– and ultra-real (like infra-red and ultra-violet). They can be appreciated by ordinary thought and are indistinguishable from those objects normally perceived by the senses, like things that are "visible", "audible", "touchable", etc. Bion was attempting to describe the existence of a domain pertaining to reality, unknown but approachable by **intuition**, only if special preparations were made. When he argues about the existence of a psychoanalytic domain with its particular realities, he is obviously referring to phenomena such as **hallucinosis, O** and **acts of faith.** He said:

> . . . unquestionable, constant, subject to change only in accordance with its own rules even if those rules are not known. These realities are "intuitable" if the proper apparatus is available in the condition proper to its functioning . . . The conditions in which the intuition operates (intuits) are pellucid [*see* **transparence**] and **opaque.** [1992, p. 315]

The main opacities that prevent the intuition of reality correspond to understanding, **memory,** and **desire.** Such opacities act like **turbulences** that obstruct transparence of an **unsaturated psycho-analytic listening** that eventually will allow communion with **O.** In order to avoid such opacities a permanent, continuous and lasting discipline must be established (*ibid.*). (*See:* **beta-space**)

Altered focus: Concept used in group dynamics related to the different vertices or perspectives someone might choose to observe or conceive a situation, like using different microscope lenses to investigate a thick section, implying that the instrument of observation is a variable model of the structure of the situation being observed. It should be differentiated from "binocular vision". *See:* **Dependent basic assumption, Reversible perspective, Groups, Basic assumption, Binocular vision.**

---

[8] See: López-Corvo 1992, 1994.

A-morph: *see*: **Noösphere**

Analogy: Bion (1977a) used the term "analogy" in order to emphasize the importance of the relationship between objects, instead of the objects themselves: "confusion can occur because attention is given to the two images used in the analogy, and not, which is the important point, the relationship between them" (p. 26). The problem of being abstract to the point of being incomprehensible could be overcome by being concrete, but the conflict then is that it could be misleading. "The importance of the analogy is not the similarity of one thing to another, but the relationship between the two" (Bion, 1974, p. 19). *See*: **Emotional links, Attacks on linking, Binocular vision.**

Analytic: Kant has distinguished between analytic and **synthetic** propositions, just as he also differentiated **a priori** from **empirical** propositions. An analytic proposition implies that something can only be known by experience, for instance, to say that "the Angel Falls is a very tall fall", means that it has been seen. A synthetic proposition, on the other hand, is one in which the predicate is part of the subject, for instance, "a fat man is a man", or "a white building is a building".

Analytic situation (setting): In Bion's language it represents the background or the setting where **transformations** (or "the process" in classical analysis) would take place:

> What I mean by "receptor" or "field" or "ground" can be most simply grasped by **analogy** with painting in which the ground for the transformation would be the canvas on to which the transformation was projected [be it **projective transformations** or **rigid movement transformations**] . . . I propose to discuss the problem of the ground for projective and rigid motion transformations as if it were stable and corresponded to what is regarded in classical analysis as the analytic situation. [1965, pp. 113–114]

It would correspond to categories D1 or E1 of the Grid. *See*: **Transformations, Projective transformations, Rigid movement transformations**

Animate and inanimate, difference between: Bion (1962) referred to enforced **splitting** associated with a disturbed relationship with the breast or its substitutes (p. 10). When **envy** obstructs the relationship with the good breast, provider of **love**, understanding, solace, knowledge, etc., just as Klein (1946) described it during the **paranoid–schizoid position**, the persecutory **anxiety** present cannot obstruct the physical need for sucking that could jeopardize the infant's life. "Fear of death through starvation of essentials" said Bion, "compels resumption of sucking. A split between material and psychical satisfaction develops" (1962, p. 10). This situation leads to an enforced splitting between physical need for survival on one hand, and psychic satisfactions on the other; a condition achieved by destruction of α-**function**.

> This makes breast and infant appear inanimate with consequent guiltiness, fear of suicide and fear of murder [it is easier to destroy something inanimate than something alive] . . . The need for love, understanding and mental development is now deflected, since it cannot be satisfied, into the search for material comforts. [*ibid.*, p. 11]

Psychotic patients or the **Psychotic part of the personality**, could change an animate object into an inanimate one, or into the "**thing-in-itself**" or **beta-elements**, as Segal (1957) has described it in her concept of "**symbolic equation**".

Another **vertex** to consider was discussed by Bion in his book *Cogitations*, where he reflects on the attack made by the baby on those objects linked with displeasure and with the consequent need to placate them by means of idealization, due to guilt and persecutory anxiety. Idealization is achieved through future transformation into worshipped objects, for they acquire supra-human attributes which, according to Bion, are achieved precisely because they are dead. Bion says:

> Contrary to common observation, the essential feature of the adored or worshipped object is that it should be dead so that crime may be expiated by the patient's dutiful adherence to animation of what is known to be inanimate and impossible to animate. This attitude contributes to the complex of feelings associated with fetishism. [1992, p. 134]

In other words, the establishment of a useless dependency on those objects would pay off the crime perpetuated through the attack on the good objects. These objects however, being inanimate (dead) are believed (invented) to be animate but, for this same reason, are not capable of giving anything; for instance, expecting a miracle from a figure made of plaster. **Fetishism** and some people's religious faith can be explained in this way. In other words, in the same way as the inanimate becomes animate, the contrary also takes place; that is, the animate becomes inanimate. It seemed that the "life" stolen from live objects as a way to control them and avoid separation anxiety ("heterophobia"), would later be projected into dead (inanimate) objects that have been given life and have been idealized. Guilt would be expiated, as Bion has said, by trying to obtain protection as well as trying to obtain a miracle from something that doesn't even have a life. *See*: **Proto-real objects**.

Animism: A state that contrasts with the difficulty of conceiving others and oneself as living beings. It is distinguished by the need to give living objects qualities of death and *vice versa* (1962, p. 9). *See*: **Fetishism; Proto-real objects; Animate and inanimate, difference between**.

Anxiety: "All anxiety is related ultimately to The Anxiety, which has two roots" (1992, p. 207): (1) the contents of the **Oedipal** situation, which has as its **"scientific deductive system"** the **Theorem of Pythagoras**; (2) the fear produced by the Kleinian **"Positions"** that have as their scientific deductive system **Euclid**'s theorem of **Pons Asinorum**.

A priori: According to Kant, it represents a proposition that, even if it could be elicited by experience, once known, it could be thought of as having a basis other than experience. Russell (1945) says:

> A child learning arithmetic may be helped by experiencing two marbles and two other marbles, and observing that altogether he is experiencing four marbles. But when he has grasped the general proposition, "two and two are four" he no longer requires confirmation by instances. [pp. 706–707].

Apparatus for thinking: *see*: **Thinking, apparatus for**.

Apparatus of perception: *see:* **Perception, apparatus of.**

Arm that fell off, dream of the: *see:* **Significant dreams.**

Arrogance, curiosity and stupidity: These concepts are based on Bion's article "On arrogance" (1957a, pp. 86–92) presented at the International Congress of Psychoanalysis in Paris, July/August, 1957. He considers the occurrence of these three forms of behaviour, "arrogance, curiosity and stupidity" in the same person, as the expression of a "psychological disaster." When pride appears within an individual who is dominated by the life **instinct**, pride becomes self-respect, but if the death instinct predominates pride then becomes arrogance. In order to make clear the relationship between these three concepts, he considers the **Oedipus myth** from a perspective where the sexual crime is regarded as a secondary element. The central crime then is Oedipus' arrogance in "vowing to lay bare the truth at no matter what cost" (*ibid.* p. 86); insisting that Tiresias reveal the secret about the plague of Thebes. It could be argued that Oedipus, dominated by his stupidity, could have believed, because of his arrogance, that he was free from any wrongdoing or from any possible sin.

A similar mechanism could have been present in the mind of many dictators, such as Hitler for instance, whose stupidity and arrogance forbade him from seeing that it would be impossible to take over the whole world, of Gaea, as a simple metaphor for his mother. Bion considers that, in practice, the analysis of these persons may seem superficially to follow the patterns that we are familiar with in the treatment of neurosis, while in reality, the lack of improvement in spite of the analytical work that is done, could represent the evidence that we might be dealing with a true psychological disaster of such magnitude, that it may as well correspond to a psychosis. A possible complication results from the possibility of a **transference** collusion between the patient's curiosity, and the curiosity normally present in the analytical procedure, which the patient could experience as an intrinsic component of the "disaster", or as an expression of some kind of perverse **acting-out**; a situation, Bion alerts us, that could be difficult to avoid. In this case, the orientation of the analysis might be analogous to the treatment of a **psychotic** patient: investigation of

projective identifications, confusional states, depersonalization, and **delusions**.

Bahía (1977) introduces a relationship between the analyst's **negative capacity** and his omnipotent and arrogant curiosity, the wish to know the truth at any cost instead of being tolerant with "no-knowledge" (–K). In a sense, this could also represent the analyst's attachment to his/her own desire, which could be extended to the level of omnipotent curiosity, meaning a true stupidity.

About Bion's work on arrogance, Meltzer (1978) ironically commented: "Certainly, for instance, the reading of the paper 'On Arrogance' at the Paris congress struck many people as a shocking display of the very hubris Bion was describing" (p. 31).

Articulation: In an undated note written in *Cogitations* (1992), Bion explained its **meaning** as:

> . . . it is a name for the process of bringing elements together, integrating them, so that the combined parts form a complex whole. The meaning I attach to the word will be clear if its use is contrasted with that of "**agglomeration**" . . . [p. 158]

Perhaps here could be inferred the notion of the "**selected fact**" taken from Poincaré, that Bion would use so extensively later on.

Assimilation:[9] Bion gives this concept exactly the same sense given to the digestive **function**, such as "assimilation of sensuous impressions", but emphasizing also that he does not employ it as a "technical term" (1992, p. 157) Assimilation is well preserved within the

---

[9] Similar to Bion, Piaget also used the digestive apparatus as a model to understand the mind. Piaget introduced the existence of two functions: (a) Organization, and (b) Adaptation. Any act by a living being implies a certain degree of organization: from a protozoa's simple act of phototropism, to the more complex act of mathematical calculus. Adaptation entails a dynamic and progressive process that also involves two functions: (a) Assimilation; and (b) Accommodation. Assimilation represents the act of incorporating an external reality inside mental schemata that is already there. Accommodation, on the other hand, represents the change that the schemata must suffer in order to assimilate the new experience.

"Non-psychotic part of the personality", but it is destroyed by the psychotic part. This destruction does not impede that incorporated but non assimilated sensuous impressions could be stored within the self as **things-in-themselves** or foreign bodies, that could be used as material for discharge. Bion states that,

> The objects formed by the process that excludes assimilation are amenable to the usages of a personality employing projective identification and its introjective counterpart, but do not lend themselves to any function other than evacuation and return. [*ibid.* p. 161]

Destruction of the capacity to assimilate could be the product of the superego's sadistic and fragmentary attacks under the dominion of the death **instinct**, producing a mental state similar to the physiological state of starvation, together with an increased fear of imminent annihilation (*ibid.*, p. 164).

Bion remarks that people often refer to these stored objects, shaped outside the process of assimilation or "unassimilated sense impressions", with names usually given to words in common use. They are not names of feelings but they are contained in these words, which are felt as if they were feeling themselves. "The words employed for this purpose are those used in articulated speech to express relatedness, such as 'and', 'with', 'in', 'outside' and all verbs" (*ibid.*, p. 160). Patients might try to evacuate these objects because of accretions of stimuli, by means of muscular movements, changes in mien, changes in posture or attitude.

> What appears to be an articulated sentence is an **agglomeration** of objects, and is therefore not to be distinguished from the agglomeration manifest to the analyst as apparently inarticulate or incoherent. [*ibid.*, p. 161]

Predominance of life over death instincts, leads towards dominance of the impulse to **repair** the capacity for assimilation, something observed in the patient's use of verbal expressions that could be used for the construction of dream thoughts and dreams, as well as communication or association. These verbal **statements** are capable of articulating with each other, are not suitable for projective identifications and represent transformations still in the process of moving towards greater transformations, according to the assimilation of future sense impressions.

Asthma: Bion writes a short note about asthma, in *Elements of Psychoanalysis* (1963), when trying to explain the Grid with the use of models other than the one provided by the digestive tract, such as respiratory, auditory, and tactile. He says: "It is worth noting that clinical manifestations of asthma become psycho-analytically more meaningful if their relationship to the respiratory model for thinking–feeling is recognized" (p. 96).

At-one-ment: A term created by Bion to represent a fusion with the other, as a form of "incarnation", "embodiment" or "incorporation" (1965, p. 163). It could be equivalent to what has been defined as "empathy", but much more complex. He describes it as a form of relationship with **O**, something possible only when the final becoming of the **transformation** in O is reached: $T\beta \rightarrow O$ ($= T\beta O$). This kind of open **intuition** intended towards a communion or fusion with the **truth**, should be distinguished by the analyst from sensuous greed and gratifications where **memory** and **desire** are present. "The experience of at-one-ment *resembles* possession and sensuous fulfilment", says Bion (1970, p. 33). In other words, memory and longing dominated by the pleasure principle, will always be directed towards something gratifying that will **saturate** the mind and forbid the necessary freedom and nakedness required to be in touch with the **thing-in-itself** or at-one-ment. Bion states: "The evocation of that which provided a container for possessions, and of the sensuous gratifications with which to fill it, will differ from an evocation simulated by at-one-ment" (*ibid.*). He also refers to the existence of what he calls a "**constellation**", a function that will facilitate the precipitation of a constant conjunction and will act as a form of catalyser to facilitate the fusion with O or at-one-ment, or transformation of $O \rightarrow K$.

In summary, at-one-ment during the analytical session represents an "embodiment" with O, with the thing-in-itself or the truth, achieved without memory and desire, different from the kind of at-one-ment observed between a couple who love each other, but whose embodiment is based on memory and desire and is determined by the pleasure principle. Some remembrances might surface in a form Bion distinguishes by the name of "constellations", but they evolve on their own, forced by the associations produced by a constant conjunction that will ease the process of at-one-ment.

Attacks on linking (or that which joins): Bion mentioned this concept for the first time in 1957 (1967, p. 48), as an attempt to understand why **psychotic** patients or the **psychotic part of the personality**, always present a certain **consciousness** of reality, notwithstanding the extreme attack made on their verbal thinking. Bion felt these attacks were oriented not so much against reality itself, but against **verbal thought**, which according to Freud (1911), represents the existing relationship between reality sense impressions and consciousness, that is, between external and internal realities; this is why, if this link is destroyed, thought and object relations are disturbed, but consciousness of reality remains.

Bion used attacks and **splitting** on the "primitive breast or penis", as paradigmatic of all attacks made on links, and also described the mechanism of **projective identification** as the way the mind tries to free itself from fragments resulting from such attacks (1967, p. 93). *The main contribution on this subject consists of the emphasis made on the link and not so much on the object, as was previously expressed by Klein.*

Attacks on the link are originally made during the paranoid–schizoid **position**, which is controlled by **part-objects**, whose relations are established not with the shape of the breast, but with its contents, not with anatomy but with physiology, with its functions, such as nutrition, loving, hating, poisoning, etc. It represents a more dynamic than static condition (*ibid.*, p. 102). This kind of part-object relationship with himself and with others explain expressions

> ... such as "it seems", which are commonly employed by the deeply disturbed patient on occasions when a less disturbed patient might say "I think" or "I believe". "When he says 'it seems' he is often referring to a feeling—an 'it seems' feeling—which is a part of his psyche and yet is not observed as part of the whole object".
> [*ibid.*, pp. 101–102]

For some patients projective identification becomes the only form of link or **communication** that they have access to in order to make themselves understood. They are usually patients who when babies, experienced "**nameless terror**" of dying, which was not well taken or contained by their mothers. Afterwards, these feelings changed to hatred and were experienced in the **transference** as if they were not well understood, that the analyst was someone who neither accepted their complaints, nor alleviated them. "Thus" said Bion, "the link between patient and analyst, or infant and breast, is the mechanism of projective identification" (*ibid.*, p. 105). In extreme cases, primitive **envy** and hatred is changed into greed, which ends devouring the patient and the analyst's minds, with the use of **acting-out**, delinquency or suicide threats (*ibid.*, p. 106).

Another important link destroyed by envy is the relationship between both parents, something observed in attacks on "that which joins" the couple, as well as their creativity and achievements, experienced also in the incorporated image (*ibid.*, p. 99), which is then internally attacked with mechanisms of "self envy" (López-Corvo, 1992, 1994). **Judgement** as well as curiosity, also represents possible targets for fragmentation and evacuation that will interfere with the **capacity to learn** (*ibid.*, p. 103). *See*: **Emotional links, L, H, K, –K, –L, Maternal reverie** and **Nameless terror.**

Attention: According to Freud (1911), it represents, together with **action, notation, judgement**, and **thought**, one of the functions used by the ego to reach consciousness of reality.

> A special function was instituted which had periodically to search the external world, in order that its data might be familiar already if an urgent internal need should arise—the function of *attention*. Its activity meets the sense-impressions half way, instead of awaiting their appearance. [p. 220, original emphasis]

Bion has used this concept, together with those mentioned above, as part of the **horizontal axis** of the **Grid**, in order to structure particular qualities and functions of the mind.

Awareness: *see*: **Conscious awareness.**

Axiomatic algebra: *see*: **Psychic mathematics.**

Axiomatic deductive system: *see*: **Scientific deductive system.**

Axis of uses: *see*: **Grid, horizontal axis of the.**

B

Babel Tower, myth of the: *see*: Tower of Babel, myth of the

Basic assumption (ba): Bion uses this to represent emotional complications, which appear at a given moment in a rather automatic, involuntary and unavoidable manner within a **working group** (W), changing its direction and determining how it will function subsequently (1948b, pp. 105, 117). Bion describes three kinds of ba: "**dependence**", "**pairing**" and "**fight–flight**." All ba have a leader, although in the pairing **group** it would be "non-existent", i.e. "unborn": the leader may not be identified with a person, but with a metaphor, an **idea** or an **inanimate** object; whereas in the dependent group, sometimes the leader may be filled by the history of the group or "the **bible**" (*ibid.*, p. 155).

Because of circumstances related to its own dynamics, a group could change from one ba to another, while the other two ba remain hidden or latent (*ibid.*, p. 97). The surfacing of a ba can be appreciated because of the kind of **emotions** present that act as the "cement" that keeps the group assembled; for instance guilt and **depression** in the dependent group, Messianic hope in the pairing group, anger and hate in the fight–flight group (*ibid.*, p. 166). The change from one ba to another is promoted by the failure of the defences present in the manifest ba, unable to deal with **anxiety** induced by mechanisms of disintegration always present in the group. This situation will encourage the need to make use of other defences present in the latent ba (*ibid.*, p. 163), perhaps because at that moment the defences present in the ba that has been chosen, "appear far more to have the characteristics of defensive reactions to **psychotic** anxiety" (*ibid.*, p. 189).

There are no conflicts about the predominance of one ba over the other, because the main line of divergence is always with W (work group) (*ibid.*, p. 96). During the course of one hour, for instance, a therapeutic group could be dominated by several ba, or perhaps one ba would take over the group for several months. The communication between members of the group is instantaneous, regardless of cultural differences or incapacity to form **symbols**, and can be achieved following a mechanism Bion referred to as "**valence**", or the tendency of an individual to "combine" with the group, depending on a specific ba (*ibid.*, pp. 151–152). The dominating ba represents what Bion has described as the "**establishment**", which might be present in any existing social structure.

As already stated, a ba changes depending on the way the predominant defences from this manifest ba fail, giving place then to other anxieties related to a latent ba. There are, however, other varieties Bion has referred to as "**aberrant forms of change**", linked to the dominating ba and the presence of an external group.

Brown (1985) established a relationship between the three forms of ba and the psycho-sexual stages of evolution described by Freud. According to him the dependent ba would represent a form of **regression** to the "oral dependent" phase characterized by the interaction present in the baby–mother dyad; the fight–flight would equally be a regression to the "separation–individuation" period related to the anal stage, and finally, the pairing group would indicate a regression to the phallic or Oedipal stage (p. 198).

Other researchers in the area of group therapy, such as Turquet or Lawrence *et al.*, have attempted to create new forms of basic assumptions. Turquet (1974), for instance, defined the "Oneness basic assumption" (Oba), which could be translated as a kind of unity, referring to the members of a group who "seek to join in a powerful union with an omnipotent force . . . to be lost in oceanic feelings of unity." Lawrence, Bain and Gould (1996), on the other hand, have suggested the presence of a fifth ba they refer to as "Meness" (baM), which they define as a basic assumption completely opposed to Turquet's "oneness", and representing the tendency of the members to prevent the formation of the group, for they fear they might "disappear" in the group or be persecuted by it.

See: **Work groups, Dependent ba, Flight–fight ba, Pairing ba, Schism, Oscillation of Dba, Valence**.

Beckett, Samuel: From the beginning of 1934 to the end of 1935, Bion analysed this Irish writer and 1969 Nobel Prize winner, something never mentioned by him in his autobiography (Bion, 1982, 1985). According to Anzieu (1986) perhaps both men might have influenced each other, as some kind of "imaginary twins", for they had many things in common: French Huguenot ancestors who escaped to England because of religious persecution, "schizoid and narcissistic" features, as well as making use of culture as a "continent" to deal with **psychotic** components. Perhaps, says Anzieu, if someone had asked Bion about his motivation to write he would have given the same answer Beckett did: *"Bon qu'á ça"*, meaning: "I am only good for that".

Bléandonu (1994), on the other hand, stated that Beckett's therapy helped him not only to understand himself better but also to show more of himself in his writings, even though he had to discontinue it prematurely because of the consolidation of a negative therapeutic reaction:

> Beckett could not progress until he could acknowledge his "addictive" relationship to his mother. Nine years older than Beckett, Bion, who was still in therapy with Hadfield, became, in the **transference**, the writer's older brother Frank (it was in his bed that "Sam" [Beckett] sought refuge from his nocturnal panic attacks before coming to London). The two men shared many intellectual interests, especially literature. At times they discussed, even argued about, the nature of the creative process. According to Beckett, the "analysis" was limping along ... he could not make a choice between Bion and his mother. His body somatized, producing boils, tremors and an anal abscess. Beckett announced his intention of stopping at the end [around Christmas] of 1935. [p. 45]

Beta-elements: (β-**elements**): These represent sensual impressions identical to what Bion, following Kant, has called the **thing-in-itself**. He described them as ". . . objects compounded of things-in-themselves, feelings of depression–persecution and guilt and therefore aspects of personality linked by a sense of catastrophe" (1963, p. 40).

At the beginning he referred to them as "indigested or non-dreamed facts" that have not been transformed by α-**function** (1992, p. 64), and later on: "unreal or dead objects" in contrast with α-elements, to which he referred as "alive and real objects" [1992, p. 133). Bion has also defined them as ". . . objects compounded of things-in-themselves, feelings of depression–persecution [as seen in the **paranoid–schizoid position**] and guilt and therefore aspects of personality linked by a sense of catastrophe" (1963, p. 40). Finally, in an undated note in *Cogitations*, he called them "β-elements" (1992, p. 181).

At the beginning all sensuous impressions belong to the **proto-mental system** incapable of discriminating between mental and physical impressions. Beta elements *are not synonymous with mental pathology*, instead they represent a type of non-verbal **communication**, perhaps an intuitive one, commonly used by children (1974a, pp. 127–128), by the **psychotic part of the personality** or by **psychotic** patients. Because these individuals lack α-function in order to work through (digest, metabolize) **abstractions**, they use beta elements that cannot be intellectually conceptualized and are thus communicated by mechanisms of **projective identification**. Bion says:

> Beta-elements are a way of talking about matters which are not thought at all; alpha-elements are a way of talking about elements which, hypothetically, are supposed to be part of thought. The poet **Donne**[10] has written "the blood spoke in her cheek . . . as if her body thought!" This expresses exactly for me that intervening stage which in the **Grid** is portrayed on paper as a line separating

---

[10] *Her pure and eloquent blood*
Spoke in her cheeks, and so distinctly wrought,
That one might almost say, her body thought. ["The Second Anniversary. By occasion of the religious death of Mistress Elisabeth Drury," poem written by British poet John Donne, 1572–1631].

beta-elements from alpha-elements. Note that I am not saying that it is either beta or alpha, but the line *separating the two* which is represented by the poet's words. [1990, p. 41)

If α-function is troubled and therefore inoperative, sense impressions as well as **emotions** remain untouched and become β-elements, which cannot be used to produce **dream thoughts**. Instead they are evacuated through projective identifications that discharge the mental apparatus from accretion of stimuli and influence as well as the configuration of **acting-out**. Such discharges can take place through muscular movements or facial expressions, etc. or can also be used in some kind of evacuative thought good for manipulation (1962, p. 6).[11] Even though they can be stored they do not represent **memories** like α-**elements** do, but represent "undigested facts", and in contrast with them too, they are not felt to be **phenomena** but things-in-themselves. Beta-elements cannot become unconscious and therefore cannot be repressed, suppressed nor used to **learn from experience**.

The breast provider of love, security and wisdom, can in some cases generate such cruel **envy** in the baby, that it could induce him to attack the breast furiously and thus generate a conflict between the need to suck in order to survive and fear of retaliation. According to Bion, in those cases the only way out would be to attack the alpha-function, which would make both, the breast and the baby, feel like inanimate things (*see*: **animate-inanimate**) where the homicidal or suicidal destructive impulses remain present. When envy and aggression disturb the baby's relationship with the breast, there comes a point when the baby must continue sucking in order to avoid death. The fear provoked by the destructive power of envy induces **splitting** between *psychic* and *material* aspects, that is, between the need for affection and the need for sustenance respectively. This split makes him mistake the need for affection for accumulation of material things, which represent β-elements. When the patient lacks the α-function that enables him to discriminate the animate from the inanimate, he then turns to a

[11] Green (2001), has argued, referring to the Internet, that this form of communication "reminded him too much of a hypothetical channel through which beta-elements were discharged" (Personal communication).

greedy accumulation of material things and a continuous search for material comfort, considered by Bion as real representatives of β-elements. Because he lacks:

> ... the apparatus, α-function by which he might understand his predicament. The patient greedily and fearfully takes one beta-element after another apparently unable to conceive of any activity other than introjection of more beta-elements. [1962, p. 11]

This can be observed in the consulting room, for instance, by the interest the patient shows towards the material objects around him, such as furniture, the couch, etc. It can also be observed by the fact that the patient is not capable of conceiving either himself or the ones who surround him as live persons. Some patients frequently come to consult under the following model: they feel themselves to be machines, they do not know how well they function, and since the analyst must know better they ask for help in much the same way a mechanic fixes real machines.

β-elements are saturated as are **bizarre objects**, but they differ from them in that they only contain sense-impressions while the latter also include ego, and especially superego, aspects (*ibid.*, p. 26). In some situations β-elements can be changed into α-elements, as can be observed, for instance, during the **maternal reverie**: ". . . the fear [of the baby] is modified [by the mother] and the β-element thereby made into an α-element" (1963, p. 27). "It is tempting to suppose", says Bion further on, "that the transformation of β-element to α-element depends on ♀ ♂ and the operation of Ps$\leftrightarrow$D depends on the prior operation of ♀ ♂" (*ibid.*, p. 39). The β elements are dispersed, but they can reach cohesion through Ps$\leftrightarrow$D or through a **selected fact**, unless a container ♀ is found by the patient, that compels cohesion of the β-elements to form the contained ♂ (*ibid.*, p. 40), a change that Bion explains through "psycho-mechanic" mechanisms. [*ibid.*, p.84] *See*: **Grid, vertical axis**.

A process of elaboration of these concepts, as well as of alpha-function and alpha-elements, can be read in *Cogitations* (pp. 62–68), written in 1959. There Bion identifies alpha-function with **dream work** and beta-elements with "indigested facts that have not been dreamed" (1992, p. 64). Such constructions about alpha and beta-elements could be interpreted as an extension of "secondary and primary precesses" respectively, as they were described within classical theory.

Green (2000) compares Freud's concept of "unconscious Id impulses" with beta elements. He states:

> The main difference between Id and unconscious is that in Freud's thinking there were no representations of the Id. The Id was made of impulses—a concept very close to Bion's beta elements. He was aware of that. The main difference between Bion and Freud could be that for Freud the drives always had their source in the most inner part of the body, whereas for Bion beta-elements may arise from external stimuli ... [p. 115]

These statements could be questioned, because Klein and Bion, as opposed to Freud, believe that impulses and objects are not separable, one is the "corollary" of the other. There is no such thing as an impulse free of an object representation, therefore, even beta-elements as things-in-themselves, as the ineffable, endure the implicit presence of an object. How then can impulses be projected? How can an object-free impulse be projected? When Bion compares beta elements with sense impressions, he is referring to an object's sense impressions. That is why, as Green expresses it, these elements "arise from external stimuli".

Beta-screen: *see*: **Screen of beta-elements**.

Beta-space (β-space): According to Bion it represents a mental **space** of "unthoughts", "unthinkable **thoughts**" and thoughts "without a thinker" (*see*: **"wild thoughts"**). A mental domain that extends in **time, space** and style in such a manner that it could only be explained (or thought by a thinker) using astronomical analogies. In this universe there are also "constellations of **alpha-elements**" capable of composing

> ... **universes of discourse** that are characterized by containing and being contained by terms such as, "void", "formless infinite", "god", "infinity". This sphere I shall name by borrowing the term, **noösphere** ... but as I wish to avoid too great a penumbra of associations, particularly those activated by the term, "sphere", I shall employ a sign that is as devoid of meaning as I can make it

(compatible with retention of its capacity for communicability) Σ (**sigma**)." [1992, p. 313]

What eventually would make a difference to the outcome of all these constellations, would be the presence of a "thinker" containing an **alpha-function** capable of transforming, or not, any of these wild thoughts or unthinkable thoughts, or using "lost" or wild alpha-elements that eventually might allow an illumination by O as a "formless infinity".

Bible, the: Name used by Bion to refer to the manner in which a **dependent group** behaves when trying to use past references or the history of the **group** as an abstract entity to depend on, usually when the group therapist refuses to promote dependency by disregarding the role of a leader.

> The group resorts to bible-making when threatened with an idea the acceptance of which would entail development on the part of the individuals comprising the group. Such ideas derive emotional force, and excite emotional opposition, from their association with characteristics appropriate to the **pairing-group** leader. [1948b, p. 155]

See: **basic assumptions, dependent group**.

Binocular vision: The use of vision as a regulating or integrating **element** can be found in Bion's article "**The Imaginary Twin**" (1967, p. 3), where he refers to the way the "visual concern" experienced by three of his patients represented "the emergence of a new capacity for exploring the environment" and to resolveearly conflicts that had always been there, although its observation was obstructed by the lack of intellectual perception and the conflict brought by the phantasy of the "imaginary twin". Bion said:

> I have wondered whether the psychological development was bound up with the development of ocular control in the same way that problems of development linked with oral aggression co-exist with the eruption of teeth. [1967, p. 22]

Elsewhere, Bion (1962) states that Freud's position considering consciousness as a sense organ of psychical qualities, although true, was incomplete, because psychoanalytic vision required not only the presence of consciousness, but of the unconscious too:

> The model is formed by the exercise of a capacity similar to that which is in evidence when the two eyes operate in binocular vision to correlate two views of the same object. The use in **psychoanalysis** of **conscious** and **unconscious** in viewing a psychoanalytic object is analogous to the use of the two eyes in ocular observation of an object sensible to sight. Freud attributed this function, the sense organ of psychical quality, to consciousness alone [1962, p. 86]

The interaction of analyst and analysand could also act as a binocular vision (1965, p. 74).

In "**Transformations**" (1965), Bion puts forward arguments about the "**reversible perspective**", where a patient could be observed to alter his attitude towards an object by changing his **view-point**, representing a procedure that involves **splitting** in **time** and **space**, because in this circumstance the patient and the analyst's time–space dimensions are completely different. Reversible perspective can be understood as a kind of binocular vision that will be dealt with and modified, paradoxically with the help of the analyst's binocular vision.

There is also a binocular vision between the *presence* and the *absence* of an object represented for instance by a **point**, that is, the place where the object was but no longer is, which can be observed in language with words that signal the objects, or symbols that represent them, but are not the real object. This form of binocular vision is absent in **psychotic** patients or in the **psychotic part of the personality**, because **thinking** is dominated by **symbolic equations**.

Bion makes observations about binocular vision in relation to time and space dimensions, like keeping one eye in the present and another in the past or in the future. He differentiates, for instance, between a patient who is conscious of his "past" that no longer exists, as can be observed in the **transference**, and the mathematician who is unconscious of a "future" discovery that has not yet come to pass. To represent these two positions he develops a scale, which at one end represents the past, and at the other the future. He gives the unconscious a sense, thus:

—————>   <—————   —————>

unconscious and unconscious; reciprocally, conscious and
<———

conscious. The "state of mind of the mathematician unaware
of mathematical formal artifices can then be represented by
—————>

unconscious and that of the disturbed patient [who expresses
frustration intolerance about the absence of the breast can also
            <———

be represented] by conscious (1965, p. 85). The sense of the arrows
can also symbolize the denial of the present, because the patient
will try to search in the past for the scent of the absent breast with
his conscious, while the mathematician would keep the level of
future knowledge in his unconscious; this could be represented
with a point "where the present used to be." *See*: **Analogy, Links,
Attacks on linking, Reversible perspective, Intra-uterine life, No-
breast, Point, Symbolic equation.**

Bishop George Berkeley: *see*: **"Ghosts of departed quantities"**

Bizarre objects: Are seen in **psychotic** patients, and are made of
particles that once free from the mind, become encysted in external
objects and will either contain these objects or be contained by
them, in the sense of the **container–contained** ($♀$ $♂$) theory. These
objects differ from beta–elements because in their structure they
also have, beside these later elements, ego and superego traces
(1962, p. 25). "Each particle", says Bion, "is felt to consist of a real
external object which is encapsulated in a piece of personality that
has engulfed it". The external object then acquires the characteristics of the projected particles; for instance, if the object is a gramophone into which visual aspects have been projected, the psychotic
patient will feel that when the gramophone is working, it will also
be watching him, or listening, if the part projected is auditory (1967,
pp. 39–48). At the same time, the chosen object can control the function that contains it and, because these personality particles can be
felt as prototypes of ideas—and then words—external ideas and
objects become homologous to such a point that the capacity to
make symbols becomes impossible. Instead, as Segal (1957) has
described it, the patient equates, but does not symbolize.

See: "**symbolic equation**". The patient now moves in a world made out of **bizarre objects**, which are ordinarily used as **dream furniture**. Another consequence would be that when psychotic patients discover that things are ruled by natural laws and not by the omnipotence of their mental functioning, they become puzzled. Something similar happened to a catatonic patient who felt that when he joined his thumb and forefinger, the world would move, birds would fly, people would breathe and so on. These objects make up the dream material present in **delusions** (1967, pp. 81–82). On the other hand, within the non-psychotic part of the personality, these bizarre ". . . objects, primitive yet complex, partake of qualities which in the non-psychotic personality are peculiar to matter, anal objects, senses, ideas and superego" (*ibid.*, p. 51).

Bride's Chair theorem: *see:* **Theorem of the Bride's Chair**

C

Caesura: Greek and Latin related word, describes a short break or pause made on certain occasions in verse. In "Inhibitions, Symptoms and Anxiety", Freud (1926) states: "There is much more continuity between **intra-uterine life** and earliest infancy than the impressive caesura of the act of birth would have us believe" (p. 138). Bion extends the metaphor to include the existence of a threshold that unites/separates or separates/penetrates different dimensions described as similitude or differences; for instance, the resistance in psychoanalytic **communication** (1987, p. 298), the interaction between the mouth and the breast, intrauterine and adult lives, between the individual and the couple or between oriental and occidental cultures. Bion says:

> Picasso painted a picture on a piece of glass so that it could be seen on both sides. I suggest that the same thing can be said of the caesura: it depends which way you look at it, which way you are travelling. Psychosomatic disorders, or soma-psychotic—take your choice—the picture should be recognizably the same whether you look at it from the psychosomatic position, or from the soma-psychotic position. [*ibid.*, p. 306]

In relation to time Bion formulates:

> ... the patient may express a fear of the future which has many of the characteristics of a past which one thinks he could not possibly remember; nor can he remember the future because it has not yet happened. These things, so faintly expressed, may in **truth** be very powerful. I can imagine that there may be **ideas** which cannot be more powerfully expressed because they are buried in the future which has not happened, or buried in the past which is forgotten, and which can hardly be said to belong to what we call "thought". [1977a, p. 43]

Then he questions:

> Can any method of communication be sufficiently "penetrating" to pass that caesura in the direction from post-natal conscious **thought** back to the pre-mental in which thoughts and ideas have their counterpart in "times" or "levels" of mind where they are not thoughts or ideas? That penetration has to be effective in either direction. It is easy to put it in pictorial terms by saying it is like penetrating into the woman's inside either from inside out, as at birth, or from outside in, as in sexual intercourse. [*ibid.*, p. 45]

Bion speculates that many incidents in the mind of patients, just as Freud expressed in relation to birth, might be strongly influenced by what could have happened during their intra-uterine life. He concludes:

> So. . . .? Investigate the caesura; not the analyst; not the analysand; not the unconscious; not sanity; not insanity. But the caesura, the **link**, the synapse, the (counter-trans)-ference, the transitive–intransitive mood. [*ibid.*, p. 56]

Calculus: Bion used it as part of H category, the last one in the "**vertical axis**" of the **Grid**, signifying how a **scientific deductive system** could be represented using algebraic calculus. Different signs are brought together in the algebraic calculus according to certain rules of combinations, for instance: $(a + b)^2 = a^2 + b^2 + 2ab$, which may be successively replaced by numbers following the scheme provided by this statement, a formula that will also retain a certain capacity for saturation (1963, pp. 24–25). Bion established a line of comparison between the latent content—for instance the latent content of a **dream**—and algebraic calculus, in the sense that both could be regarded as the starting point of an expansion (like free association in dreams and the successive expansion of mathematical formulas, like replacing letters with numbers) that is coherent within itself and is often found to be applicable to data of an empirically verifiable kind (1992, pp. 127–130).

Differential calculus, introduced by Galileo, Newton and Descartes, results in a satisfactory instrument useful to deal with **K**, mainly in its inanimate dimension, but it is inadequate to induce growth. It only allows accumulation of knowledge about knowledge or increment of K, but never of **O**.

Castration: Bion argues that true castration is the one the Id carries out against the ego, similar to Klein's (1931) description of the sadistic attacks made by the child, in his own phantasies, against his mother's body. Bion also refers to extremely sadistic attacks made against consciousness attached to sense organs, as well as functions such as **attention**, **notation**, **judgement**, capacity to tolerate **frustration**, and motor discharge or **action**, and most of all, the attacks made on **thinking** as seen in psychotic patients.

Catastrophic change: A concept that shows some resemblance to "catastrophe theory", introduced by René Thom, a French mathematician who refers to abrupt changes between two stable states, as a theory to explain many situations involving a rapid change of behaviour such as occurs when an attacking animal turns to flight or when a stock market crashes.

Bion relates "catastrophic change" to "subversion of the order or system of things; it is catastrophic in the sense that it is accompanied by feelings of disaster in the participants . . . [and that] it is sudden and violent in an almost physical way" (1965, p. 8). It usually occurs when a change that has taken place cannot be contained, following the container/contained theory. For instance the case of a borderline patient who, during analytical treatment, improves to the point of building up **psychotic** symptoms, which induces alarm in other people, such as the family physician, relatives and even lawyers who get involved. Bion discriminates between a pre-catastrophic and a post-catastrophic period, and evaluates the transformation between the two in three main aspects: (a) subversion of the system; (b) violence; and (c) **invariants**.

First of all there is a subversion of the system because the **analytic** setting changes from one to different persons. (a) The first or pre-catastrophic one is characterized by being theoretical, without **emotions**, devoid of major changes, and with a predominance of hypochondriacal symptoms. (b) The nature of its violence is confined to **interpretations** and analytical insight, some kind of "theoretical violence". In the post-catastrophic period, by contrast, the violence is obvious and it is present in the patient and the analyst. Hypochondriacal[12] elements however are less evident. (c) Regarding the **invariants** present in the **transformation**, Bion highlights that the patient's hypochondriacal symptoms during the previous stage have become external, for they have been transformed into suffering and anxiety (impending law-suits, mental hospitals, certification, etc.) suffered by the family, the patient and the analyst during the post-catastrophic stage. Processes during this catastrophic change correspond to the patient: Tp, $Tp\alpha$, $Tp\beta$, which represent the analyst's major preoccupation, although he also should consider his own: $T\alpha$, $Ta\alpha$, $Ta\beta$, as well as T (public), (1965, pp. 8–11) (*see* "abbreviations" at the beginning of this dictionary).

Transformations from an old system into a new one can take place without the existence of a catastrophic change; for this to happen the old system must transform and adapt to the new one. When the contrary takes place, the catastrophic change would be represented by the injury the new truth might create on the old one that has not adapted (Grotstein, 1981, p. 24).

Causality, theory of: Refers to a cause–effect correlation, or necessary sequence of events, following rational means. Corresponds to a **definitory hypothesis**, or category 1 of the **Grid** (1965, p. 79). Bion follows Hume's postulates that deny a theory of causality, because there is not a logical rationality between two events, but some kind of initial accident that turns into a compulsion afterwards. Hume conceived as a **constant conjunction** this determinant relationship of causality, where one event follows another without any logical presupposition (*ibid.*, pp. 64–65). One difficulty of this system is that it fails to discriminate between a **deductive scientific system** and

---

[12] In the text "hypochandriachal" is written several times instead of "hypochondriacal".

animism, that is, between **depressive** and **paranoid–schizoid positions.** Bion introduces the existence of two opposite systems, one related to −**K** considered as pseudo-causation, and another related to **K** or causation proper. For instance, pseudo-causation could be a chain of β-elements, or situations related to absence of objects, the "presence of an absence", like minus breasts (*see*: **point**). Bion explains:

> The patient's attention passes from one β-element to the next, all linked by a chain of pseudo-causation to deny that their "cause" or genesis lay in the destruction and dispersal of their common origin. [1965, p. 79]

Points in a line, meaning a continuous chain of events, could geometrically represent both, causation and pseudo-causation (*ibid.*, pp. 79–80).

Circle: Bion uses it as a geometrical visual image, similar to the **point** or the **line,** all considered analogous to a **pre-conception,** although belonging to category H of the **Grid,** because they represent algebraic **transformations** (1965, p. 100). Bion uses the circle as a pictorial representation of the mind. He states:

> The circle, useful to some personalities as a visual image of "inside and outside", is to other personalities, notably the **psychotic,** evidence that no such dividing membrane exists. [*ibid.*, p. 82]

It could be speculated that he is phenomenologically conceiving the mind as similar to the Möbius strip.

A line that cuts a circle, says Bion (similar to the relationship between an object and the mind), has the following possibilities:[13] (i) *Real and distinct* (or *actual and separate)*: inside the circle, in the internal world; would represent a relationship in which analyst–analysand work harmonically in search of **O** and its transformation in **K.** (ii) *Real and coincident* (or *actual and coincident*): when the line is a tangent equally inside and outside of the circle. It represents a relation dominated by feelings of omnipotence and idealization resistant to change. (iii) **Conjugate complex:** when the line

---

[13] See figure in **Complex conjugate.**

is completely outside the circle. Represents narcissism: a mirror representation in which the external is compensated by the internal; for instance, an analyst–patient interaction dominated by a **reversible perspective** (*ibid.*, p. 83).

The movement of a line around a circle, from a position inside to merely tangential touching it and then completely outside, represents a transformation. "In the domain of thought," says Bion, "where a straight line can be regarded as lying within, or touching or wholly outside, a circle, a transformation has been effected" (*ibid.*, p. 83). *See*: **line, point, conjugate complex, no-thing, no-existence, no-breast, ←↑, ↑→** .

Circular argument: Bion states "that probably any logical argument is essentially circular" (1997, p. 18). An argument of this kind can be seen in the patient who says that he feels angry because he is depressed, and when asked why is he depressed, he then answers, because he is angry. Bion classifies the "argument" in relation to the "size" of its circularity:

> I decided that the difficulties that arose depended (to extend the use of the circle as a model) on the diameter. If the circular argument has a large enough diameter, its circular character is not detected and may, for all I know, contribute to useful discoveries such as I understand the curvature in **space** to be . . . Conversely, the diameter can be so reduced that the circle itself disappears and only a **point** remains. [1997, p. 18]

A **psychotic** patient became very disturbed immediately after his twenty-two-year-old younger brother committed suicide. A very important problem with this patient was, as is often observed with psychotics, the difficulty in following the bizarre sequence of associations in his discourse. Some time later it turned out that this patient felt so close to this brother because he was trapped inside a very powerful dilemma, as a consequence of two different experiences in his life. When he was thirteen and his brother eleven, he accidentally shot him with a home-made rifle. Although he became very ill he survived. It was then understood that the confusion in his manifest discourse was the consequence of some kind of monologue. For instance, he would say one word trying to express a wish, and it was immediately followed by another word that was an anticipation of what he felt the Other—the interlocutor—wished to say. It was an attempt to avoid the aggression from the projections of a very sadistic superego. Apparently he was trapped between two different moments in his life: the present time when his brother was dead because he had committed suicide, and the past when the patient was the one who shot him but he had survived. In his monologue it seemed as if he was endlessly saying: "I shot my brother, but he didn't die, but he is dead, but I didn't shoot him" and so on. Such splitting of time was his manner of dealing with the persecutory anxiety induced by his fratricidal impulses present in the **transference** (Lopez-Corvo, 1994). The diameter reduction of the circular argument between these two incidents was so small and so fast, that it interfered with the patient's discourse making the dialogue absolutely incomprehensible.

Bion also adds:

> There is implicit in this [in the diameter size] the possibility that there must be distance between the correlated statements if meaning is to be achieved. If "madness" is feared, the operation that leads to meaning is avoided. The circular argument must therefore be of small diameter to preclude the conjunction of meaning and a feeling of madness. [1997, p. 20]

In other words, the diameter's size represents a defence against the awareness of madness: if the diameter is small there is less possibility for consciousness of being sick and less danger of **acting-out**; but if the diameter is greater and the argument acquires a sense that could lead to awareness of madness, there is then the danger of **acting-out** such as suicide.

Claustrophobia–agoraphobia: Bion says little about agoraphobia or claustrophobia; he associates them with **acting-out** using the theory of **container–contained**. Agoraphobia represents a contained outside a container, while claustrophobia represents the opposite: a contained trapped inside a container.

> Acting-out, as it is ordinarily understood, takes place "in" the analysis and analysis is then itself a part of acting-out . . . When a patient can be said to be acting-out the analysis is "in" a situation of which the boundaries are unknown. If the behaviour characterized as

"acting-out" is brought to the analysis it can be accompanied by claustrophobic symptoms in the patient. [1970, p. 110]

When the patient's acting-out is contained by the analysis as a container, the patient could feel trapped.

Clouds of probabilities: Represents an **abstract** and cryptic visual **model** Bion used just once to represent questions taking place during the session between the analyst and his patient and *vice versa*. He might be referring to a model of **psychoanalytic listening,** of "searching for a **meaning**" to take place, one of which, the **transformation O → K** could be obtained by means of an **act of faith,** similar to the model of **hallucinosis** he described in relation to **psychotic** patients.

In this model Bion imagines the existence of two **points,** one corresponding to "clouds above" and another he refers as a "hot-point in a summer's day" located below. He considers also the tension between both points. The entire model would fit in category C of the **Grid.**

At a given moment the tension could change from clouds of probabilities to clouds of possibilities, doubts, certitudes, depression, guilt, hope, fear, etc.; while the hot-point could correspond, for instance, to the analyst or the patient's genitals, dress, positions, an insect in the room, or some other location that might acquire relevance during the session. Bion compares the visual model (it could be also odoriferous, audible, etc.) with a **geometrical** model of points and **lines,** but this, he said, could be less open, more **saturated.** The important thing, he adds, is for the model to remain unsaturated "searching for a meaning": (Ψ (ζ)) (1965, pp. 117–118). *See*: **Saturated–unsaturated elements, Psi, ζ, Preconception.**

Cogitations: According to Francesca Bion, "*Cogitations*" represents the **name** given by Bion to his "own **thoughts** transferred to paper." It is also the name of a posthumous recollection of some of Bion's manuscripts (1992, p. vii). Bion's daughter, Parthenope, said that these notes were perhaps written with the purpose of **publication** at a given time, because she cannot otherwise explain why he took them with him when he moved from England to Los Angeles, and then brought them back again ten years later when he went back to England. There are also paragraphs where Bion approaches the reader directly. In this sense Green (1992), had said:

> Compared with Bion's published works, the Cogitations are thrilling to read and often less difficult to assimilate, because the author's formulations are less condensed and because he makes us witnesses to the process of the unfolding of his thought. We literally follow him. [p. 585]

Commensal relationship: Represents a **container–contained** ($♀$ $♂$) form of interaction, in which two objects share a third to the advantage of all three, for instance the relationship between a child (1) and his mother (2), where both can benefit from each other in experience as well as mental growth (3) (1962, p. 91); or the thinker who contains an idea or an invention with a purpose that is beneficial for both, the inventor and his invention. In the first place there is the sum of all the $♂$ represented as: $♂ = (♂ + ♂ + ♂)$, meaning a continual series of doubts (ideas, inventions, etc.) or variables, that are linked by emotions and could be best condensed as: $♂n$. These contents would introduce themselves (*see*: **wild thoughts**) in successive containers = $(♀ + ♀ + ♀)$ that could be better represented as $♂n + ♀n$. The possibility of learning from experience will be based on these successive fusions and integration, of $♂n + ♀n$, that should also remain open, free of rigidities and always ready for any future assimilation. Any individual whose mind works in this manner will display a capacity to retain knowledge and experience, be able to use his past experiences and be receptive to new ones. (*ibid.*, pp. 92–93). *It is obvious that K levels will depend on this kind of commensal relationship.*

Besides the commensal form of $♀$ $♂$ relationship, Bion also described the **symbiotic** and the **parasitic** one. *See*: **Container–contained, Symbiotic, Parasitic.**

Common sense: From Bion's statements about this concept, four different points of view can be conjectured: (1) a conception established from a **public** or social **vertex**; (2) a private, individual or narcissistic vision; (3) a perceptive–cognitive vertex; (4) a perceptive–**emotional** point of view.

(1) It represents a sense that is common to more than one person, or a sense used for recognition of a **fact** by more than one observer, something often used in psychoanalytical presentations (1963, p. 10); it is related, according to Bion, with concepts such as a '**selected fact**', or a '**link**' that unites facts having a deep but hidden **analogy** (1992, p. 18).

(2) Common sense could also be used from a private vertex within the individual, like "an adequate description covering an experience felt to be supported by all the senses without disharmony" (*ibid.*, p. 10). For instance, the sudden and unpredicted tactile contact with fur gives rise to the **thought** of an animal that can be confirmed visually, and finally reaches a consensus or a common sense agreement about what kind of animal the fur belongs to. It is common sense that allows the conclusion that the observed facts are really facts. Common sense would be absent in the **psychotic part of the personality**, when the delusional patient seems to have a feeling or a belief that although compatible with his own **delusion**, lacks the logical "sense" common to the rest of the observers.[14] Bion introduced this concept when he referred to his **theory of thinking**. There he said:

> The failure to bring about this conjunction of sense-data, and therefore of a commonsense view induces a mental state of debility in the patient as if starvation of **truth** was somehow analogous to alimentary starvation. [1967, p. 119]

(3) All the examples provided so far, from public as well as private points of view, belong to a cognitive vertex.

(4) In relation to a "common *emotional* vision", equivalent to a vision of common sense, Bion states:

> . . . a sense of truth is experienced if the view of an object which is hated can be conjoined to a view of the same object when it is loved and the conjunction confirms that the object experienced by different emotions is the same object. A correlation is established. [*ibid.*]

---

[14] I have referred to a similar aspect by the name of "schizoid secret", using as a paradigm the narrative of "Eleusian mysteries" (Lopez-Corvo, 1990, 1994).

This correlation corresponds, for instance, to a child's understanding that hated and loved aspects of the mother are one and the same.

Common sense or the capacity to maintain an agreement with the tenet that dominates a **group**, would be indispensable to survive within that group because, as Bion explains, the individual's welfare is secondary to the group's survival: "Darwin's theory of the survival of the fittest needs to be replaced by a theory of the survival of the fittest to survive in a group" (1992, p. 29). If the individual cannot maintain a common sense with the group, he would have to face his fear of the group, that is, to privilege narcissism over **social-ism**. When there is no common sense, there is the risk of experiencing phantasy as a fact, a sort of narcissism that would make **public-ation** impossible, because if published it would never be scientific (*ibid.*, p. 24). According to Bion, a private fact is made public within the person

> . . . when it has become a matter of common sense; that is, all his senses combine to give the same information . . . Private knowledge becomes public knowledge when the common sense of analyst and analysand agree that the perceptions of both indicate that some **idea** corresponds to an external fact independent of both observers. (*ibid.*, p. 197)

Although patients have common sense, usually they do not make good use of it: generally, common sense is the least common of all senses. The **interpretation** represents a public-ation of the analyst's private knowledge to his patient, a translation of thought into **action** and a truth shared because the common sense present in both would, in the long term, allow the cure to take place.

Nebbiosi & Petrini (2000) have introduced the **hypothesis** that common sense is what allows a contact between two persons. When contact is feared common sense is attacked giving place to megalomania, indolence and **psychosis**, but if contact is tolerated, group **communication** and sharing of knowledge and experience is possible (p. 167).

Communicable awareness: With this term Bion describes a mental state signifying to "have **knowledge**" or to "know something about":

> "Knowledge" has no meaning unless it means that someone knows something, and this . . . is an assertion of relationship . . . The term, "knowledge", I propose provisionally to employ to describe a state of mind indissolubly associated with a relationship between communicable awareness on the one hand, and the object of which the person feels thus aware, on the other. [1992, p. 271]

Bion prefers "communicable" instead of "**consciousness**", because it is possible to know something and **communicate** it without being conscious of it, or the opposite, to be conscious of something but not be able to communicate it. *See*: **Conscious awareness (Cs)**, **Awareness**.

Communication: Bion described it as the capacity to make public (*see*: **public-ation**) a private knowledge (1963, p. 92). When the analyst makes an **interpretation**, the facts implicit in it are no longer private (1965, p. 31); also, when the analyst tries to make the unconscious conscious, he is also making something private public. In the process of communication there is a complex chain of events that go from the unknown, the ineffable or **O**, to the final transformation that Bion has referred to as Tpβ (*see*: **transformation**). Take for instance, the relationship established between a landscape, the painter who reproduces it and the public capable of responding to a conveyed emotion when admiring the piece of art (*ibid.*, p. 32); similarly, the public reaction towards the presentation of a psychoanalytic paper could be related to the emotion elicited in the session at the moment of transformation of O into **K**.

Bion refers to every analyst's need to forge a private language to fabricate the interpretation, avoiding **saturation** presented by some words already worn-out by use, such as sex, fear, hostility, **transference**, etc.; or technical terminology that is usually indistinguishable from jargon, "just noises, "learnèd nonsense" (1987, p. 315).

> I think that each analyst has to go through the discipline—which cannot be provided for him by any training course that I know of—of forging his own language and keeping the words that he uses in good working order. [*ibid.*]

Complex conjugate: In mathematics a complex conjugate is represented by a pair of complex numbers whose imaginary parts are identical but differ only in sign, for example, 6 + 4i and 6 – 4i are complex conjugates. Or in simple words, they are like a mirror image of each other, a concept Bion has used to represent narcissism geometrically: –2 would be the mirror image of +2.

He gives the example of a straight line, (representing an object) which cuts a **circle** (symbolizing the mind) in two different points that could be represented as **point-pairs** (*see* figure): (1) *real and distinct*, or *actual and distinct*: inside the circle, in the internal world, would represent the analyst–analysand relationship working harmonically in search of **O** and its transformation in **K**. Inside and outside are distinguished, in a manner that the place where the object (i.e. the breast) was represented as –. (minus point), and the place where the object is: .+, coincide. (2) *Real and coincident*, or *actual and coincident*: when the line is a tangent equally inside and outside of the circle. Represents a relationship dominated by feelings of omnipotence and idealization resistant to change. (3) *Complex conjugate*: when the line is completely outside the circle. It corresponds to a narcissistic, or a mirror representation where the external is compensated by the internal; for instance, an analyst–patient interaction dominated by **reversible perspective** (1965, p. 83). *See*: **point-pair**

Concept: It represents a developmental level thinking process corresponding to category F of the **Grid's vertical axis**. Concepts are saturated elements, thoughts or fixed conceptions. *See*: **Vertical axis, Realization, Thinking, apparatus for; Thinking, theory of.**

Conception: It represents a developmental level thinking process, corresponding to category E of the **Grid's vertical axis**. Because it is the product of a combination between a **pre-conception** and a **realization**, the conception remains in **constant conjunction** with a satisfactory emotional experience (1967, p. 111). The conception could be considered as a variable that has been replaced by a constant. For instance, if a pre-conception of the breast is represented by the formula $\Psi(\zeta)$, where ζ (*see*: **psychoanalytic element**) is an empty or unsaturated (*see*: **saturated–unsaturated**) element waiting to mate with a realization with the real breast, once this realization takes place, ζ would be replaced by a constant or a **concept** (it would be set, fixed). However, because the realization is never absolute, it would allow new conceptions to remain open for further realizations and new conceptions to take place (1963, pp. 23–24). This theory reminds us of Piaget's mechanisms of "**assimilation** and accommodation". *See*: **Realization, Pre-conception, Saturated–unsaturated elements, Thinking, apparatus for; Thinking theory of, Vertical axis.**

Conjecture: From Latin *conjectura*, or act of *conjicere*, to throw together, to combine. A doubtful opinion founded on weak probabilities, supposition, presumption, **hypothesis**. In science, all experimental **truth** goes through a conjectural phase.

Conscious awareness (Cs): Originally Bion identifies "conscious awareness" with the "**apparatus of perception**". In 1956 he said:

> . . . attacks are directed against the apparatus of perception from the beginning of life. This part of his personality is cut up, split into minute fragments, and then, using the **projective identification**, expelled from the personality. Having thus rid himself of the apparatus of *conscious awareness* of internal and external reality, the patient achieves a state which is felt to be neither alive nor dead. [1967, p. 38, my italics)

This is a confusion Bion seems to have had in mind when he wrote his "commentary" (*see*: Bion, 1967) around nine years later in 1965. Here he said that it would be a mistake to use his 1956 remarks as

> C category formulations and used by the reader as "**disclosure models**". They are to be read, forgotten, but permitted to reappear, as part of the evolution peculiar to a particular psycho-analytic **emotional** situation. [*ibid.*, p. 154]

Discrimination is attempted afterwards when he tries to use geometrical abstractions in order to represent aspects of the mind and to differentiate between "being aware" and "being conscious". The former he represented with the letters Cs or the sign $\pm$ ← ↑, and would mean almost the opposite of the latter. "Being conscious" would be equivalent to the definition given by Freud (1926), of a "sense organ for the perception of psychic qualities"; being aware or Cs, on the other hand, implies a condition similar to the phototropism present in an insect, or the awareness (alertness?) of a predator looking for its prey, or someone in search of an "absent breast"; something Bion has represented as –. (minus point), or the place where the object was (*see*: **no-object, point**). ← ↑ symbolizes a direction contrary to that one normally followed by the vertical (from A to H) and horizontal (from 1 to 5) axes of the **Grid**: ↓ →, and it is equivalent to A1, that is, to the category occupied by β-elements, but not so much by a β-element as such, but to its concept, something belonging not to A1 category but to D1, D3 or D4. Cs and ← ↑ would be inseparables and amount to an unsaturated constant conjunction (Ψζ) that continuously seeks saturation, like "hunger" looking for food.

> This "consciousness" is an awareness of a lack of existence that demands an existence, a thought in search of a meaning, a definitory hypothesis in search of a realization approximating to it, a psyche seeking for a physical habitation to give existence, ♀ seeking ♂. [1965, p. 109]

-← ↑ implies a category C3, and may be personified by a non-existent "person"

> whose hatred and envy is such that "it" is determined to remove and destroy every scrap of "existence" from any object which might be considered to "have" any existence to remove. Such a non-existent object can be so terrifying that its "existence" is denied, leaving only the "place where it was". [*ibid*., p. 111]

See: **No-thing, No-breast, No-existence, Point.**

Consciousness: Bion's contributions are based on Freud's (1926) definition of consciousness as a "sense organ for the perception of psychical qualities." Following Bion's **"thinking theory"**, consciousness is an organ that depends on α-**function** to convert sense information into α-**elements**, in order to provide the mind with material to fabricate **dream-thoughts**, as well as the capacity to sleep, to be awake, to discriminate between being conscious or unconscious and to achieve a sense of self-awareness. For Bion this level of **abstraction** is originally obtained from **maternal reverie**. A baby's rudimentary consciousness is not associated with its unconscious, all self-impressions are of equal value, they are all conscious, and it is the mother's capacity for reverie, which functions as a receptor organ, where all sensations that feed the baby's consciousness will be originally processed (1967, p. 116). The baby's rudimentary conscious is not able to process its sense information, that should be evacuated inside the mother, and it will depend on her own α-function, if they are changed into α-elements or not. "By definition," says Bion, "the term conscious relates to states within the personality; consciousness of an external reality is secondary to consciousness of an internal psychic reality" (1965, p. 86).

Conscious–unconscious, relation between: In *Learning from Experience*, Bion (1962) stated that Freud's theory (1911) about consciousness being the only sense organ for the perception of psychical qualities, was not satisfactory. His argument was not against the validity of such asseveration, but against the fact that it did not discriminate between the different kinds of interactions that take place between the **conscious** and the unconscious. According to Bion, the correct **model** would be depicted by the existence of a capacity similar to the one given by **binocular vision**, whereby two views of the same object are correlated. In **psychoanalysis**, the use of both conscious and the unconscious to look at a "**psychoanalytic object**" is similar to binocular vision. In order for images to superimpose without generating double vision, one must look inwards with the unconscious eye, with the same eagerness consciousness looks outwards.

In the first place, the existing relationship between the pre-conscious and the unconscious is a **container–contained** relationship (♀ ♂) (similar to the one observed between the baby and the breast). In other words and following Bion, it would represent the interaction between a **pre-conception** and its **realization**, which results in a **conception**. The baby's instinctive need, similar to the unconscious, represents a biological **truth**, which is universal, predetermined and unchangeable. The main differences in the interaction between "container" and "contained" would be determined by the oscillations (plus + or minus –) within the **maternal reverie** and never by the baby's biological demands. The contained (♂) (or unconscious) is always the same; what changes is the container's (♀) (or conscious) attitude towards it. The fact that the truth could be well received or might represent a threat will not depend on the truth in itself, but on the one who receives it or disregards it. Such a difference would be the consequence of consciousness being dominated either by the normal or by the **psychotic part of the personality**.

Bion established the existence of a special entity between the unconscious and the pre-conscious, whose particular configuration and physiology would depend on the mind being dominated either by: (a) normal aspects; or (b) the psychotic part of the personality. In the first situation he described the existence of a "**contact barrier**", representing a structure composed by the proliferation of coherent and continuous **alpha elements**, demarking contact as well as separation between conscious and unconscious and discriminating outside from inside realities. It will perform as a kind of permeable membrane whose nature will depend on how the supply of α-elements is established, and on how they relate to each other.

If, on the other hand, the mind is controlled by the **psychotic** part of the personality, then the structure of this intermediary entity between conscious and unconscious would be organized as an **agglomeration** of **beta-elements**, he referred to this as a "**screen of beta-elements**", placed between the unconscious and the conscious and responsible for a state of confusion similar to **dreams**, as well as for the possibility of massive projections of beta-elements. These elements might induce **emotional** changes in the analyst that could determine the profile of the **countertransference** and the architecture of the **interpretation**. *See*: **Alpha-elements, Beta-elements, Alpha-function, Contact barrier, Screen of beta-elements, Agglomeration, Binocular vision, Container–contained, Maternal reverie**.

Constant conjunction: A **concept** Bion borrowed from the philosopher David Hume, to explain how an object or a fact points to another, although the ideas implicit in both are not at all related. It seems as if there is nothing logical to explain their relationship, which bears more towards a **causality** or cause–effect relation, where both were linked by experience, by accident and remain associated. Two elements are in constant conjunction, said Hume, when we infer one from the other not by reason, but from the particular experience that surrounded them, although we might fail to penetrate inside the logic of such conjunction. This concept is different from the determinism described by epigenesis (Waddington, 1957; Piaget, 1971), where fatalism is present in the progression of elements in a **narrative**, a history, or a **myth**, or in biological or geometrical structures, in the sense that each step is indispensable to the sum of the preceding steps although they are independent from the initial one. For instance, if we recite the alphabet, letter N would not be present at the beginning at all, at the level say of C, but once we reach letter M, N will be a determinant and compulsory step. In other words, the relationship is not based on chance, like the constant conjunction, it is part of a narrative where one event follows the other (like the **Oedipus myth**) fatalistically.

For Bion, constant conjunction has a **meaning** that could be represented as **Ps ← → D**, that is, according to him, it is, together with the **selected fact**, what determines the interaction between the **paranoid–schizoid** and the **depressive positions** (1965, pp. 80, 108).

The term is first mentioned in **Cogitations** in a note headed "Scientific Method" dated January 10th, 1959 (p. 13) and afterwards in "A Theory of Thinking" (1962 in *Second Thoughts*, 1967). However, it is not used in *Learning from Experience* (1962) or *Elements of Psycho-Analysis* (1963) in spite of its importance for the understanding of concepts such as "**model**", "**scientific deductive system**" or "**narrative**" and its difference from the interaction of paranoid–schizoid and depressive positions.

Constellation: An obscure concept seldom used by Bion, who described it as a term that "represents the process precipitating a constant conjunction." (1970, p. 33n) He refers to the analyst's preparation to listen to the patient without **memory** or **desire**, in order to allow a state of **at-one-ment** with the patient's discourse and for **O** to take place. The analyst will avoid remembering or desiring, but "a relevant constellation will be evoked [instead] during the process of at-one-ment with O, the process denoted by **transformation O →** **K**" (*ibid.*). It seems from this description, that "constellation" is a precursor or a catalytic state reached by the analyst while listening to the patient without memory or desire, that will allow the precipitation of constant conjunctions, in order to reach a condition of at-one-ment with O. In other words, it represents the paradox of allowing memories or associations (constant conjunctions) to take place, while avoiding remembering them. *See*: **Memory, Desire, Act of faith, O, At-one-ment, Transformation of O →K.**

Contact-barrier: In order to depict what he thought was an entity composed by the proliferation of coherent and continuous **alpha-elements**, Bion used the same term Freud used to describe a neuro-physiological unit known later as the synapse. The contact-barrier is supposed to be located amid the conscious and the unconscious, demarking their contact as well as separation between each other and discriminating outside from inside realities. It will perform as a kind of permeable membrane whose nature will depend, on how the supply of α-elements is established, and on how they relate with each other. **Alpha-function**, during wakefulness or when sleeping, changes sense impressions, related to an emotional experience, into alpha-elements. These elements as they proliferate, may cohere, agglomerate, get sequentially ordered to give the appearance of a narrative, get logically or even geometrically ordered (1962, p. 17). According to the nature of the transition from conscious to unconscious and *vice versa*, the contact-barrier could affect memory and the characteristics of some particular memories. It also defines the nature of defences, deciding the way consciousness behaves in relation to the unconscious, either repressing it or allowing it to become conscious and to be used as a thought that might reveal the **truth**.

Investigation of **psychotic** patients, or on the **psychotic part of the personality**, allowed Bion to become aware of a kind of conscious and unconscious interaction different from that observed in neurotic patients, basically a lack of resistance about unconscious elements becoming conscious, as well as a disturbance in memory processes. Such observations induced Bion to create another psychological construct he referred to as the "screen of beta-elements" or "**Beta-screen**".

Meltzer (1978) associated contact-barrier with Klein's concept of "**unconscious phantasy**" (pp. 41–42), although it could also resemble the notion of "defence" in classical theory. Unconscious phantasy, on the other hand, could be related to the concept of O introduced by Bion.

Container–contained, interaction: The clinical notion of this theory seems to have been mentioned for the first time when Bion, in his 1959 article "Attack on Linking", refers to the mother's aptitude to deal with the baby's "primary aggression and envy". Bion used several words to describe the mother's reaction: "unreceptiveness", to "remain balanced", "comfortable state of mind" and finally, when describing the **transference–countertransference** interaction with a patient, he says: "Projective identification makes it possible for him to investigate his own feelings in a personality powerful enough to *contain* them." (1967, p. 106, my italics).

The concept of "container–contained" corresponds to an abstraction **model** of psychoanalytical **realizations**, representing a **psychoanalytic element** to which Bion bestowed the signs of ♀: 'container' and ♂: 'contained', meaning feminine and masculine respectively, but without having a specific sexual connotation (1970, pp. 106). They are linked, according to the pleasure principle, to objects or concepts such as vagina–penis, mouth–breast, thinker–idea, or to models such as 'evacuation–retention', 'remembering–forgetting', etc. (*ibid.*, p. 29). The preference about when to use this model is similar to the decision of when to "include" or "exclude" something, and related to questions like "what?", "where?", "when?", or why is something included or excluded? Bion describes three different kind of links between container and contained: (a) **commensal**, (b) **symbiotic**, and (c) **parasitic** (1970, p. 95–96; 1962, p. 91).

Because of **alpha-function** operations, a baby is capable of incorporating relations of the kind present in ♀ ♂. One word could contain a **meaning**, or the opposite: a meaning could contain a word; the relationship between the two will be established following one of the forms mentioned above: "Commensal" will mean that both, container and contained benefit from each other; for instance an invention could benefit from a thinker and *vice versa*. Or it could be 'symbiotic', and then one will destroy the other, for instance the word *testify* was originally represented by Egyptian hieroglyphics with the picture of male genitalia, meaning that only men, having testicles, were qualified to bear witness. Today the meaning of the word still remains, but the concept that originally contained it disappeared. Finally the relationship could be "parasitic" where both, ♀ ♂ would destroy each other, for instance a relationship dominated by envy and revenge, that at the end will only have $-K$ as a result.

Using Jaques (1960) notion of **"integrative reticulum"**, which describes the existence of a complex mental schema that will help the mind finally to acquire the idea of a total object, Bion explains how growth, intricate and successive, between container and contained, achieves such levels of abstraction that allows the possibility of **learning from experience**. Development follows the evolution of Klein's **paranoid–schizoid** and **depressive positions**, and will require at a given moment, the presence of a **"selected fact"**. Contents ($\male$) characterize doubts, questions or variables linked by emotional experiences, that successively add to each other within the containers ($\female$), in a continuum that could be portrayed as $\male^n + \female^n$, corresponding to a process that at the end will guarantee growth and capacity to learn from experience. This learning will depend on the capacity of $\female^n$ to integrate and to keep open at the same time, free of rigidity and ready for further assimilations. An individual in whom this mechanism operates will be capable of preserving knowledge and experience, and capable of using his past experiences as well as being receptive to new ones (1962, pp. 92–93). Therefore, the level of **K** will depend on this kind of "commensal" relationship, for instance, the successive complexity of new **hypotheses** that will form systems and later on **deductive scientific systems**. Bion also relates the apparatus for thinking to **I** (Idea), assuring that the material out of which the apparatus is formed and has to deal with, is I (1963, p.31).

There is on the other hand, as was stated previously, a $\male$ $\female$ situation completely dominated by **envy**, where the result will not be K but $-K$. Under these circumstances the baby splits and projects its feelings of fear inside the breast together with envy and hate, a condition that obviously will prevent the appearance of the $\male$ $\female$ commensal relationship that will have K as a product. In this condition it is felt that the breast enviously removes all goodness and valuable **elements** that could metabolize the baby's fear of death, and in its place forces back inside denigrated residues that will determine the manifestation of a **nameless terror**, a kind of container–contained provision that Bion represents as $-K$. This condition becomes very serious when the breast not only is unable to neutralize the wish to die, but removes the wish to live (1962,

pp. 97–99), represented again by Bion as **(minus)** $-\sigma \; \female$ and qualified as a **without-ness**, meaning:

> . . . an internal object without an exterior. It is an alimentary canal
> without a body. It is a super-ego that has hardly any of the charac-
> teristics of the super-ego as understood in psycho-analysis: it is a
> "super" ego. It is an envious assertion of moral superiority without
> any morals. In short it is the resultant of an envious stripping or
> denudation of all good . . . and will continue this process till $-\sigma \; -$
> $\female$ represents hardly more than an empty superiority–inferiority
> that in turn degenerates to nullity. [1962, p. 97]

Co-operation: A form of voluntary relationship, conscious or
unconscious, that can prevail among members of a **Work group**
(W). The organization and structure induced by "co-operation" in
the **group**, would stimulate further co-operation. It is equivalent to
the concept of **valence** within the group dominated by a given **basic
assumption**.

Correlation: From Latin *correlatio*, meaning the character of two
correlative terms, where one cannot take place without the other.
There is a correlation, for instance between slim and fat, husband
and wife, etc. From the point of view of mathematics, it corresponds
to the rigid relationship presented by two variables that will occur
in a way not expected on the basis of chance alone. In geometry, for
instance, two quantities are correlated when the value of one variable determines the other; for instance, the diameter is correlated
with the surface of the **circle**. Bion introduces the possibility of
using "correlation" in **splitting**, as observed in **reversible perspective**, where the two fragmented parts correlate with each other. It
could also be observed in addictive behaviour, where the perverse
aspect correlates with the part that due to guilt, repents. There is
correlation in **binocular vision**, between conscious and unconscious, **common sense** and selected fact, **between projected and
introjected identifications**, etc. (1965, pp. 66–67).

Countertransference: From his experience with **groups**, Bion introduced the importance of the use of countertransference to formulate an **interpretation**:

It could be justly argued that interpretations for which the strongest evidence lies, not in the observed facts in the group but in the subjective reactions of the analyst, are more likely to find their explanation in the psychopathology of the analyst than in the dynamics of the group. [1948b, pp. 148–149]

Bion anticipated what later on would be expressed more concisely by Heimann (1950), Racker (1953) and Grinberg (1957) among others, on the important role played by **projective identification** in the structuring of countertransference. He said:

It is my belief that these reactions are dependent on the fact that the analyst in the group is at the receiving end of what Melanie Klein (1946) has called projective identification ... the experience of countertransference appears to me to have quite a distinct quality that should enable the analyst to differentiate the occasion when he is the object of a projective identification from the occasion when he is not. The analyst feels he is being manipulated so as to be playing a part, no matter how difficult to recognize, in somebody else's phantasy. [1948a, p. 149]

About this last aspect, Bléandonu (1994) adds:

When the **concept** of countertransference began to appear in the psychoanalytic literature of the 1950s, Bion had encountered the phenomenon a good ten years earlier. His writings on psychosis, in their originality and their density, are immediately distinctive. [p. 108]

In 1953, in his article "Notes on the theory of **schizophrenia**" (1967, pp. 23–35), Bion stated that the "Evidence for interpretations has to be sought in the countertransference and in the actions and free associations of the patient. Countertransference has to play an important part in analysis of the schizophrenic ..." (*ibid.*, p. 24). Fourteen years later in **Cogitations** (1992), in a note dated March 1967, he talks about the importance of experimenting with persecutory as well as depressive feelings, during the analytical session, before producing the interpretation:

I suggest that for a correct interpretation it is necessary for the analyst to go through the phase of "persecution" even if, as we hope, it is in a modified form, without giving an interpretation. Similarly, he must pass through the depression before he is ready to give an interpretation . . . I am fortified in this belief by the conviction that has been borne in on me by the analysis of **psychotic** or borderline patients. I do not think such a patient will ever accept an interpretation, however correct, unless he feels that the analyst has passed through this emotional crisis as a part of the act of giving the interpretation. [1992, p. 291]

Later he said: "We may assume that what the psychoanalyst says about the analysand is likely to be true of the psychoanalyst himself" (*ibid.*, p. 361).

During his conferences in Brazil in 1974–75 (1987, p. 26; 1974, pp. 87–88, 189), Bion distinguished between the conscious feelings the analyst experiences towards his patients and therefore can be used to build interpretations, and those feelings the analyst is not aware of and therefore cannot be used, unless they become conscious. *It is to these last feelings that Bion has referred as true countertransference.*

In one of his supervisions in Brazil in 1975, one of the presenting analysts expressed his difficulty in communicating with one of his patients: "I was never sure if the difficulty of establishing contact lay with me or with the patient." Bion answered the following:

That is always worth considering. But here again I think there is a fallacious argument because analysts think that they can use a countertransference. That is an inaccurate way of thinking. You can use a *feeling* you have, but countertransference you cannot use. By definition I cannot do anything about my countertransference; there is nothing to be done with it except to go to an analyst and get analysed. But most of us have to put up with the fact that there is no analyst to whom we can go. [1987, p. 26]

Similar expressions were used the previous year in Rio de Janeiro:

Countertransference is a technical term, but as often happens the technical term gets worn away and turns into a kind of worn out coin which has lost its value . . . *The theory about a countertransference is that it is the* **transference** *relationship which the analyst has to the patient without knowing he has it* . . . One cannot make use of one's countertransference in the consulting room; it is a contradiction in terms. To use the term in that way means that one would have to invent a new term to do the work, which used to be done by the word "countertransference". It is one's unconscious feelings about the patient, and since it is unconscious there is nothing we can do about it. [1990, pp. 122, my italics)

And some time later while in São Paulo, when someone asked him about the analyst making use of the countertransference to build the interpretation, Bion said:

I think it would be better to get another analyst, because the ana-lytic interpretations which are stimulated by countertransference have a good deal to with the analyst. If the analysand is lucky they may also have something to do with the analysand. Sooner or later, an analysis which is based on the countertransference will come to disaster, or at any rate failure, because all the interpretations will have little to do with the analysand and a great deal to do with the analyst. In physical **medicine** this would become apparent fairly early if the surgeon operated on the strength of countertransference and not on the strength of the anatomical and physiological find-ings. [*ibid.*, p. 191]

He also refers to the danger of counter-acting, for instance in relation to malignant murderous and sadistic **hate** devoid of insight that the patient might induce in the analyst. According to him, the lack of insight, or resistance to using it by the patient, could pro-voke similar feelings in the analyst, for instance: "damned-if-I'll-give-an-interpretation" feeling. "Why should I give him an interpretation without being given what I call 'evidence'?" (1992, p. 301). He continues as if talking to himself:

I feel a deep lethargy. I cannot see my way, and when I cannot see my way I feel no **disposition** to act as if I could, or in a way that would give substance to a reassuring phantasy that I could. *I do not know.* Nor does anyone else. It is absurdly simple really—unless one wants to complicate it. When there is nothing to do—don't do it! [*ibid.*, pp. 301–302].

It is difficult not to question the conflict, not to say confusion, Bion presents to his readers, when comparing all these remarks about countertransference, with his description of what an **act of faith** or becoming **O** consists of. One could ask the following question: Is there any sufficiently analysed analyst free from countertransference feelings, in the sense expressed by Bion, who therefore knows that when he makes an interpretation in a "state of **hallucinosis**", is "enlightened by O" or makes use of an "act of faith", he is not dealing with his own countertransference? It is possible that Bion might have discriminated between a "pathological" component, corresponding to "countertransference proper", and a "normal" one related to O and to the act of faith. Although conceptually different, such statements might be related to the demarcation made by Gitelson (1952), between the analyst's reaction to the patient as a whole (or the "analyst's transference"), and the reaction to partial aspects of the patient (or the "analyst's countertransference"); a delineation widened by Racker (1953) when he differentiated between "concordant" and "complementary" forms of countertransference.

Crossroads: Bion uses this word to designate the crossing of the roads in Thebes where **Oedipus** slays his father. It represents action or column 6 of the **Grid**. The problem, says Bion, would be to know

> ... what impulses must dominate when **thought** is translated into **action**, or from meditation into decision, or from one state of mind into another ... This struggle may be regarded indifferently as taking place within the psyche, outside it, or tangentially ... [1965, pp. 95–96]

Bion relates the "crossroads" to the paradigmatic **emotion** in all **transformations**; emotion in the sense of the **violence** implicit in the Oedipal murder, be it real or fantasy, which he symbolizes also as the penis' transformation from child to adult, represented as the "no-penis." *See*: **Conjugate complex**.

Cs: *see*: **Conscious awareness**.

Cure, the: **Psychotic** patients might use mechanisms of **splitting**, **evacuation** of the sense organs and **hallucinations** as the expression of "an ambition to be cured", a condition that will make these symptoms appear as creative activities (1967, p. 68). The "curing process" in these patients can be seriously affected by "**secondary splitting**", that is, by the repression of defences just when the

depressive position has been initiated during analytical treatment ending up in a regression to a **paranoid–schizoid** massive splitting. Dreams can be useful tools as reliable indicators of progress, in the same way they are in the analysis of non-psychotics, for instance when images of "total objects" come into view (*ibid.*, p. 80). A change to the depressive position could be rather traumatic and often induces regression or secondary splitting, with all the danger that this implies, including suicide or the impossibility of recovery (*ibid.*, pp. 80–81).

D

Dba: *see:* **Dependent (group) basic assumption.**

Deductive axiomatic system: *see:* **Scientific deductive system.**

Definitory hypothesis: Name used by Bion to designate column 1 of the **Grid**. It represents the potentiality of all distinctions as yet undeveloped, like a **group** or a conjunction needing to be bound by a **name**. It always presupposes a negative element because if we assume that something *is*, in some ways we are also assuming that it might *not* be, in another way; if we say this dictionary is about Bion we are implying that it is not about somebody else (1970, p. 24). We could imply that something is in the same manner we could imply that it is *not*, a condition that will allow an opening or the possibility to infer one or the other. For instance, if a person is capable of tolerating **frustration**, there is no **reason** for that person not to assume the possibility that something is, an attitude that will allow for it to become an **unsaturated pre-conception** open for saturation. But if on the contrary frustration intolerance is "excessive", then the individual may react against that "something" to deny and destroy its existence. A **model** could be the baby unable to tolerate weaning because being restricted by the loss of the breast, it cannot accept what is left of that loss. If the patient does not tolerate the definitory hypothesis, the pre-conception cannot be reached, something that could correspond in the Grid to D4 (1970, p. 16).

Bion has also used an ironic publication of Bishop George Berkeley about Newton's differential calculus, to emphasize this aspect of the negative element in the definitory hypothesis, using the Bishop's expression of "**ghosts of departed quantities**" (1965, pp. 157–158).

A word, like "daddy", could represent a group of facts that remain together within the word, in **constant conjunction**. Therefore, daddy could stand for a definitory hypothesis because of the group of situations that implicitly is holding together. From a mathematical point of view, says Bion, "one" (1) being the negation of the group, could be equivalent to a negative hypothesis, to a void of hypotheses; or the other way around: "the negative quality of the definitory hypothesis is a denial of the group" (1965, p. 150). Bion invented the concept of psychic **turbulence** to describe a state of expectancy and relinquishment, equivalent to column 1 of the Grid.

Ferreira (2000) suggested that what Bion said about definitory hypothesis implicitly carries the existence of three subdivisions: (a) the definition of the concept; (b) the negative aspect of that definition; and (c) the annihilation of the definitory hypothesis. (p. 186) *See*: **Grid, horizontal axis. "Ghosts of departed quanti-ties", Psychological turbulence**.

Déjà vu: Short-lived experience concerning a reduplication of **memory**. Bion tries to explain it using what he calls "fundamental rules in the use of **dreams**" or **myths**: (1) all dreams have only one **interpretation** and only one; in other words, the representations or **alpha-elements** that support dreams or myths, follow an order according to a particular **constant conjunction**; (2) every dream has a corresponding **realization** representing (like the realization of a wish) a purpose, which is usually so insignificant or so uncommon that it never takes place, but on some occasions, when the resemblance between the content of a dream and a conscious purpose is so alike, the person has the impression that what has been dreamt has been fulfilled; a mechanism observed in the **phenomenon**

known as *déjà vu*. Bion also said that **alpha-function** has two **meanings**: one will be to store up a **narrative** in the form of memories corresponding to a real experience that could be used to build a dream, and another one, experienced in dreams as well as when awake, corresponding to a *déjà vu*. [1992, p. 230)

Delusion: Represents the mechanism used by **psychotic** patients to interact with their **bizarre objects**; that is, the way in which they are "**contained**" by them, or they "contain" them (1967, p. 82). Delusions are usually associated with **pre-conceptions** in search of **conceptions**, because of their mating with **realizations** that do not approximate to pre-conceptions closely enough as to **saturate** them, but do approximate closely enough to give rise to a conception or a mis-conception. Normally, "the pre-conception requires saturation by a realization", says Bion, "that is *not* an **evacuation** of the senses but has an existence independent of the personality" (1965, p. 137). In other words, reality should be sensed as it is by its **primary qualities**, and should not be confused with projections or evacuation of the senses.

Denude: Bion used it to signify impoverishment of the personality associated with hostile and destructive impulses such as **envy**. He differentiates it from "negative **growth**" which is more related to attacks on reality or on knowledge ($-\mathbf{K}$).

Dependent basic assumption (baD): The **basic assumption** of this **group culture** stands for the ambivalence experienced between the need to create a leader on whom to depend, and at the same time the feeling that he cannot be trusted. The need to establish an individual relationship with the leader prevails, because he is felt to be the only one able to **cure** or to provide solutions. The **model** is similar to the doctor–patient or the teacher–pupil relationship. The leader could be any member of the **group** that might be willing, and at other moments, the history of the group is considered as the "**bible**". The power placed on the leader is felt to come from **magic** and not from science. Frequently, **silence** is used to try to deprive the therapist, the "scientist", from the material he might have required for his "investigation", in order to maintain the illusion of the magician. Some members consider the group to be a religious sect; also, the greed of the group might contrast with the individual's needs (1948a, pp. 74 and 78). Feelings of guilt because of greed and **depression** predominate (*ibid.*, p. 166).

Bion refers also to a variant or *dual* of baD, representing some kind of **reversible perspective**, where a group dominated by baD defends itself from the therapist's attitude of not taking responsibility for the group, by doing exactly the inverse, that is, they protect and nourish the therapist who refuses to look after them (*ibid.*, pp. 119–121). Another important aspect is the tendency of this type of group, if allowed to evolve spontaneously, to choose the sickest member as a leader, something frequently observed in many countries or in religious sects (*ibid.*, pp. 121–122). *See*: **Basic assumptions (ba)**, **Pairing ba (Pba)**, **Flight–fight ba (Fba)**, **Oscillation of baD** and **Group, Group culture**.

Depression: Bion says little about clinical depression: "Depression represents the place where the breast or any other lost object was", while the "space is where depression or any other **emotion** was" (1970, p. 10).

Depressive position (D)-paranoid–schizoid position: *see* **Depressive position**.

Desire: It is the product of an unsatisfied or **non-saturated** idea, related to the future just as **memory** is to the past, although both are linked with past sense experiences (1970, p. 45). Bion explains that the concept of wish he is interested in, does not refer to simple reminiscences or anticipations, but is related to experiences acquired through sense impressions, which are already formulated and represent evocations of feelings that contain pleasure or pain, belong to category 2 of the **Grid** and are used for **transformations** of O into K. For instance, like the wish to **cure** the patient or the need to remember **theories** that will interfere with the access to an **act of faith** representing the ultimate reality, the unknowable **truth** or O (*ibid.*, p. 30). If the psychoanalyst does not free himself from memory and desire, he faces the risk of inducing in the patient the fantasy of being **prisoner** inside the analyst's wish (*ibid.*, pp. 43–43). This is something often observed in "false-self" pathology.

Bion confesses:

For example, I think it a serious defect to allow oneself to desire the end of a session, or week, or term; it interferes with analytic work to permit desires for the patient's cure, or well-being, or future to enter the mind. Such desires erode the analyst's power to analyse and lead to progressive deterioration of his intuition. [*ibid*, p. 56]

Disclosure Model: Concept used once by Bion in 1965 when he made written comments to re-evaluate previous papers, published again in 1967 under the heading of *Second Thoughts* (1967, p. 154). "Disclosure model" was a concept coined by archbishop of Canterbury Ian T. Ramsey to describe **abstract models** used to cross meanings from one kind of observation with another one. Some of the examples he used were the discoveries of such things as "a **circle** also being a polygon with an infinite number of sides", or in relation to what is involved or to the kind of commitment implicit in a disclosure such as a surgeon finding a friend on the operating table, or even more, finding his wife. It would be like invoking an insight, a disclosure of meaning or the existence of givenness of something not appreciated previously. A certain relationship between this concept and the **selected fact**, can be evoked. *See*: **Cs**.

Dismantling: Term used by Meltzer to describe a special form of defence observed in autistic and obsessive patients, which he differentiates from mechanisms of **splitting**, where aggressive impulses are used for the purpose of destroying **linking**. A process of dismantling is characterized by an immediate and transitory suspension of mental activity, overall the **attention**. It takes place in a rather more passive than active way, like a wall that crumbles away slowly through the force of time, weather, fungi, and so on, but which could restore itself suddenly; similar to those little toys that remain upright by the tension of a thread that secures the pieces of wood together, but could tumble down if pressure is applied underneath the base and would recover its posture again once the pressure was released. Because aggression is absent, persecutory **anxiety** is also insignificant. A good example can be observed in the incapacity of autistic or obsessive patients to distinguish a person from an **inanimate** object as a consequence of dismantling or suspension of attention, which allows them to **denude** individuals from their living presence or to reduce them to a simple **non-existence**. There is a quote from Bion in relation to **psychotic** patients, in which autism is not mentioned, that shows great resemblance to what is said by Meltzer, but since Bion wrote it in a note dated 1960, nineteen years before Meltzer published his investigation on autism, it is worth reading it.

> **Evacuation** of **emotion**, evidenced by the absence of all connections that *are* emotions, leads to disintegration of the patient because that which holds the objects together is no longer available. This differs from splitting in that it is a passive falling apart of the objects. [1992, p. 161]

The absence of violence referred to by Meltzer in this kind of defence, seems more obvious in autistic rather than obsessive patients, in whom passive aggressive mechanisms are present. Dismantling is more often observed in Anglo-Saxon than in Latin cultures.

Displacement: Bion refers to displacement in time, from past events to some other situation in the immediate present, like the one observed for instance, in the **transference**. He says:

> What seems to have happened is that the immediate cause is suppressed, perhaps before it has become clear to the patient that he has [not][15] been stimulated at all [that nothing has happened]. And at once the old "**memory**" is substituted for the awareness of the current event. The subject of the early story becomes the main character, after the patient, in the current day-dream, which has been drawn across to shut out the thinking proper to the immediate reality situation. Is not this account sufficient? [1992, p. 137]

Another explanation provided by Bion is related to mechanism of **projective identification**, for instance, when a present event is projected on to someone in the past, presently absent in **time** and **space**. At the end he asks:

> In short, is it not possible that the mechanisms that Freud describes as peculiar to **dream-work** are in reality found to be operating over a wide area of the psyche and in a great number of different functional fields? [*ibid.*, pp. 137–138]

---

[15] In the original, the negative particle "not", was omitted, however since it seems not to make sense without it, it has been considered a mistake.

Disposition: Any given mental state or attitude, present in any individual as a consequence of a series of internal and external circumstances that would compel that person towards that particular way or disposition.

> A man may be disposed to **envy**, or to **violence** of **emotion**, or to regard **truth** or life highly, or to be intolerant of **frustration**. Whatever it is that causes him to be so disposed, I shall call his state of mind at the **time** he is so disposed, his "disposition". [1992, p. 262]

Dissociation: Bion used this term to describe **fragmentation** in less disturbed pathologies such as neurosis (hysteria), different from **splitting** used to illustrate minute fragmentation as observed in more severe pathologies like **psychosis** or in the **psychotic part of the personality**. Dissociation will depend on primary **verbal thoughts** that could be used, as Freud expressed it, by the body and the organs as a form of language.

Distance: Bion used the term to describe something unknown, to see coming, like the **"ghosts of a departed quantity"**, or the distance that there once was but is no longer there. He represents it by the following formula: Distance = $\Psi(\zeta)$, where (ζ) = a non-existing quantity, or where the quantity used to be or will be, but never where it is presently, like an **unsaturated** element, "an evanescent increment or departed quantity". He associates distance with **transformation** in **O**, for instance, the distance (ζ) that could exist between O and Tβ, or in other words, the **time** it will take the analyst to know (**K**) what the patient is saying, to be illuminated by insight, or for O to take place; and the time it will take before the next O takes place in the mind of the patient or the analyst. He distinguishes between one direction from the position of "not-knowing" (K), or "not-becoming" (O), to the position of "knowing" or "becoming"; and the *opposite direction*: from "knowing" or "becoming" to "not-knowing" or "not-becoming" (O or K), and so on:

> **Transformations in K** may be described loosely as akin to "knowing about" something whereas **Transformations in O** are related to becoming or being O or to being "become" by O. The *"distance"* (ζ) between O and Tβ may be artificially described in a series of stages.

Assuming a direction O→ Tβ, O can be said to "evolve" by (a) becoming manifest (or "knowable") TβK→ (b) by becoming a "reminder", an "incarnation" ... → (c) by becoming TβO or "at-one-ment". Assuming the reverse direction Tβ → O [1965, p. 163, my italics).

See: **Hyperbole**.

Donne, John: British poet (1572–1631), quoted by Bion from a short strophe of his poem "The Second Anniversary. By the occasion of the religious death of Mistress Elisabeth Drury":

Her pure and eloquent blood
Spoke in her cheeks, and so distinctly wrought,
That one might almost say, her body thought.

See: **Beta-element**.

Dream furniture: Constitutes an ambience structured by "things" similar to **bizarre objects**, which according to Bion represents the world of **psychotic** patients. Would be composed by a diffusion of sensuous particles, **ideas** or words, which being projected inside some external objects, will encyst them, either containing or being contained by them and will provide them as well with the characteristics of the projected part. For instance, if what has been projected is "sight" or "hearing", the object in question would be experienced as looking at or listening to the person. These objects represent the furniture that normally would form **dreams**, but with psychotic patients, however, it will be part of their everyday life.

Dreams: Considered a category in the **vertical axis** of the **Grid**, together with **dream thoughts** and **myths**, corresponding to row C. "They are", says Bion, "private myths" (1963, p.92), and represent an

> ... **emotional** experience ... that is an attempt to fulfil the functions which are incompatible; it is in the domain of the **reality principle** and the pleasure principle, and represents an attempt to satisfy both. That is to say, it is an attempt to achieve **frustration** evasion and frustration modification and fails in both (1992, p. 95)

Something related to Freud's statement about dreams representing wish satisfaction, a concept many psychoanalysts disagree with and Bion considers rather irrelevant. He also states that the dream manifests contents corresponding to a "narrativized collection of visual images" or **alpha-elements** organized following a **constant conjunction** (*ibid.*, p. 233).

The "sense" of a dream he explains as follows:

> One of the reasons why sleep is essential is to make possible, by a suspension of **consciousness**, the emotional experiences that the personality would not permit itself to have during conscious waking life, and so to bring them into reach of dream-work-α[16] for conversion into α-elements and a **narrative** form, consecutive and dominated by a causation-theoretical[17] outlook, suitable for being worked on by conscious rational processes of **thought**. [*ibid.*, p. 150]

Also:

> ... the core of the dream is not the manifest content, but the emotional experience; the sense data pertaining to this emotional experience are worked on by a-function, so that they are transformed into material suitable for unconscious waking thought, the dream-thoughts, and equally suitable for **conscious** submission to **common sense**. [*ibid.* p. 233]

Bion is in agreement with Freud's remark that dreams are guardians of sleep, but he differs from him on the role given to "dream-work", in that it is able to discriminate between sleeping and waking activities:

> But *Freud* meant by dream-work that unconscious material, which would otherwise be perfectly comprehensible, was transformed into a dream, and that the dream-work needed to be undone to make the now incomprehensible dream comprehensible. [*ibid.*, p. 43]

Bion thinks that it is the conscious and not the unconscious material, which is subject to dream-work, that makes it more satisfactory for storage and more suitable to be used in the transformation of the

---

[16] Afterwards Bion changes "dream work-α" to "α-function".
[17] See **Causality, theory of.**

paranoid–schizoid into the **depressive position**: "*Freud* says Aristotle states that a dream is the way the mind works in sleep: *I* say it is the way it works when awake" (*ibid.*). Bion insists that the dependence of waking life on dreams has been overlooked, for dreaming is indispensable for the storage of sense impressions acquired when awake that will then become the "contents of **memory**" (*ibid.*, p. 47).

Alpha-function, states Bion—previously known as "dream-work-α"(*ibid.*, pp. 43–49)—is necessary for the formation of dreams, which have a similar "censorship" and "resistance" function in the creation of a barrier ("**contact barrier**"), necessary to keep the unconscious from becoming conscious and to preserve the individual from a **psychotic** state: "the ability to 'dream' preserves the personality from what is virtually a psychotic state" (1962, p. 16). In this theory, dreams create the basis for a structured **thinking** that allows alpha-function to create alpha-elements.

In relation to psychotic patients, Bion compares their dreams with a hallucinatory process where the bizarre behaviour in the consulting room can be used as associations to understand the dream content, which is usually announced but never referred to, by this kind of patient (1967, p. 78). Such lack of association represents the **transference** of a hallucinated breast "that gives no milk" (1992, p. 141). Narrating a dream verbally would require a capacity to tolerate temporality as well as **causality** (*ibid.*, p. 1). Bion compares the difficulty in narrating a dream with the **phenomenon** of "**invisible–visible hallucinations**", affirming that it will take many years of analysis for these patients really to report a dream, because very often what they might be saying is that their **apparatus of perception** is compromised by trying to expel something. In this case dreams would be a "nocturnal **evacuatory** process" of the mind trying to get rid of any unpleasant thing the individual feels it has incorporated during the day, something similar to the excretory function of the bowels. Bion also insists on the relevance of vision as a mechanism of excretion, often used by psychotic patients to expel image-**ideograms** of some dreams, analogous to the means used by visual **hallucinations** (*ibid.*, pp. 66–67). Dream thoughts could also represent the undigested aspect of some event, which after being dreamed might appear as if it has been digested, a process that will allow **learning from experience**. Dreams seem to work in a manner similar to the digestive apparatus, and to analyse them would mean to examine the content of the ingested food. Different from Freud, Bion did not consider dreams to be the satisfaction of repressed impulses, but as a process of digestion of the individual's particular **truth**, something absolutely essential for the **growth** of the mind, like food is for the growth of the body. In this sense it could be said that dreaming represents a mechanism by which conscious **lies**[18] are made obvious and truth is revealed.

The presence of total objects in dreams can indicate a manifestation of mental growth, a mechanism that should be considered because

> The "peculiarity" of the dream to the psychotic is not its irrationality, incoherence, and fragmentation, but its revelation of objects which are felt by the patient to be whole objects and therefore fit and proper reason for the powerful feelings of guilt and depression which Melanie Klein has associated with the onset of the depressive position. [1967, p. 80]

Bion proposes some fundamental rules about dreams and myths: (a) "All dreams have only one **interpretation** and only one", that is, all representations or alpha-elements that organize a dream, follow an order according to a particular constant conjunction. (b) "Every dream has a corresponding **realization**, which it therefore represents." The realization would be similar to the satisfaction of a wish, but it would be so rare that it will usually never take place, with the exception of a few times when the dreamer has the illusion that the dream has come true; a mechanism also described as **déjà vu**:

> In a dream an act *appears* to have consequences; it has only sequences. What is needed is a spatial model to represent a dream. [1992, p. 1]

(c) ". . . certain factual experiences will never be understood by the patient, and therefore will never be experiences from which he can learn, unless he can interpret them in the light of his dream or the myth . . ." (1992, pp. 230–231). *See*: **Insanity, realization of,**

---

[18] Latin had provided the same basic root to mind (*mentis*) as well as to lying (*mentior*), perhaps meaning that 'the mind lies'.

Evacuation, Dream work, Dreams furniture, déjà vu, Meaningful dreams.

Dream-thought: Bion uses this concept in the same manner Freud did. In a footnote written in 1925, Freud said:

> At bottom, **dreams** are nothing other than a particular **form** of **thinking**, made possible by the conditions of the state of sleep . . . The fact that dreams concern themselves with attempts at solving the problems by which our mental life is faced is no more strange than that our conscious waking life should do so. [1900, pp. 506n–507n]

And in another footnote, from 1914:

> Thus the dream's function of "thinking ahead" is rather a **function** of preconscious waking **thought**, the products . . . **phenomena**. It has long been the habit to regard dreams as identical with their manifest content; but we must now beware equally of the mistake of confusing dreams with latent dream-thoughts. [*ibid.*, p. 580n]

Dream-thoughts, disinvested from idiomatic expressions, are visual metaphors presented as **symbolic** representations of disturbances presented during **dream-work**. They are usually made of condensations, **displacements**, and fragmented childhood **memories**, usually of a visual kind. The concrete content of dream-thoughts is gathered and elaborated during the mechanism of regression during the dream-work, leaving the analytical work to reconstruct the **links** that were destroyed during the dream-work.

Dream-work (α): The name "dream-work-α" was used by Bion originally to describe a combination of Freud's concept on "dream-work" proper, and what later became Bion's **"theory of functions"**, including α-**function** as well as **reverie** capacity, and **alpha and beta elements**. Although Bion agrees with Freud about the relevance of **dreams** in preserving sleeping in that they discriminate between sleeping and waking activities, he disagrees with him on the role of dream-work:

> But *Freud* meant by dream-work that **unconscious** material, which would otherwise be perfectly comprehensible, was transformed

into a dream, and that the dream-work needed to be undone to make the now incomprehensible dream comprehensible. [1992, p. 43]

The main difference with Freud's concept of dream-work hinges on Bion's notion that it was conscious, not unconscious material—as Freud had stated—that was subject to dream-work. The conscious material is stored as **memory** and later used to create dreams as well as to make **transformations** from the **paranoid–schizoid** to the **depressive position**. "*Freud* says Aristotle states that a dream is the way the mind works in sleep: *I* say it is the way it works when awake." (*ibid.*, pp. 43, 47)

Originally Bion referred to "dream-work-α"[19] but later on he changed it to merely "α" in order to avoid confusion with Freud's original idea (*ibid.*, p. 73); however, he continued using it in the same manner even after making such a remark. The term "α-function" was used for the first time in **Cogitations**, in a note possibly dated at the end of the sixties, which allowed Bion finally to discriminate between dream-work proper and α-function. To construct this concept Bion used Freud's "Interpretation of Dreams" (1900) and "Formulations on the Two Principles of Mental Functioning" (1911), as well as Klein's notion of guilt, superego and paranoid–schizoid and depressive positions. Before he distinguished this function from dream-work, he stated that a series of steps were essential for this function to operate: (a) to pay attention to sensuous impressions; (b) to store these impressions in the memory; (c) to change them into "**ideograms**"; and (d) depending on which principle dominated the mind, either to store them and to remember them if **reality principle** dominated, or to expel them under the ruling of the pleasure principle.

See: **Alpha-function, Alpha-elements, Beta-elements, Dreams, Dream-thoughts**.

Dream-work-α: *see*: **Alpha-function** and **Dream-work**.

---

[19] A month after suggesting the name of "dream-work-α" Bion changed it to just "α", in order to avoid confusion with Freud's original concept of "dream-work", although he felt it was too abstract.

Dual: *see:* **Reversible perspective.**

Dual of Dependence group, the: *see:* **Dependent basic assumption (baD)**

Dynamic links: Changes between categories A and H of the **vertical axis** of the **Grid**, could be of two kinds: mechanics and dynamics. Mechanical links correspond to the structure ♀♂, where a pre-conception (row D), for instance, is contained in a **conception** (row E), and this one in turn is contained in a concept (row F), and so forth. Dynamic links on the other hand, are reached by means of **H**, **L** and **K** elements. The benignity of the operation ♀♂ will depend on the nature of the dynamic link; the degree of persecutory anxiety, for instance, will be related to the interaction between the envious attacks (H) and the love relationship (L) directed towards the breast (1963, p. 34) *See:* **Link.**

E

Eckhart, Meister: *see*: Meister Eckhart.

Emotional links: Among all the possible emotional links (envy, gratitude, depression, sex, guilt, etc) that relate the self to itself and to other persons, Bion has chosen three: love (L), Hate (H) and knowledge (K). Such a selection, says Bléandonu (1994),

> . . . of L, H and K is motivated not by the need to represent the total-ity of emotional facts of the session but by the need for a key which, like a musical key, can give the value of the other elements which combine to create a statement. [p. 161]

These links signify relationships between animated objects and are considered by Bion as hypotheses+ or psychoanalytical ele-ments that portray constant conjunctions and contain all the other emotions (1963, pp. 249–250; 262–270). Each link represents what-ever it is that it should represent, although there are situations in psychotic patients or the psychotic part of the personality, where the word is no longer the representation of a thing, but the thing in itself or, following Segal (1957), a symbolic equation.

Links perform like hypotheses expressing a constant conjunction between feelings related or not to the senses: (a) "those represented by terms that are succinct hypotheses of constant conjunction of certain sense impressions", for instance to say "I hate the sea", the sea is perceived by the senses; (b) those represented by terms that are succinct hypotheses of the constant conjunction of impressions not related to the senses—for example, "I hate **depression**", depression does not have taste or odour (1992, pp. 266–267).

In cases of a wrong representation the K link might correspond to −**K** (minus K), analogous to −H or −L, although −L is not the same as H or *vice versa*. Different from physical things, psychic qualities have no sensual information; **anxiety** for instance, has no smell or taste. In this sense, Bion suggested that hypochondria might represent an attempt to establish a link with a psychic quality, when substituting physical sensations with sense information that are absent in psychic quality. Communicating with patients presents similar limitations: how do we know what patients are talking about if their anxiety has no physical qualities? The only reference we can depend on in these cases is our own, because there is no odour or taste to compare them with.

L and H may very well represent the classical notion of life and death instincts, whereas K could represent the epistemophilic instinct introduced by Klein. *See*: **L, H, K, −K (Minus K), −L (Minus L), Catastrophic change**.

Emotions: Bion represents them as Love (**L**), Hate (**H**) and their corresponding negatives: −**L**, −**H**; although −L is not equivalent to H, perhaps it could be more related to "indifference". In classical psychoanalysis they correspond to the concepts of sexual and aggressive drives. Together with knowledge (**K**), Bion regards them as passions (1963, p. 4), as well as **links** that unite persons, hypotheses or psychoanalytic elements.

Emotions deform the outline of ideation (**I** or K) (*See*: **Grid**), in a fashion similar to the one observed when a reflection on the surface of a lake is distorted by the breeze, or any other incident that produces a **turbulence**. Emotions represent complications that take place during the progress of any process dominated by ideation, as can be observed during the psychoanalytic process, which is eminently cognitive. However, during this process, emotions could act as undesired but unavoidable complications, in both the analyst and patient, in the form of **transference** and **countertransference**, that will induce true turbulence in the form of a **catastrophic change** during the process of insight.

Bion questions whether the Grid can be used for situations different from K: "It is a part of common experience that strong feelings of love and hate affect ability to discriminate and learn" (1965, p. 70) The Grid, oriented towards knowledge similar to psychoanalysis, will be disturbed like the surface of a lake, with the presence of emotions. In the horizontal axis a feeling of love could correspond to category 1, as a definitory hypothesis (*ibid.*).

Using the notion of turbulence and catastrophic change, Meltzer (1986) has defined the emotional experience as:

> . . . an encounter with the beauty and mystery of the world which arouses conflict between L, H and K, and minus L, H and K. While the immediate meaning is experienced as emotion, maybe as diverse as the objects of immediate arousal, its significance is always ultimately concerned with intimate human relationships. [p. 26]

Empirical: An empirical preposition represents what can only be known with the help of sense perceptions, by ours or those of some one we trust. Historical **facts**, the law or geographical descriptions, for instance, belong to these categories. *See*: **A priori**.

Enforced splitting: Described by Bion as a form of **splitting** resulting from a disturbed relationship with the breast, when the baby feels forced to choose between the need to suck in order to survive, and the threat of envious attacks against the breast and fear of retaliation. The dread of the destructive power of **envy** induces a splitting of the mind between psychical needs, such as love, understanding, and solace, on one hand, and material needs on the other. This splitting provokes a confusion between the need for affection and accumulation of material things as a representation of β-elements. When the person lacks an α-function to help him discriminate between **inanimate and animate** things, he then resorts to acquiring material things, one β-element after the other, endlessly (1962, pp. 10–11). This form of behaviour can be observed in the consulting room, in the interest some patients convey about material things, such as the furniture, finding it difficult to conceive themselves as "alive" persons, as well as other people who surround them. They usually come for consultation thinking of themselves as a sort of machine that is not performing properly, although ignoring its mechanism and expecting the analyst to know best, like a good "mechanic" who could fix any wrongdoing.

Envy: Bion's conception of envy is very similar to Klein's. In **Cogitations** (1992) he states that envy plays a very important role in **psychotic** patient's projections:

> *Envy* contributes to the belief that external objects are the patient's **thought**. Since he cannot admit dependence on an external object, he claims (in order ultimately to escape feeling envy) that he is, like the breast that feeds itself, the producer as well as the consumer of that on which he depends for this life. [1992, p. 120]

And some time latter:

> **Splitting** of the breast enables the infant to take the milk without understanding its dependence on the breast and the indulgence it extends to him. Such understanding involves hate and envy, and these impel attacks on the apparatus of understanding[20] to prevent the stimulation of envy—envy thus destroying envy. The attacks mean that *in effect* the breast as a source of understanding, the "mental" breast, is felt to be destroyed since no apparatus to understand it means no understanding of it, and so no "it" to understand. [*ibid.*, p. 188]

At a given time he also alludes to mechanisms of "self-envy" (Lopez-Corvo, 1992, 1994); for instance, when referring to the analysis of a patient in his article "Attacks on Linking" (1959), he said:

> This recurrent **anxiety** in his analysis was associated with his fear that envy and hatred of a capacity for understanding was leading him to take in a good, understanding object to destroy and eject it— a procedure which had often led to persecution by the destroyed and ejected object. [1967, p. 97]

---

[20] It is quite possible that the "apparatus of understanding" represented at this time what later on he named "apparatus for thinking thoughts".

And a bit further on, more explicitly:

> I said that he felt so envious of himself and of me for being able to work together to make him feel better that he took the pair of us into him as a dead piece of iron and a dead floor that came together not to give him life but to murder him. [*ibid.*]

Bion considers the existence of a primary and essential **form** of envy, capable of explaining the incapacity observed in psychotic patients to achieve satisfaction, even with the use of **hallucinations**, a mechanism based on the omnipotence of being able to provide anything, while in reality it provides nothing at all:

> Apparently [patient] X can get nothing from analysis. In feeling it is a hallucination in which he cannot have either love or hate, I am an object manipulated—like a masturbatory object—to obtain gratification but which yields none. Why is this? Does it mean that envy is primary and precludes the possibility of any gratification, even hallucinatory gratification? (1992, p. 112)

Establishment: Is defined by Bion as:

> that body of persons in the State who may be expected usually to exercise power and responsibility by virtue of their social position, wealth and intellectual and emotional endowment . . . I propose to borrow this term to denote everything from the penumbra of associations generally evoked, to the predominating and ruling characteristics of an individual, and the characteristics of a ruling caste in a **group** . . . Because of my choice of subject it will usually be used for talking about the ruling "caste" in psycho-analytic institutes. [1970, p. 73]

He also differentiates between the group and the establishment: while the main purpose of the former is to produce the **mystic**, the intention of the latter is to maintain the continuity of the group. The establishment, in other words, represents the dominant **basic assumption** (ba) that imposes itself on other basic assumptions, regardless of the group being social or therapeutic.

The advent of the genius, **mystic** or messiah is established, at least from a religious **vertex**, on the separation and preservation of such separation, between god and men, by means of mechanisms of idealization towards god and devaluation towards men. Bion describes the relationship between the group and the mystic, as a kind of **container–contained** interaction according to **commensal, symbiotic** or **parasitic** forms of associations. Paradigmatic of these dynamics are the events that surrounded the lives of Jesus and Freud, who were well appreciated while alive by their disciples as ordinary people, but were so idealized after death, that any form of criticism was unsustainable and considered a sign of heresy (1970, pp. 76, 80–81). Bion describes three progressive stages in the interaction between the group and the mystic: (1) In the first stage there is not a real confrontation between god and men because there are no differences among them. (2) During the second stage, there is a contrast between the infinitude of god and the finitude of men. (3) In the third stage, some individuals, particularly mystics, need to reaffirm a direct experience with god of which they have been, and still are, deprived by the institutionalized group (*ibid.*, p. 77).

The **communication** between the mystic and god takes place according to certain models; for instance, in the case of Christianity it is achieved by means of a "light" or a "voice". "It is significant", adds Bion, "that psychoanalysts seeking direct access to an aspect of **O** . . . conduct their affairs through language", but lacking certain sensuous support, such as **memory, desire** or understanding (*ibid.*, pp. 81–82). Followers of the mystic, who feel close to him, can demonstrate their divine origin by means of an "inalienable element" which is part of the deity, but resides within themselves and allows them to represent the establishment. The description of these dynamics is very clear and easy to follow (*see*: 1965, Chapter 7). It can be interpreted as a direct allusion to the hierarchy established within the IPA, many institutes and local associations, as well as the psychoanalytic Congresses, something possibly experienced by Bion in the British Psychoanalytical Society. *See*: **O, Mystic, Commensal, Symbiotic, Parasitic**.

Euclidian geometry: Euclid lived in Alexandria between 323 and 285 BC. Although some of his contributions are still relevant in the field of mathematics, most of his postulates related to geometry are considered inexact and have been abandoned since the nineteenth century. His work covers five axioms and five "commune notions" where he described the **point**, the **line** and the **circle**, which Bion has used, together with other geometric schemes related to projective transformations, spatially to represent myths, conflicts, symptoms, personality characteristics, patient–analyst interaction, etc. He justifies the importance of such concepts on the basis that geometry originally represented an **abstraction** from the **realization** of external **space**, and could then find its realization again in the **mental space** whence it originated. This means that geometry was initiated from practical needs, for instance having to measure the surface of a portion of land, where calculation of a triangle's surface was very useful. Afterwards, mathematics became very abstract, losing the initial connection with the human needs that originally gave them meaning (1963, pp. 88–89; 1992, pp. 203–204). "My suggestion", says Bion, "is that its *intra-psychic* origin is experience of 'the space' where a feeling, **emotion**, or other mental experience was" (1965, p. 121) (*see*: **mental space**). Bion uses geometric elements to represent biological realities such as emotions, no-emotions or anxieties of **psychotic** intensity, for instance the point (.), the line (___), ←↑, ↓→, <-.— and <-.—↑. The last four symbols represent backward movements through the axes of the **Grid** of the "line" meaning "no-penis" or the "**point**", meaning "**no-breast**".

Following Plutarch, Bion associates the **Oedipus myth** with a right-angled triangle, not only because of the triangulation of the myth, but also because of the ancient Greek's description of the triangle as a "**three-kneed-thing**" and equal legs. Onians (1951)—who could never be accused of supporting Freud's theories on sexuality—argued that the knees were frequently associated with the genitals in early Greek literature. "This has made me look", says Bion, "at Euclid's Fifth Proposition in a new light. It also makes one inclined to attempt a revaluation of the question traditionally attributed to the Sphinx" (1992, p. 202).

Bion introduces a distinction between geometric and **mathematical elements**, whereas the former are primarily associated with presence or absence, existence or non-existence of the object, the latter are related to the condition of the object itself: be it a whole, a fragmented, a total or a partial object. Also, while a "geometric space" would be associated with depression (absence–presence, separation), mathematical elements would be related to persecution and to Klein's **paranoid–schizoid position** (1965, p. 151).

Throughout a great part of his work, Bion insisted on the great advantages that the substitution of mental abstractions for geometric elements would represent for psychoanalysis. Describing what he called "the infinite universe of projection" in psychotic patients, he argues:

> For the investigation of this mental state the patient cannot, but the analyst can, employ points, lines and space. The geometer has used them for the investigation of three-dimensional space and, by the substitution of algebraic geometry for the figurative geometry of Euclid, has been able to extend his investigation to multi-dimensional space and leave Euclidean space to be used for psychological preparation for the non-Euclidean geometries now available. [1970, pp. 14–15]

Meltzer (1978), when comparing the book *Transformations* with *Elements of Psycho-Analysis*, explains the difficulty the reader has to face when dealing with mathematical signs used by Bion:

> In the present work no such hope sustains us in the face of the proliferation of mathematics-like notations, pseudo-equations, followed by arrows, dots, lines, arrows over (or should it be under?) words and not just Greek letters but Greek words. How are we to bear such an assault on our mentality? [p. 71]

See: **horizontal axis, vertical axis, Grid, Conscious awareness, mental space.**

Evacuation, process of: Mechanism used by **psychotic** patients or by the **psychotic part of the personality**, to expel **split**-off parts of the **mental apparatus** using different paths, in order to inoculate external objects (*see*: **bizarre objects**). According to this, eyes, for instance, could suck or eat, sight might be expelled through the anus or the skin and thrown away in a corner of the room, words could be seen, as could odours or other sensations (*see*: **hallucinations, delusions**). The process of evacuation could represent a mechanism to free the person from bad objects, as was originally explained by Klein. In this sense, satisfaction of a need could be equivalent to evacuation of that need. For Bion, these objects capable of being evacuated correspond to β-**elements** (1962, p. 59). *See*: **Projective identification, Maternal reverie, Beta-elements.**

Evolution: Bion distinguishes between evolution and **memory**. He defines the former as those experiences where some kind of **idea** or pictorial impression, based on experiences that do not have a sense impression but could be expressed in terms derived from sense impressions, can suddenly and unexpectedly take place or "float" in the mind; for instance to say: "I see", meaning that I intuit through a visual image. Memory, on the other hand, implies a "conscious attempt to remember something". What Bion attempts to say is that while listening to the patient's discourse, instead of remembering or wishing something, the analyst should wait with the mind open like a white sheet of paper, completely unsaturated until something "evolves" by itself and suddenly and unexpectedly floats. *See*: **memory, desire, psychoanalytic listening, O, Act of faith, K**.

Excessive projective identification: Expanding Klein's statement on "excessive projective identification", Bion in 1962 added: "I think that the term 'excessive' should be understood to apply not to the frequency only with which **projective identification** is employed but to excess of belief in omnipotence" (1967, p. 114). Meaning that "excessive" should be defined not only in relation to the quantitative but also to the qualitative aspects of the concept, to the power of omnipotence carried by the process and experienced by the receptor. Two years previously, in a note dated August 1960, Bion said that "excessive projective identification" could also refer to the 'exclusion' of other methods (function?) such as "**dream-work-α**", a term he later changed to **α-elements**. It could be questioned, however, why he did not consider the exclusive use of β-**elements** in projective identification, as "excessive" too? Although he had defined these elements previously he did not mention them again at this time. *See*: **dream-work-α, evacuation, beta-elements**.

F

Factor: Word of Latin origin meaning "the one who makes", "the author". In arithmetic it signifies each of the numbers gathered to obtain a product. From a wider conception, it represents each of the **elements** that contribute to an end result or **function** of those elements. The analysis of these factors, known as "factor analysis", represents a method of assessment of the interaction between variables in a table of **correlations**. From this point of view, Bion's **Grid** stands for a factor analysis of a correlation between **thought** evolution, represented by the "genetic" or **vertical axis** on one hand, and those functions of the mind that make use of that evolution, also referred to as "uses" or the **horizontal axis**, on the other. Bion presupposes the existence of factors in the personality able to combine to produce stable entities that he refers to as "functions of the personality" (1962, pp. 1–2) He states:

> "Function" is the name for the mental activity proper to a number of factors operating in consort. "Factor" is the name for a mental activity operating in consort with other mental activities to constitute a function. Factors are deducible from observation of the functions of which they, in consort with each other, are a part . . . Factors are deduced not directly but by observation of functions (*ibid.*)

For instance, in Bion's "psychoanalytic theory of functions", represented by Ψ (ζ), ζ represents a factor, or **unsaturated** element, or **preconception**, in search of a **realization** to build a **concept**.

Facts: External things about which we can do nothing and in consequence are not material for analysis, such as physical appearance, financial situation, etc. (1987, p. 143).

Facts not digested or dreamt: Name initially used by Bion to call β-**elements**. The initial development of these ideas as well as the concept of function and α-**elements** (the latter identified as "**dream-work** α), can be read in **Cogitations** pp. 6–8, in a note dated August 10th, 1959. *See*: **Beta-elements, Evacuation, process of, Projective identification, Psychotic and non psychotic part of the personality**.

Falsehood: Different from the truth, falseness requires a thinker or a **thought** inside a **content** (1970, p. 117). A genuine example of **O** based on falsehood and **lies could never exist**, because O represents the absolute truth of any object (*ibid.*, pp. 30, 117) *See*: **lie, O, Truth, Wild thoughts**.

Fascination: Although Bion does not elaborate further, he relates fascination to "repetition compulsion", referring to the masochistic need of a patient to search compulsively for punishment as a way out from guilt. He said: "the more profitable the more guilty and the more likely to be "fascinated"—being fascinated meaning what we would call repetition compulsion" (1974a, p. 98).

Fba: *see*: **Fight–flight (group) basic assumption**

"Felt need": A concept Bion once described in relation to "**resistance**". It represents a **countertransference** resistance experienced as a need or wish to act something out. Bion illustrated its meaning in relation to **dream interpretation**, stating that resistance in **dream-work** is a compound of two **elements**:

> resistance, as described by Freud; and a felt need to convert the conscious rational experience into **dream**, rather than a felt need to

convert the dream into conscious rational experience. The "felt need" is *very* important; if it is not given due significance and weight, the true dis-ease of the patient is being neglected; it is obscured by the analyst's insistence on interpretation of the dream. [1992, p. 184]

See: **Resistance**

Fetishism: Bion introduces the **idea** that fetishism might depend on the **form** that guilt, resulting from the feeling of attacking and destroying some objects, can be expiated by attempting unsuccessfully to revive these objects with **magic**. He explains it in the following manner: the baby dominated by the pleasure principle, would be surrounded by gratifying and alive **proto-objects**, while those objects that frustrate would be "non-existent". If intolerance to **frustration** increases, either because the level of tolerance decreases or aggression from the surrounding objects increases, or both, the need to be free from displeasure forces the baby to attack the mental apparatus responsible for the transformation of sensuous impressions into material suitable for dream thoughts, a condition that will have as a consequence that **thoughts**, not having an apparatus to process them (think them), would change into "things" (or β-**elements**). An excess of these "dead proto-objects", plus the need to placate them, induces idealization and future **transformation** into objects of adoration, providing them with super-human attributes precisely because *they are dead*.

> Contrary to common observation, the essential feature of the adored or worshipped object is that it should be dead so that crime may be expiated by the patient's dutiful adherence to animation of what is known to be **inanimate** and impossible to **animate**. This attitude contributes to the complex of feelings associated with fetishism. [1992, p. 134]

In other words, crime will be paid for by the useless dependency on those objects that by being inanimate (dead) are believed (invent them) to be animate, but because of this, they are not capable of providing anything, for instance believing that a simple statue is capable of making miracles. Fetishism as well as all religious beliefs can be explained in this manner. *See*: **Animate–inanimate, difference between, Magic, Thinking apparatus for, Proto-real objects.**

Flight and fight basic assumption: The **basic assumption** of this **group culture** stands for the need either to fight or fly from something, regardless of what might be involved; for instance the army. The **group** requires and searches for a leader capable of fulfilling the need either to fight or fly; usually individuals with paranoid traits who defend themselves from internal persecution by projecting the "enemy" outside (1948b, p. 73).

Feelings of anger and fear predominate (*ibid.*, p. 166), although Bion states that in this ba, panic, as well as the uncontainable need to escape, is in reality the same. "Panic" said Bion, "does not arise in any situation unless it is one that might as easily have given rise to rage" (*ibid.*, p. 179), that together with fear does not offer a readily available outlet:

> ... **frustration**, which is thus inescapable, cannot be tolerated because frustration requires awareness of the passage of **time**, and time is not a dimension of **basic-assumption phenomena**. Flight offers an immediately available opportunity for expression of the **emotion** in the fight–flight group and therefore meets the demand for instantaneous satisfaction—therefore the group will fly. Alternatively, attack offers a similarly immediate outlet—then the group will fight. [*ibid.*, pp. 179–180]

The group will then follow any leader capable of facilitating either immediate flight or fight. *See*: **Basic assumptions, Dependent basic assumption, Pairing basic assumption, Groups, Valence.**

Forms, theory of; or Platonic forms: The word "form" (μορφω) has been used to translate Plato's concept of "**Idea**" (ιδεα), a Greek word akin to concepts such as "look at", and extended to words like "sort", "kind" or "type", similar to the Latin word *species*, but different from the English notion of idea. What is called Plato's "theories of Forms" refers to the existence of a type or sort of "something" that exists independently whether or not something of that kind exists. For instance, the idea of a book does not have a sensory form, however it is a possibility present in any book, but only one book in particular, for example book X could change into a "**phenomenon**" and become recognizable by the senses as book X, that will represent a **realization**. Bion uses this notion to explain the **transformation** of **O** into **K**, or from **noumenon** to phenomenon, by means of a realization. In a similar way, O could be conjured up by the senses as a possibility within an individual, but could only be formulated once it is touched by a special event, a realization.

Bion states:

> As I understand the term, various phenomena, such as the appearance of a beautiful object, are significant not because they are beautiful or good but because they serve to "remind" the beholder of the beauty or the good which was once, but no longer is, known. This object, of which the phenomenon serves as a reminder, is a form. [1965, p. 138]

Bion declares that Plato presaged the **pre-conception** as well as Klein's notions of the "internal object" and his own concept of "inborn anticipations."

Platonic Ideas and Forms are "noumena", and phenomena are things that present themselves to the senses. Kant refers to "phenomena" as everything that appears in our perception and has two aspects: (a) what belongs to the external object that he refers to as "sensation"; (b) what belongs to our apparatus of perception and is capable of ordering what is perceived, something he refers to as the "form". Noumena, on the other hand, are objects of which we have no sensible intuition and hence no knowledge at all, they are **things-in-themselves**, and in a positive sense, could be conceived of as objects of intellectual **intuition**, a mode of knowledge that man does not possess. The form, says Bion, could also be presented in mystical terms like God in the **Godhead**, considered as a "spiritual substance, so elemental that we can say nothing about it" (1965, p. 139). "In this view", continues Bion, "God is regarded as a Person independent of the human mind . . . The phenomenon does not 'remind' the individual of the Form but enables the person to achieve union with an incarnation of the Godhead, or the thing-in-itself." Forms and Incarnation give the

> . . . suggestion that there is an ultimate reality with which it is possible to have direct contact although in both it appears that each direct contact is possible only after submission to an exacting discipline of relationships with phenomena, in one configuration, and incarnate Godhead in the other. [*ibid.*]

Bion presents a similar mechanism in relation to the concept of O. *See*: **Godhead, Phenomenon, O, Meister Eckhart, Noumenon, thing-in-itself.**

Fraunhofer, lines of: Joseph von Fraunhofer was a German physicist who, in the nineteenth century, classified dark lines of absorption in the solar spectrum, a condition previously discovered by William Wollaston. The absorption bands represent different wavelengths of elements present in the atmosphere of any planet capable of reflecting light.

Bion uses the Fraunhofer lines as a "rudimentary" metaphor, where the dark bands represent interferences or **turbulences** in the mind, contrasting with transparent bands indicating areas of **communication** or **at-one-ment** with the other. **Memory, desire** and understanding can be equated with opaque bands interfering with the analyst's **intuition** (1992, pp. 315–316).

Frustration, tolerance or intolerance of: When any wish conceived as a **pre-conception**, meets with the **realization** of an absent breast, depending on either genetic or acquired potentials, there are three possibilities: (a) Frustration is tolerated and the "absence" is changed into **thoughts** that modify frustration making it more tolerable. At the same time, the **conception** mating with a realization, be it negative (no-breast), or positive (good-breast), will make it possible to **learn from experience**. (b) If frustration imposed by reality is not tolerated, the mind attempts to evade as well as to dispose of the bad experiences represented by bad internal objects, by means of massive **projective identifications**. Frustration intolerance could block the development of thoughts and the capacity to think. (c) An intermediary position related to omnipotence and **omniscience**. Bion said:

> If intolerance of frustration is not so great as to activate the mechanisms of evasion and yet is too great to bear dominance of the reality principle, the personality develops omnipotence as a substitute for the mating of the pre-conception, or conception, with the negative realization. [1967, p. 114]

Such omnipotence involves omniscience as a substitute for learning from experience, making discrimination between **true** and **false** a rather dictatorial and arbitrary decision based on what is believed to be morally right or wrong; as can often be seen in many fanatical individuals. Omniscience can also be responsible for a lack of preoccupation for life, for it makes individuals incapable of discriminating between **animate and inanimate** objects, humans and machines, in relation to others and to themselves, in relation to murderous or suicidal impulses (1992, p. 248).

Functions, theory of: From Latin *functio* meaning "to perform". "Theory of function" is employed in several fields such as biology, psychology or mathematics, with different connotations. In psychoanalytic practice, the use of functions allows the construction of transitory **models**, similar to Bion's invention of the **concept** of "α-function", useful for describing some clinical observations without having to create new **theories** to the detriment of those already existent. Function and **factor** are mathematical terms used by Bion in his attempt to make psychoanalysis an empirical verifiable theory. Bion presupposes the existence of factors in the personality able to combine to produce stable entities he refers to as "functions of the personality" (1962, pp. 1–2); although a function could be considered a factor of another function of higher hierarchy or greater degree of sophistication. Bion's "psychoanalytic theory of functions" or simply "function", is represented as a "psychoanalytic theory of personality" symbolized by the Greek letter Ψ (Psi) (1962, p. 89). "**Thought**" and "α-function" are factors of Ψ. Factors could be represented by unsaturated elements symbolized by Greek letter ζ in $\Psi(\zeta)$, representing a **pre-conception** in search of a **realization** to build a **concept**.

He states:

> "Function" is the name for the mental activity proper to a number of factors operating in consort. "Factor" is the name for a mental activity operating in consort with other mental activities to constitute a function. Factors are deducible from observation of the functions of which they, in consort with each other, are a part . . . Factors are deduced not directly but by observation of functions. [*ibid.*, pp. 1–2]

Functor: Bion uses the **concept** succinctly as representing **elements** that could be considered both variables and constants: "They are variables or unknown in that they are replaceable. They are constants in that they are only replaceable by constants" (1962, p. 90): for instance, elements present in the **container–contained** interaction.

G

Generalization: Similar to **abstraction**, it represents a process according to which, **saturation** of an unsaturated element is bound with something in order to consolidate the gain and avoid losing the experience by dispersion or destruction of its components (1963, p. 85), similar to the mating of a **pre-conception** with a **realization** to create a **conception**. For instance, the notion of an **idea** is consolidated when it is bound with a word or some other sign, as observed in Hume's concept of **constant conjunction**, or in Freud (1911) when he said that **thoughts** acquire new **qualities** perceptible to consciousness, once they are bound with the rest of words (p. 226)

Genetic axis: *see*: **Grid, vertical axis of the**.

Genius: *see*: **Mystic**.

Geocentric theory: *see*: **Heliocentric theory**.

Geometric space: Stands for a **space** where a psychoanalytic empirical observation of an emotional event could find a representation when replaced by constant geometric values, for instance the **point** or the **line**, illustrating an "empty space, where the object was", or element -←↑ signifying the existence of a "greedy non-existing object". This is extremely important in most of Bion's contributions: he often argued that if geometry, as **Euclid** postulated, was origi- nally used to represent realizations in geometric space of feeling and human aspirations, it should not be odd for him to try the opposite:

> . . . if it is accepted that geometric space affords a link between unsophisticated emotional problems, their unsophisticated solu- tions and the possibility of their restatement in sophisticated terms admitting of sophisticated solutions, then it may be that musical and other artistic methods afford a similar link. [1965, p. 125]

See: **conscious awareness, space.**

"Ghosts of departed quantities": Expression used by Bishop George Berkeley (1685–1753), in his ironical criticism of Newton's presentation of the differential calculus, published in 1734 under the suggestive name of: "The Analyst, A Discourse addressed To An Infidel Mathematician". He said:

> And what are these fluxions? The velocities of evanescent incre- ments. And what are these same evanescent increments? They are neither finite quantities, nor quantities infinitely small, nor yet nothing. May we not call them the ghosts of departed quantities . . .? (Quoted by Bion, 1965, p. 156.)

Newton's differential calculus represents a **definitory hypothesis,** while Berkeley's ironical criticism can be considered as the *negative* side of that definitory hypothesis, which might be conceived as a "ghost of a departed quantity". Bion states also, that Newton's scientific contribution represents a **transformation of K** corre- sponding to column 1 of the Grid, while the Bishop's criticism was expression of fear about a **psychological turbulence**, and would correspond to column 2 of the Grid: "transformations in K are feared when they threaten the emergence of **transformations in O.** This can be restated as fear when $T\alpha \rightarrow T\beta = K \rightarrow O$." (1965, pp. 157–158). *See*: **Definitory hypothesis, Horizontal axis, Transformation of K, Transformation in O, Psychological turbu- lence, O.**

Gnomon: Early Pythagoreans used the so-called *gnomones* (γνωμωνεζ) meaning "carpenter's squares", to designate odd or even **numbers** represented by dots (perhaps pebbles) in the shape of a square. When Bion (1965, pp. 93–94) states that he will "add a 'gnomon' to the previous figure", he means that by adding dots in the shape of a square (right and upper sides), he will increase the quantities in a form seen in the figure on p. 93: from 1 to 4, to 9, to 16, and to 25. It was also a graphic way of representing square numbers with pebbles, because all of these numbers are squares: 2^2, 3^2, 4^2 and 5^2.

| 1 | 2^2 | 3^2 | 4^2 | 5^2 |

Bion uses this notion as a symbolic representation of **growth**, of accumulation, or adding something "to something or someone not specificied" (*ibid.*, p. 94).

Gnomon is also the name given to the pointer in a sundial, perhaps because of its square shape. *See*: **Growth**.

Godhead: As a proof of his theory of **O**, Bion used several hypotheses: (a) Kant's **concept** of **noumenon** or the unknown (or the **preconception**, the **thing-in-itself**, the ineffable, etc.) which could only be **intuited**, and the **phenomenon** (**conception**, object, breast, etc.), as the end result of a mating or **realization** between the noumenon and a particular object; (b) **Aristotle's theory of form**, which could be considered as the opposite, because now the phenomenon acts as a reminder of an abstract and idealized concept considered as the Form. Bion also presented some strophes from Milton's *Paradise Lost* as a paradigm of Aristotle's theory; (c) the Godhead, as it could be inferred from descriptions made by **Meister Eckhart**, Blessed John Ruysbroeck, as well as St. John of the Cross's description of his union with God in "The Ascent of Mount Carmel".

From a religious vertex the Godhead represents the "three-in-one" or Trinity and can be defined as the essence or divine nature of a person or a thing, which has been considered as reason for adoration. Bion borrows this concept as stated by Meister Eckhart, or St. John of the Cross, to explain the meaning of the ineffable, the unknown, the *aprioristic* notion of the object (the breast), the thing-in-itself, the pre-conception or O. According to Eckhart, the distinction between God sensed as "spiritual substance, so elemental that we can say nothing about it" and the Godhead where God "Incarnates" as the Trinity, is a phenomenon men can witness. In this sense, God would be the ineffable, the unknown, equivalent to O, that when incarnated (realization) produces the Godhead, trinity, phenomenon, pre-conception or **K**, analogous to the relation between the baby's need to suck and the breast. God and Godhead are different from each other like Paradise and the earth, the former is **action** but not the latter; equal to K and O, where the former is a form of **knowledge** that implies action, but O is a form of knowledge that emanates existence (1970, p. 88)

"Form" and incarnation—like O and K—suggest the existence of an ultimate reality that could be known only by submitting it to the rigour of a special discipline, such as phenomenology, religion or **psychoanalysis**. Bion quotes St. John of the Cross in "The Ascent of Mount Carmel":

> The first (night of the soul) has to do with the **point** from which the soul goes forth, for it has gradually to deprive itself of **desire** for all the worldly things which it possessed, by denying them to itself; the which denial and deprivation are, as it were, night to all the senses of man. The second reason has to do with the mean, or the road along which the soul must travel to this union—that is, **faith**, which is likewise as dark as night to the understanding. The third has to do with the point to which it travels—namely, God, Who, equally, is dark night to the soul in this life. [quoted by Bion, 1965 pp. 158–159]

In relation to psychoanalysis Bion emphasizes the importance of discipline that demands a particular way of **listening** to the patient without **memory**, desire or understanding in order, like Saint John of the Cross, "gradually to deprive itself of desire for all the worldly things", to become in O, "which is as dark as night to the understanding" (*ibid.*, 139).

See: **O, Form, Phenomenon, Noumenon, Thing-in-itself, Realization, Meister Eckhart, K, Ultimate reality, Psychological turbulence, Memory, Desire.**

Grid, the:

	Definitory Hypothesis	ψ[21]	Notation	Attention	Inquiry[22]	Action . . . n	
	1	2	3	4	5	6	
A β-elements	A1	A2				A6	
B α-elements	B1	B2	B3	B4	B5	B6	. . . Bn
C Dream Thoughts Dreams, Myth	C1	C2	C3	C4	C5	C6	. . . Cn
D Pre-conception	D1	D2	D3	D4	D5	D6	. . . Dn
E Conception	E1	E2	E3	E4	E5	E6	. . . En
F Concept	F1	F2	F3	F4	F5	F6	. . . Fn
G[23] Scientific Deductive System		G2					
H Algebraic Calculus							

---

[21] Perhaps Bion borrowed the sign ψ from the expression *proton pseudos*: "πρῶτον" (*proton*) = first; and "ψευδος" (*pseudos*) = false, to lie; possibly taken from Aristotle's Prior Analytics (Book II, Chapter 18, 66a) which deals with false premises and false conclusions, asserting that a false statement is the result of a proceeding falsity ("*proton pseudos*"). It was used by Freud (1886) in the "Project for a Scientific Psychology", to describe the importance of lying in hysterical patients. Strachey added that a Viennese physician, Max Herz, used the same term in a similar context, in a paper previously read at a congress where Freud was the secretary. (p. 352*n*)

[22] In the first Grids this column was named "Oedipus" instead of "Inquiry" (Bion, 1997p. 7).

[23] In the original Grid, files G and H were not present.

Grid, amalgamation of the: Represents the intention to unite both, the "genetic" or **"vertical axis"** and the **"horizontal axis"** or "axis of uses", by providing double attributes to some categories, for instance the **pre-conception**, which could represent both the use that can be given to a certain **statement**, as well as the genetic stage to that same statement. It would be appropriate, says Bion, to ask whether research would gain and the Grid be enhanced, if the uses and genetic stages were to be put together. In this way, for instance, columns 4 and 5 could amalgamate and be represented by the term pre-conception. At the end, Bion (1965) questions such a procedure because it would create confusion by making unnecessary a series of concepts, such as β-elements, dreams, concepts, etc. [p. 43].

Grid, as a psychoanalytic game: Bion presents the possibility of using the grid to play a psychoanalytic game, to use it in a kind of analytic make-believe in which the experiential aspect would be less determinant. He associates this "imaginative exercise" with the "activity of the musician who practises scales and exercises, not directly related to any piece of music but to the *elements* of which any piece of music is composed" (1963, p. 101).

Grid, functioning of the: The construction of the Grid, perhaps based on Mendeleev's Periodic Table, represents Bion's attempt to cross the genetic evolution of **thinking**, on the one hand, with the mind that contains and uses such evolution or transformation, on the other. He refers to it as "an instrument for classifying and ultimately understanding [psychoanalytical] **statements**" (1997, p. 13), or as a "convention for construing psycho-analytical **phenomena**. But if an analyst uses this convention he entertains a **pre-conception** of which the Grid, as printed or written, is a representation" (1963, p. 98).

The Grid usually moves from left to right and from top to bottom as thinking progresses in degrees of sophistication both in the use as well as in the level of abstraction and organization. In this way it could be said that, on a structuring level, the vertical axis follows the progressive movements of Klein's positions: **PS↔D**, while the uses, or horizontal axis, follows the mechanisms of the **container–contained (♀ ♂)**, in the sense of a mind that contains.

The Grid is described as a manifestation of the development of **K**, which is consonant with the purpose of the psychoanalytical process. "The analyst must decide whether the idea that is expressed" said Bion, "is intended to be an instrument whereby feelings are communicated or whether the feelings are secondary to the **idea**" (*ibid.*, p. 96). At the beginning he refers to **I** (idea) and later on, after he starts to use the theory of **transformation**, he changes to K. **Emotions** might disrupt the cognitive purpose of the analysis, just as the wind would disrupt the surface of a lake creating **turbulence**; the only difference would be that in the Grid both emotional and cognitive aspects are mutually affected by each other (1965, pp. 70–71).

In *Elements of Psycho-Analysis* (1963), Bion gives the impression of sometimes solving, and other times not, the "mysteries" of the Grid. He does it by bits, inducing great expectation in the reader. Some of these difficulties can be observed, for instance, when he attempts, unsuccessfully, to evaluate the Oedipus myth using the **horizontal axis of the Grid**. There he admits the possibility of having forced things by inventing pre–conceptions, and he apologizes:

> It is not my object to establish an exact correspondence ...
> Therefore to make the correspondence between the horizontal axis
> and the elements of the myth appear to be exact would be a falsifi-
> cation that obscured the nature of the myth. [1963, pp. 65–66]

The Grid's level of abstraction makes it elusive and mysterious, like something that cannot be grasped.[24] Understanding the Grid is only possible through practice, using it for what Bion has created it for; such as trying to introduce into it the content of a session, or when an analyst wishes to do some "home-work" by extra analytic meditation about a session, or wishes to enhance his intuitive deductive capacity, or simply because he is doubtful about the preciseness of the work he is doing and wishes to refer it to the Grid. The use of the Grid during the analytical session is obviously not recommended (1963, p. 73; 1977a, p. 3). On the other hand—and

---

[24] See for instance, Chapter Seventeen of *Elements of Psycho-Analysis*.

this is very important—the fact that the Grid's categories can be used in order to classify the content of a session implies that in some way we are dealing with psychoanalytic elements or "molecules".

Francesca Bion (Bion, 1997) summarizes the possible uses of the Grid in the following way:

1. to keep the analyst's intuition in training;
2. to help in impressing the work of the sessions on the memory;
3. to increase the accuracy of observations;
4. to make it easier to bridge the gap between events of an analysis and their interpretation;
5. as a "game" for psycho-analysts to set themselves exercises as a method of developing their capacity for intuition;
6. to help in developing a method of written recording analogous to mathematical communication, even in the absence of the object;
7. as a prelude to psycho-analysis, not as a substitute for it;
8. to provide a mental climbing-frame on which psycho-analysts could exercise their mental muscles;
9. as an instrument for classifying and ultimately understanding statements. [p. 5]

The Grid combines two main axes that cross each other: the Horizontal axis, marked 1 to . . .*n* columns, which represents the "mind" that "uses" thoughts and the elements in the Vertical axis. The Vertical axis consists of eight levels of evolution (A to H) showing the genetic development of thinking, from the most primitive aspects to the more complex ones. According to Bion, in the horizontal axis the terms are the same, but they can be used differently, while in the Vertical one the terms vary, but have the same use (1963, p. 87). The Grid contains **elements** that represent ideas (*I*) and feelings that can be placed inside its categories and, in turn, be capable of forming **psychoanalytic objects**.

Throughout different expositions Bion shows an ambivalent attitude towards the use of the Grid. At the beginning he frequently seems optimistic and stands up for its value. Nevertheless, at some other points, especially towards the end of his life, he seems pessimistic about its significance. In 1974, at the Rio de Janeiro conference, Bion said:

The Grid is a feeble attempt to produce an instrument. An instrument is not a theory. It is made up out of theories, just in the same way as a ruler, which is marked in inches and centimetres, has been made in conformity with a number of theories. But the ruler can be used by different people for all sorts of purposes. When I was a boy at school the teacher would say, "hold out your hand" and then use the ruler to strike the palm . . . That is about all I can claim for the Grid. Some people may be able to use it for different purposes . . . I think it is good enough to know how bad it is, how unsuitable for the task for which I have made it. But even if it inflicts a certain amount of mental pain I hope you can turn it to good account and make a better one. [1974a, p. 53]

Later on, by 1977 he says: "Nevertheless, its use [of the Grid] has made it easier for me to preserve a critical and yet informative, illuminating, attitude to my work" (1977a, p. 6). In the same year, in New York, he stated: "As soon as I had got the Grid out of my system I could see how inadequate it is . . . the satisfaction does not last for long" (1980, p. 56). When asked if it was difficult, he answered: "Not for me, only a waste of time because it doesn't really correspond with the facts I am likely to meet" (*ibid.*).

Grid, horizontal axis: Bion refers to it also as the "uses" or "schematic" axis. It represents the "mind" that "contains" thoughts, that allows them to evolve (**Vertical axis**) and uses them according to the circumstances. "The columns in this axis" says Bion, "represent the functions that a statement is being made to perform. The statement may be an oracular pronouncement, an announcement of the theme of the session . . ." (1963, p. 71). This axis is considered to be incomplete $(1 - \ldots n)$, which means it can eventually be extended. The formulations on this axis are always the same, the only thing that varies is the use that they are given. For instance, statement X could be a formulation considered to be a "**definitory hypothesis**" (column 1) used as defence, as a lie (column 2), recognized as a repetitive behaviour (column 3), that eventually might determine a certain kind of **acting-out** (column 6). The meaning varies according to the use that has been given to it, which in turn depends on the category, or column, where the formulation has been placed. The mechanism by which transition from one use of this axis $(1 \text{ to } \ldots n)$ is transformed into another seems to depend on container–contained mechanisms, while its dynamics are based on pleasure and pain (*ibid.*, p. 34).

Column 1 represents a series of definitions of various uses, such as a **myth**, or the content of a session that could represent a "definitory hypothesis", denoting that facts in it are bound by a **constant conjunction**, that they are meaningful, but have no meaning, and very important, that they are limiting because the present constant conjunction excludes all the other previously recorded. If I say "cat" for instance, such a term will represent a preposition or a constant conjunction that joins hair, colour, eyes, lives, etc.; it will be so restrictive that it will exclude all other animal characteristics,[25] it would be unique because it will exclude any other previous constant conjunction that, even if it might have represented something, will have no meaning. The content of a session constitutes a definitory hypothesis and at the same time it also represents the **transformation** of an emotional experience **O**, into a final product (Tβp), which once presented in a session and understood by the analyst will help to construct the interpretation. This also represents a definitory hypothesis that excludes any other previously given interpretation and will correspond to the analyst's final transformation product (Tβa) up to that particular moment. Ferreira (2000), introduces the possibility of subdividing this column into three parts: (a) the definitory hypothesis as such; (b) the negative aspects of the definition; (c) the annihilation of the hypothesis.

Column 2, as well as row C, could have its own grid. It is used as a false statement with the purpose of providing the patient with a theory that will act as a defensive barrier or a resistance against feared feelings or ideas, and thus oppose the appearance of a **catastrophic change** (1977a, pp. 5–6). In classical theory, column 2 would correspond to "resistance" in the patient and **countertransference** resistance in the analyst. According to Bion, in a rather abstract way, there could also be some sort of meta-defence by which, for instance, an idea, a myth or a dream corresponding to C2, would act as a defence against another idea that in turn was acting as a defence against yet another one. Or in other words, C2

---

[25] "Carried to extremes", says Bion (1963), "the term 'cat' is merely a sign analogous to the **point** as the 'place where the breast used to be' and should mean the 'no-cat' ".

would be used to inhibit a G2 (1963, p. 80). Bléandonu (1994, p. 166), suggests that this column, designated by Bion with the Greek letter ψ, could be related to the *proton pseudos* (πρῶτον ψευδος), a concept used by Freud parodying Aristotle to refer to the "first lie" present in a hysterical patient.[26] Bion distinguishes between falsities and lies:

> The false statement being related more to the inadequacy of the human being, analyst or analysand alike, who cannot feel confident in his ability to be aware of the 'truth', and the liar who has to be certain of his knowledge of the truth in order to be sure that he will not blunder into it by accident. [1977a, p. 5]

Columns 3, 4 and 5 represent statements that are less defensive and of a more **co-operative** level during the performance of the analytical work. Column 3, for instance, uses aspects related to **memory**, or **notation** of statements that might unite or relate a given constant conjunction with other constant conjunctions previously bound and registered, and in this sense, provide relatedness and coherence that could yield meaning until then unrecorded (1965, p. 98).

Column 4 refers to what Freud defined as **attention**, especially to the way in which the analyst's **listening** takes place, to free floating attention or to the search and discovery of **meaning** (*ibid.*, p. 79). It also refers to the attention given to repetition of previous propositions or constant conjunctions.

Column 5 is related to **inquiry**, curiosity, exploration or discrimination of facts related specially with search for *moral* meaning (*ibid.*, p. 79). In the first Grids Bion referred to this column as **Oedipus**, mainly because of the tenacity with which Oedipus, according to the myth, had "inquired" about the truth (1997, p. 10) (*see*: **Arrogance, curiosity and stupidity**).

Column 6 is related to **acting-out**, in the patient as well as the analyst. According to Bion, the analysis itself could sometimes also be used as a form of **acting-out**. Muscular movements or any other form of motor discharges are important because they can be intended to disburden the mind from accumulations of stimuli

---

[26] See fn [21]

(1963, pp. 71–72) (*see*: **Projective identification**). **Functions** related to the **interpretation** also fall into this category. For example, a phobic patient says she "repeats the interpretations in her mind with the purpose of not forgetting them"; such an asseveration could represent an E6 category, but if it happens that the patient repeats the interpretation to make sure she controls and "encapsulates" them as strange elements in order to evacuate them, it would then be an A6 instead. However, it could also belong to row C if it was later found that what the patient stated was a lie, if she were to say, for instance, that she has dreamed it. Bion states:

> All Grid categories may "be regarded as having the quality of Column 1 categories in that they are significant but cannot be held to have meaning until experience invests them with it. [1997a, p. 10]

Bion proposes the use of arrows in the horizontal as well as in the vertical axis, to indicate

$$\rightarrow$$

movements along the axes. For instance, 3 would mean a notation that represents **growth**

$$\leftarrow$$

while 3 would mean notation that is growth-inhibiting (1965, p. 94).

Grid, negative: *see*: **Negative Grid**.

Grid, origins of the: "This is an instrument" says Bion (1977a) of the Grid, "for the use of practising psycho-analysts", but it is not intended to be used during the working session (p. 3), it is "intended to aid the analyst in the categorization of **statements**. It is not a theory, though psycho-analytical theories have been used to construct it, but has the status of an instrument" (Bion 1997, p. 8). Several aspects must be considered regarding the **evolution** of Bion's thinking with respect to the Grid.

(A) The first ideas about the Grid can be read in Bion's 1957 article on the "Differentiation of the **Psychotic from the Non-psychotic personalities**" (pp. 45–46), where he discusses Freud's sayings (1911, p. 220) about the relationship that exists between the sense-organs that are directed towards the external world, and of the consciousness attached to them. Freud identifies "**attention**" which searches the external world comparing what is new to what is already familiar in case an urgent internal need should arise; "**notation**" which lays down the result of this periodical activity of consciousness and contributes to memory formation; "**judgement**" which has to decide what is **true** and what is **false**; "**action**", a function directed towards motor discharge under the dominance of the pleasure principle and serving as a mean of unburdening the mental apparatus of accretions of stimuli; finally, "**thinking**", as a measure to tolerate **frustration** inasmuch as it represents a way of experimental action. Along with these **theories** the Grid's systematic, horizontal or "axis of the uses" will later be established. We can conclude that this axis represents the "mind" which "contains" thinking as well as its progressive complexity, this last one represented by the vertical axis.

In *Cogitations* (1992), dated October 11th, 1959, at the end of a brief note in which he speaks of aggressive fantasies against a colleague, Bion suddenly says: "But what of mathematics and music? Geometry is a kind of visual image; music can evoke visual images" (p. 90). In the same note he suggests in a cryptic manner that his reluctance to get into [to use] music and mathematics could be caused by lack of courage[27]; that is, to take the risk of facing the reaction that the creation of a "geometric instrument" such as the Grid would produce (*ibid.*, pp. 91, 201–202). Another important argument results from the problem faced by the analyst in finding a method,

> —If there is one—by which he can be aware that he is falling into error, and even (if possible) of what kind or error he has become the victim. The search for this method constitutes for the psychoanalyst the search for a scientific method. [*ibid.*, p. 123]

(B) Later on Bion investigates a theory about thinking and determines the genetic evolution of thought that goes from β-**elements**,

---

[27] Attempts to find answers through Euclidian geometry could be inferred from Bion's use, in this passage, of the sphinx's riddle: the animal that goes on four legs in the morning, two in the afternoon and three by night. He free-associates the notion of three with a triangle and the angles where lines articulate, with the notion of genitals as Greeks had previously speculated. Was this passage an obscure way of Bion stating that to "mathematize" psychoanalysis, courage (testicles) was needed?

which constitute entities that cannot be permeated or mutated, neutral materials that can be useful only for discharge, or the **thing-in-itself,** using Kantian language, up to the complexities of mathematical thinking (*see:* **Psychic mathematics**). Along this line he elaborates the vertical or genetic axis of the Grid.

(C) In Chapter Thirteen of *Learning from Experience* (1962, pp. 38–41), Bion argues about the need to use precise formulations that at the same time enable one to maintain flexibility of facts. Such flexibility "derives from the use of variables as **factors** that can be replaced . . . by theories and concepts of fixed value" (*ibid.*, p. 38). This would be the case throughout the use of "**Function Theory**" (as could be gathered from the notion of α-**function**) inasmuch as its principles can remain unaltered even if its factors change. He believes in the necessity of establishing a solid structure, a referential theory of psychoanalysis that is flexible in action. This concept is not at all unfamiliar, after all the plasticity of **O** results from the rigidity of the analytical setting. Bion states:

> A record of sessions that showed succinctly the progress of the analysis by representing the theories employed would thus serve a purpose that was more than an aid to the analyst's memory . . . but the central problem concerns the need for a system of notation that is valuable both for recording analytic problems and working on them . . . and that can be communicated to others without serious loss of **meaning**. [*ibid.*, p. 40]

However, Bion adds that this would not be enough because developments in **psychoanalysis** require finding a formula that stores information, as mathematical notation records facts, and provides a means for calculation. Even though Bion does not specify in these arguments that he is referring to the Grid, it is obvious that he was; something supported by Francesca Bion when she said in the introduction of his posthumous work *Taming Wild Thoughts* that, "It was written after the publication of *Learning from Experience* in which the Grid is not mentioned, although Bion had been working on the idea for some time before that" (1997, p. 3).

(D) The next step is to concretize the abstract, which Bion tries out by equating concrete and tangible functions, such as the digestive system or the baby's food ingestion, to abstract functions like

thought formation and the apparatus needed to think them. According to Bion, the digestive apparatus and the apparatus of thinking have a common origin because both have to deal with sense impressions relating to the alimentary canal: the nourishment provided, or not, by the presence or absence of milk, as well as the loving or painful sensations given by the presence or absence of the "good breast", arrive at the same time.

> The infant is aware of a very bad breast inside it, a breast that is "not there" and by not being there gives it painful feelings. This object is felt to be "evacuated" by the respiratory system [also by the skin and the digestive system] or by the process of "swallowing" a satisfying breast. This breast that is swallowed is indistinguishable from a "thought" but the "thought" is dependent on the existence of an object that is actually put into the mouth. [1962, p. 57]

In this way, the breast, or the **thing-in-itself**, is equivalent to an idea in the mind, and reciprocally, indistinguishable from the thing-in-itself in the mouth. "It is clear that we have arrived at an object very closely resembling a beta-element" (*ibid.*, p. 58).

The difference between the concrete and the abstract (*see*: **abstraction**) can be seen as follows: (a) Concrete statement: there exists a breast on which to depend in order to satisfy hunger for food; (b) Abstract statement: there exists something capable of providing—and which provides—whatever and whenever is needed. Bion concludes:

> There is reason to believe that the emotional experiences associated with alimentation are those from which individuals have abstracted and then integrated elements to form theoretical deductive systems that are used as representations of realizations of thought. There is reason for using alimentary system as a model for demonstrating and comprehending the processes involved in thought. [*ibid.*, p. 62]

Grid, vertical axis: It is formed by *non*-**saturated** elements waiting for a realization, except for row A corresponding to β elements. Each stage of this axis is a record of a previous one and a preconception of the subsequent stage. Successive growth from A to H implies a difference in degrees of sophistication instead of a difference in functioning (1963, p. 87; 1965, p. 43; 1997, p. 6), similar to mechanisms of integration and disintegration described in the Kleinian **Ps ←→D** positions, where the dynamic **links,** as well as in the **horizontal axis,** are also **L, H** and **K** elements (1963, pp. 34–35) Growth of this axis will depend on the following mechanisms: (a) psycho-mechanics; (b) an alternation of particularization and **generalization** (concretization and abstraction); (c) successive saturation; and (d) emotional drives (*ibid.*, p. 84).

(A) **Psycho-mechanics** is described as a condition that takes place in the relationship that exists between projective identification and the alternation of the paranoid–schizoid and the depressive position, in relation to K. Bion considers that fragmented bits might be capable of providing integration and solutions to problems, that will facilitate the alternation present in PS ←→D and also in ♀ ♂.

(B) Particularization and generalization processes are related to **abstraction;** that is, to a process by which an element is particularized following a realization or a saturation, from where, later on, a generalization takes place. **Naming** the process and then remembering it (**notation**), will prevent the loss of the experience by dispersion or disintegration of its components.

(C) Generalization or abstraction can be understood as a process by which an unsaturated element becomes saturated. Further details about this mechanism can be found in the corresponding entrance in this dictionary under the heading **Saturated–unsaturated elements.**

(D) Bion relates emotional impulses to a premonitory state that would represent more of an emotional condition than an ideational content which is related more to a pre-conception, although similar to a pre-conception, a pre-monition is also private and unconscious. In other words, emotions are to **pre-monitions** what ideas are to pre-conceptions.

> I do not dissociate "pre-monition" from its association with a sense of warning and anxiety. The feeling of anxiety is of value in guiding the analyst to recognize the **premotion**[28] in the material. The

---

[28] My italics. Bion uses this word without giving any definition. A few lines before this quotation he said: ". . . when a patient comes for a first consultation

premonition can therefore be represented by (Anxiety (ζ)) where ((ζ)
is an unsaturated element. [1963, p. 76]

Countertransference anxiety can become a premonition that guides the analyst in his investigation and structuring of the interpretation.

Changes between A and H[29] correspond to mechanisms of ♀♂, where a pre-conception (row D), for instance, is contained in a **conception** (row E), and this one contained in a concept (row F), and so forth. **Dynamic links** between different categories in the axis are reached by means of elements **H, L** and **K**. The benignity of the operation ♀ ♂ will depend on the nature of the dynamic link; that is, the degree of persecutory anxiety will be related to the interaction between the envious attack (H) and the love relationship (L) directed towards the breast (1963, p. 34).

Bion proposes for both, horizontal and vertical axes, the use of arrows (↓→) to indicate either progression or regression from K. A downward arrow (↓) represents a movement from A to H or a progression in the direction of K, whereas the opposite (↑) or a movement from H to A, would indicate a road to β, in the direction of fragmentation and destruction of K (1965, pp.88, 99). ↑← will represent movements contrary to the progressive movement of both axes of the Grid, a kind of minus Grid. Bion also states that any existing object corresponding to the direction of these arrows: ↑←, would represent an object considered to be violent, greedy, envious,

> ruthless, murderous and predatory, without respect for the truth, person or things. It is, as it were, what Pirandello[30] might have called a Character in Search of a Author . . . This force is dominated

---

his *premotions* give information about him that cannot be obtained from other factors" (1963, p. 75). There are doubts whether this is a printing misspelling for "premonition" or a neologism implying a condition previous to an emotional state. Similar thoughts have been expressed by Dr Elizabeth Bianchedi (personal communication).state. Similar thoughts have been expressed by Dr Elizabeth Bianchedi (personal communication).

[29] Successive growth in categories that form the vertical axis, could also be understood with the use of Piagetian constructs of "Assimilation" and "Accommodation"; although never mentioned by Bion, these are well known within the ambit of genetic epistemology.

[30] Pirandello (1996). *Six Characters in Search of an Author*. London: Penguin Books.

by an envious determination to possess everything that objects that exist possess including existence itself. [*ibid.*, p. 102]

The first row (A) of the vertical axis corresponds to β-**elements**, which cover a field of confusions[31] in relation to thought and feeling. In the domain of thoughts the confusion is between them and things, similar to Segal's concept of **symbolical equation**. In the domain of feeling it might be equivalent to the confusion between **fact** and phantasy (1963, p. 97); therefore, they could only be used in columns 2 and 6 (1965, p. 44). Beta elements cannot discriminate the animate from the inanimate, nor the subject from the object or what is moral from what is scientific; they can be used as projective identifications and have a capacity for imprisonment. (*See:* **Prisoner**)

The passage from A to B, that is, from β- to α-elements, is similar to a movement from a pre-conception to a conception and will depend on ♀ ♂. Beta elements are dispersed but could acquire cohesion by means of: (a) changes in terms of Ps ←→D; (b) according to an external organizer acting as a ♀, such as the breast, that would be a model, or some other factor that resembles a selected fact; (c) other mechanisms Bion has described as "**psycho-mechanics**". Bion says:

> The cohesion of β-elements to form ♂ is analogous to the integration characteristic of the depressive position; [while] the dispersal of β-elements is analogous to the splitting and fragmentation characteristic of the paranoid–schizoid position. [1963, p. 40)

Bion also advises that any inquiry about α- or β-elements, should always involve both of them:

> β-elements and α-elements are intended to denote objects that are unknown and therefore may not even exist. By speaking of α-elements, β-elements and α-**function**, I intend to make it possible to discuss something, or to talk about it, or think about it before knowing what it is. At the risk of suggesting a meaning, when I wish the sign to represent something of which the meaning is to be an open question, to be answered by the analyst from his own experience, I

---

[31] Although Bion refers to "confusion", I wonder whether "lack of discrimination" could have been a better term.

must explain that the term "β-element" is to cover **phenomena** that may not reasonably be regarded as thoughts at all. [1997a, pp. 10–11]

And further on,

Ideally, any meaning that the term accumulates should derive from analytic practice and from analytic practice alone. Much the same is true of the α-element, except that this term should cover phenomena that are reasonably considered to be thoughts. I would regard them as elements that make it possible for the individual to have what Freud described as **dream thoughts**. [*ibid.*, p. 11]

For Bion, β-elements represent an early matrix from where thoughts are supposed to arise. They share the quality of inanimate and of psychic objects, but without any kind of distinction between them. "Thoughts are things, things are thoughts; and they have personality" (1963, p. 22). He is referring to the qualities of omnipotent magic thinking seen in **psychotic** patients, in the psychotic part of the personality, in children and in all sorts of religious beliefs.

The second row (B) corresponds to α-elements, the product of α-function. One can question whether the inference of this function on the whole genetic evolution of this axis towards the evolution of thinking, might not justify its location at the margin of the Grid. Something of this sort could be read in Bion when he states:

By the same token [that of the **reverie** function exercised by individuals within themselves as they grow] α-function may be described as concerned with the change I have associated with the conception and the concept (E and F) as I have described these entities in my exposition. [1963, p. 27]

And further on:

All the categories in the table, with the possible exception of the row B sets, may be considered to play a part, sometimes more important, sometimes less, in any psycho-analytic material. [*ibid.*, pp. 29–30]

Row C corresponds to thought categories that could be expressed in sensuous terms, usually visual images like those that appear in **dreams**, myths, **narratives**, and **hallucinations**. Bion suggests that this category should have a grid of its own (1977, p. 3).

Row D corresponds to **pre-conceptions**, which could be conceived as similar to Kant's concept of "empty thoughts" (1967, p. 111). They represent a state of mental anticipation for some kind of realization, like the baby's expectation of the breast right after birth, or the analyst's expectation as he/she figures out the meaning of the patient's manifest content, that will in turn enable the elucidation of the **unconscious phantasy** in order to structure the interpretation. Bion represents the pre-conception with the following formula: $\Psi\ (\zeta)$, where Ψ represents an incognita, the unknown, and ζ signifies an unsaturated element, which once saturated by knowledge, becomes a conception and will hence correspond to row E.

Row E represents conceptions that result from the union of a pre-conception with a realization:

> When the pre-conception is brought into contact with a realization that approximates to it, the mental outcome is a conception. [*ibid.*, p. 111]

And also:

> In this respect it may seem misleading to describe Row E as consisting of pre-conceptions to the exclusion of the remaining rows, for they are capable also of functioning as pre-conceptions. [1997, p. 11]

In summary, a conception might be considered as a variable that has been replaced by a constant.

Row F corresponds to formulations of psychoanalytic and non-psychoanalytic theory, which intend to show scientific observations. Conceptions change into concepts by a process "designed to render it free of those elements that would unfit it to be a tool in the elucidation or expression of truth" (1963, p. 24).

Row G is of little use and must wait until the psychoanalytic **scientific deductive system** develops. Something similar could be said about row H, which also may have to wait until algebraic systems build up. This row could be important in relation to research or **publication**.

Free floating attention and relaxed unsaturated listening to the patient's material, correspond to D4, that is, "attentive pre-conceptions". The comprehension of this material would imply a movement from D4 (a pre-conception) to a conception or E4.

Searching for a confirmation, comparing one material with the other, would signify a movement towards E3 and E5. Structuring the interpretation, verbalizing impressions, integrating and so on, would correspond to F5. Lastly, when the interpretation is verbalized with the intention of affecting the patient's mind, it could be placed on G6.

Meltzer (1978) has summarized how some aspects of the vertical axis function:

> . . . the "molecules" of psycho-analysis, are seen to be compounded of elements from three rows of the grid, B, C and G, that is the sensa, or alpha-elements which have been derived from the perception of the emotional experience, the myth or dream thought in which its elements are bound, and the passion of scientific deductive system into which it would grow if allowed. [p. 67]

Group: Bion has introduced substantial theoretical and clinical changes in group therapy. His experience started with the British army during the two World Wars in which he participated, but more importantly during the second, when, at the beginning of the forties, the need to treat soldiers suffering from war neurosis induced him to investigate group techniques at the Northfield Hospital in Birmingham, England. A very important innovation was the creation of "self-interpretative" or **"leaderless groups"**, where the "abstinence law" and "neutrality" of the therapist, similar to individual psychoanalysis, were maintained. Bléandonu (1994) states that the experience at Northfield was a determinant in the later development of the "therapeutic community".

Bion attempted to solve the differences between individual and group therapy when he said:

> One disadvantage of the group situation is that seeing, say, six or ten people at the same time leads one to suppose that there are six or ten discrete personalities present. In other words, the distinct physiology of the participants is so dominant that one is liable to assume that the personality is similarly bounded by physical appearance. The "dramatic" affect of having the personalities present makes one suppose that the important thing is what any individual participant is saying or doing—another **caesura**. [1987, p. 298]

In a similar fashion he affirms that, in a group, a spontaneous and common emotional reaction can take place, that will join together several individuals at a given moment, and provide the possibility of making one **interpretation**. This is typical of a group interpretation, said Bion:

> One would have to develop a sensitiveness to what seemed to be the emotion common to the majority of the group; the group analysis would have to depend on the assessment of the "gist" of an obtruding emotion. It bears a similarity to psycho-analysis, but it is not the same thing. [1974a, p. 190]

He defined "**group mentality**" according to **basic assumptions**, as an unconscious consensus of several individuals in a group, that will involuntarily neutralize all individual aspirations (1948b, p. 59). He describes three basic assumptions (ba): **dependent (baD)**, **pairing (baP)** and **fight–flight (baF)**. There is a polarization between a group level he named "sophisticated" or "**work group**" (**W**) that operates according to reality, an idea or a conscious purpose, and another level where the prosecution of that purpose or idea is emotionally undermined, corresponding to one of the three basic assumptions previously mentioned. Depending on its own dynamics, a group could change from one "ba" to another, but onceone of them dominates and becomes manifest, the others would remain latent (*ibid.* pp. 96; 146–152). *See*: ba **Dependent**, ba **Pairing**, ba **Fight–flight**, **Proto-mental system**, and **valence**.

"**Group coming together**": When a group during therapy behaves as whole, it resembles a family organization (1948a, p. 69).

Group culture: In relation to **group** dynamics, Bion considered three entities: (a) the individual; (b) the **group mentality**; and (c) the group culture, represented by those aspects of behaviour resulting from the conflict between the dominating group mentality and the individual interest. There will be three different kind of cultures: **dependence**, **fight–flight** and **pairing** (1948b, pp. 59–61). *See*: **Basic assumptions**.

Group leader: It is established as a product of **projective identification** mechanisms; responding to the group's needs and never the other way around. It is, as Le Bon (1896) said, "an automaton who has ceased to be guided by his will", and it is precisely from this capacity that according to Bion, the **group** leader derives his power (1948a, p. 177). The possibility for a member to become the leader of the group depends on his capacity to combine instantly and involuntarily ("maybe voluntarily") with every other member of his group, as well as to fulfil the necessary requirements needed to be the leader of such specific **basic assumptions** (ba). The main difference from the leader of a **work group** (W) relies on the access this leader has to external reality, whereas the basic assumption leader is confined to his specific assumption.

Group mentality: In group dynamics Bion considered three postulates: (a) the individual; (b) the group mentality; and (c) the **group culture**. Group mentality represents the "unanimous expression of the will of the group, an expression of will to which individuals contribute anonymously (1948a, p. 59) . . . unaware, influencing him disagreeably whenever he thinks or behaves in a manner at variance with the **basic assumption**" (*ibid.*, p. 65).

Growth: At one point Bion represented it with the letter Y (1962, p. 70). It can be positive or negative: $\pm Y$, depending, in the case of a pre-conception, on the sense provided by its realization. If the direction is towards the outside, towards reality (**social-ism**), towards the **primary quality** of the object, to the breast for instance, it would be $+Y$; but if the direction is egocentric or narcissistic, the growth would be $-Y$ (*ibid.*). A 38-year-old, single patient still living with his mother, struggling with ambivalence towards an internal object we had defined as the "eternal son" ($-Y$), was trying unconsciously to sublimate his dependency creating a system of hydroponics that "was *not using* earth", as a symbolism of his mother ($+Y$).

Growth can be represented, within the tendencies of the **vertical axis** of the **Grid**, according to a greater or lesser capacity for **abstraction**. Something Bion relates to Ps$\rightarrow$D, $\female$ $\male$, and to the nature of some **myths** such as: **Oedipus**, the **Tower of Babel**, the myths of Eden and the Sphinx, all related to the fear of human knowledge ($-\mathbf{K}$), that will restrict growth ($-Y$) (1963, p. 63). The vertical axis of the Grid involves a premise of growth from A to H, which according to Bion, will depend on four aspects: (a) **psycho-mechanics**; (b) alternation of particularization and **generalization** (concretization and abstraction); (c) successive **saturations**; and (d) emotional drives (*ibid.*, pp. 84–86) (*see*: **vertical axis**). The movement in the opposite direction of the Grid, from H to A and from 5 to 1, would represent a form of negative growth that Bion represents as: ↑ ←. (*See*: **Conscious awareness** or Cs).

Criteria about growth can rest on a consensus of observation, or **common sense**, about the patient's mental development, that is, that the capacity to capture reality has increased, while the obstructive forces that had induced illusion and **delusion** have diminished (1963, p. 51). Growth is a difficult **phenomenon** to assess, for both the growing object and the object that stimulates it lack growth criteria and are influenced by the **anxiety** produced by the need to obtain "results" from the analysis. Bion suggests the use of myths (row C of the vertical axis of the Grid) such as Oedipus, the Tower of Babel, the Tree of Wisdom and the Sphinx as well as the Grid, in order to measure growth and be able to find interpretations that might illuminate some of the patient's conflicts related to mental growth. "One of the advantages of reference to the grid is that grid categorization of the patient's response to interpretation should reveal growth" (*ibid.*, p. 63n). *See*: **Gnomon**.

H

H: Is a **psychoanalytic element** taken from the word "hate" that represents, together with **L** (love), one of the passions or **emotions**, and with **K** (knowledge) a dynamic **link** that by means of **container–contained** mechanisms (♀ ♂), bound the different categories of the **Grid** (1963, pp. 34–35). Bion also considers the existence of –H, –K and –L, although –H is not the same as love. In relation to classical theory, H should be equivalent to the "death **instinct**", while L would correspond to "sexual instinct" and K to Klein's "epistemophilic instinct".

Hallucination: For Bion (1967) hallucinations represent a mechanism for unburdening the psyche by the use of the sensuous apparatus in reverse (*see*: **perception in reverse**), meaning from inside to outside instead of the other way around, as perception normally operates (p. 83). He distinguished between two forms of hallucinations, both found in **psychotic** patients: "hysterical", which contain whole objects, and "psychotic" which contain elements analogous to part-objects (*ibid.*, p. 82). The difference between the two will depend on the capacity to tolerate depression.

A psychotic patient, for instance, wishes to express a **desire** as a way to discharge his mental apparatus from accretion of stimuli, but is obstructed by feelings of impotence, **envy**, and hatred that hinder the discharge and fill him with frustration. Unable to tolerate this frustration and to unburden the psyche of destructive hate and envy, the patient might try a motor discharge instead, because during childhood and under the dominion of the pleasure principle, such discharges, like a gesture, for instance, were useful. Gestures of this kind, like changes of mien or movements that can be observed during the session, are useful for constructing the interpretation. "Experience has shown the patient" said Bion, "that action of that kind achieves its purpose far more swiftly than action directed to alteration of the environment" (1967, p. 83). However, because he is unable to use mechanisms of repression (*see*: **Projective identification**), and therefore unable to free himself from those unwanted feelings, he then makes use of massive projective identifications by virtue of which his envy and murderous hatred together with bits of his personality, are projected into the real objects, creating what Bion refers to as **bizarre objects**. These objects start to "behave" according to projections and this behaviour, perceived by the sense organs as a perception in reverse, gives place to hallucinations and **delusions;** or in other words, hallucinations are the product of a change of **vertex** (1965, p. 91). The anxiety elicited by such reversion of the system of perception, leads to a destructive attack upon the perceptual apparatus, and this in consequence increases the production of hallucinations and delusions.

Hallucinations can be used as a self-providing mechanism, because even a meal or anything needed could be hallucinated, giving place to a feeling of self-sustenance and false independence, which could be experienced by the patient as superior to psychoanalysis. The patient, according to Bion, could feel that psychoanalysis is simply a method used to steal the "sustenance provided" by the goodness of hallucinations. Failure of hallucinations to provide, because they all obviously fail, is experienced by the patient as a consequence of the analyst's envy and rivalry against the power of hallucinations.

Meltzer (1986) has summarized some of Bion's contribution on the subject:

His idea [Bion's] is that the evacuation of the stimulation is mainly in one of two forms: either it is transformed into group behaviour of the type described as the **Basic Assumption** Group mentality; or it is transformed into somatic disturbance. This latter is the basis of his theory of psycho-somatic disorders. But there is a third method of evacuation which is through the sense organs themselves, by reversing their functions so that instead of taking sensa in, they give out the data as **beta-elements** which form hallucinations. [p. 105]

See: **Transformation in hallucinosis, delusion.**

Hallucination invisible–visual: *see*: **Invisible–visual hallucination.**

Hallucinosis: According to Bion (1970), this represents a state of mind considered normal and useful (analyst) as well as pathological (patient); and represents a condition, a background, where **hallucinations** could be prompted in both, i.e. in the analyst and the patients (usually psychotics). The analyst can achieve such a state of hallucinosis by abandoning memory and desire and, with the use of an "**act of faith**", can also build interpretations. Some of these concepts were already present in his paper "On arrogance" (1957a), but *Attention and Interpretation* (1970) contains his main contributions on the subject. There he said:

> This state [hallucinosis] I do not regard as an exaggeration of a pathological or even natural condition: I consider it rather to be a state always present, but overlaid by other phenomena, which screen it. If these other elements can be moderated or suspended hallucinosis becomes demonstrable; its full depth and richness are accessible only to "acts of faith". [p. 36]

And further on:

> To appreciate hallucination the analyst must participate in the state of hallucinosis ... Before **interpretations** of hallucination can be given, which are themselves **transformations O → K**, it is necessary that the analyst undergoes in his own personality the transformation O → K. By eschewing **memories, desires,** and the operations of memory he can approach the domain of hallucinosis and of the

"acts of faith" by which alone he can become at one with his patients' hallucinations and so effect transformations O → K. [*ibid.*, p. 36]

The analyst's state of hallucinosis provides a **meaning** to the patient's hallucinations, because this condition allows a situation where sensuous impressions rule over rational thinking. Bion described a **psychotic** patient, who during the analysis felt that the analyst's words, during the interpretation, flew over his head and could be detected by what Bion felt were the patterns on a cushion, and then travelled through his eyes back to him. Bion believed that what he experienced was exactly what happened inside the patient's mind, and was possible only because he as well as the patient were in a state of hallucinosis, a situation where hallucinations could take place.

Heliocentric theory: In ancient times Aristarchus of Samos introduced the "heliocentric theory", according to which, different from what is observed by the naked eye, the earth moves around the sun and not the opposite. This **theory** seemed to have disappeared for two thousand years until Copernicus established it again, struggling against the dominion of the "geocentric theory" that was supported by the church and had dominated since the time of Aristotle. Heliocentric and geocentric are two opposed theories, the first one is true but not obvious, the second one is obvious but not true. There are still remnants from the geocentric theory; when we say for instance: "I'll see you tomorrow at sunrise". Obviously, the sun does not rise, it is the earth that moves round (1992, pp. 154–156). Similarly, in the analytic situation, a patient could be a defender of the geocentric theory, meaning a **scientific deductive system** he has used all his life, which is based on the obvious, but is not true. The analyst, on the other hand, using another scientific deductive system, for example the heliocentric theory, that is based on the truth but is not obvious, attempts to convince the patient of its effectiveness in reducing mental pain. This condition resembles the situation observed in **reversible perspective**.

A patient with an important false self pathology said very apologetically after lying down: "Yesterday when I was going to sign the document to buy the new apartment I was very anxious.

Imagine being afraid about such a foolish thing . . . I thought I was doing better, but I can see that I am still failing". According to her "geocentric" position, she presupposes "in the **transference**" the existence of an idealized model that demands from her a "not anxious" behaviour as a measure of achievement—like passing a test— or the contrary, suffering from anxiety would mean a failure. In the transference this represents her thinking that the analyst is also expecting her not to experience anxiety, and will view it as a failure, if she does. Instead of the analyst going around her (heliocentric), she goes around the analyst (geocentric). Bion believes that attempting to introduce a different scientific deductive system with the use of the interpretation, will induce **turbulence**.

Horizontal axis of the Grid: *See*: **Grid, horizontal axis of the.**

Hyperbole: A rhetorical figure used to exaggerate with the purpose of convincing; for instance saying a "goddess" to describe a beautiful woman. Bion uses it in a similar fashion to signify a **constant conjunction** that involves an exaggeration in relation to feelings such as rivalry, **transference** idealization, ambition, vigour that could induce violence and projection of objects at exaggerated **distances** (1965, p. 162). He categorized hyperbole as a "**theory of observation**" (*ibid.*, p. 160) and provides an example related to the **container–contained** ($♀$ $♂$) **model**. An **emotion** representing a contained ($♂$) could be exaggerated with the purpose of motivating a container ($♀$) to contain it: "a child cries copiously to produce a consoling mother". The container—in this case the mother—has two alternatives: (a) she could constitute into a good breast and "detoxify" the feeling; (b) she might not be able to tolerate the emotion and try to evacuate it, creating a condition that would indefinitely increase: the greater the need of the contained for the container, the greater the need of the container to evacuate the feeling, in a rather exaggerated and indefinite hyperbole (*ibid.*, pp. 141–142). In another example, a patient idealized the analyst and compared him with a soothsayer who lived in Peru many years ago, a condition that represents an exaggerated projection in time (many years ago) and distance (Peru). In the **Grid**, hyperboles could correspond to categories A (β-**elements**) also C, D or E (*ibid.*, pp. 160–162).

Hypothesis: If we can find theories, for instance **quantum** mechanics, where "statistical hypotheses" have taken the place of "empirically verifiable hypotheses", would it be possible for a theory—questions Bion—in which verification by empirical observation was replaced by "hypotheses based on idealization", to be similar to "statistical hypotheses?" He distinguishes three kinds of non-empirically verifiable hypotheses: (1) "high-level, generalized and not empirically verifiable", corresponding to a strictly theoretical statement, like a theory; (2) statistical hypotheses, deduced from conceptions based on probabilities; and (3) ideal-type hypotheses based on presumptions about situations that are supposed to exist. For instance when someone says "this year in place X there will be a day of the greatest humidity", or following Bion's example, to say "excessive splitting and **projective identification** lead to a disintegration of the personality" (1992, pp. 127–128). It is ideal in the sense that such a condition represents the maximum or the ultimate in possibilities either of "higher humidity" or "excessive projective identification". This exercise was written, according to the date of the note, on February 12th, 1960, and shows Bion's initial attempt to provide the mind with that touch of precision that was so important for him. In this sense, Bion questioned:

> How does this [his previous formulations about hypotheses] compare with the **realizations** of mathematical formulas? Before attempting an answer to this, we must consider certain similarities and contrasts that emerge by comparing mathematical formulas with dreams. [*ibid.*, p. 128]

Bion also states that one word can condense so many **meanings** that it could, just by itself, represent a hypothesis, for instance "breast" or "penis" that from a personal **point of view**, may involve a **constant conjunction** (*ibid.*, pp. 250–254).

I

Ice cream or I scream: *see*: "No-breast"

Idea (I): Is a rather ambiguous concept, sometimes considered as representing a **psychoanalytic object** composed of α-**elements** product of α-**function**; also related to **reason** (R) insofar as *I* represents a bridge between a drive and its satisfaction (1963, p. 4). A bit further, it is considered as a **function** that contains **thoughts** as factors (*ibid.*, p. 30); or representing the **horizontal axis** of the **Grid**, as well as the whole Grid: "When I use the sign *I*, I mean it to represent either the whole table or any one or more of the compartments I have distinguished by co-ordinates" (*ibid.*, p. 28); so according to Bion, *I* could be put to many *uses* that could be categorized, representing the horizontal axis; but could also develop into many *stages*, meaning the **vertical axis** (*ibid.* p. 25). In relation to **container-contained**, *I* could be either (♀ or ♂) indifferently. *See*: **I (Idea)**, **K**, **L**, **H**.

Ideogram or ideograph: Word of Greek origin: *gramma* (γραμμα), meaning "letter" or "a sign that expresses an **idea**", similar to Egyptian hieroglyphics where an image does not represent what has been illustrated but something else, like the figure of a bird meaning "small" instead of "bird". Bion uses this concept to explain aspects not implicit in manifest communication; the ideogram contains what is manifest and what is latent, "what is spoken but not articulated" (1974, p. 26). Bion tries to represent the relation between what is an unconscious latent content and the manifest variable, according to the following formula: $K(\zeta)$, where **K** is a constant and ζ an unsaturated element. Bion described a **psychotic** patient who reacted with silence to the analyst attending several sessions wearing dark glasses. Bion interpreted that perhaps the glasses, like an ideograph (K), contained several meanings (ζ): they resemble the breast, they were dark because they were frowning and angry, or were dark to be able to spy on parents' sexual intercourse, or because they were dirty and smelly, and so on (1967, pp. 57, 61).

In some patients ideograms can take the form of an "ideomotor activity", like trying with a movement or a series of movements to say something without naming it (1967, p. 54), representing an attempt to free the organism of an accretion of stimuli, or the need of the **psychotic part of the personality** "for an immediate repair of an ego damaged by the excessive **projective identification**" (*ibid.*, p. 57).

Ideomotor activity: *see:* **Ideogram.**

Imaginary twin:[32] Represents the first psychoanalytical work presented by Bion at the British Psychoanalytical Society on November 1st, 1950. There he concludes that clinical findings from three of his patients were consistent with Klein's theory about the existence of an early and pregenital **Oedipus complex**. These three patients coincide in three aspects: (a) The presence of a phantasy about a twin, either completely imaginary or taken from reality, identified with the analyst or with other internal objects, and used as an obstacle to understanding mechanisms such as **splitting** or **projective identification**. This mechanism would also represent an obsessive

---

[32] The concept of the imaginary twin reminds us of Fairbairn's (1952) concept of the "internal saboteur", of Freud's (1919) work on the phenomenon of the "double" based on Rank's (1914) contributions, and more recently, of publications such as those of Aray and Bellagamba (1971), Lopez-Corvo (1980).

defence that uses a "**personification** [as a twin] of the split–off portions of his [of the patient's] personality" (1967, p. 9). The main purpose of this form of defence would be to deal with the fear that the "alive object" that cannot be controlled, would eventually threaten with separation and exclusion. (b) Existence of **elements** related to the sense of sight and in one patient with hearing, used with the purpose of exploring the environment to solve old conflicts that were always there, but whose capacity to explore was impeded due to lack of intellectual perception and the conflict with the "imaginary twin". Bion states:

> I have wondered whether the psychological development was bound up with the development of ocular control in the same way that problems of development linked with oral aggression co-exist with the eruption of teeth. [*ibid.*, p. 22]

(c) Consequently a more precise oedipal material appeared together with a greater disposition to work with it; for instance, in the first case presented, Bion remarks that the change "from a perfunctory and superficial treatment of the oedipus situation to a struggle to come to terms with an emotionally charged oedipus complex was extremely striking" (*ibid.*, p. 21).

Meltzer (1978) suggested that perhaps at the time of this presentation "Bion . . . was experiencing a sort of psychoanalytical latency period in which dutifulness was indeed dulling his creativity" (p. 17); and then adds "a preconceived theoretical framework is imposed on rather recalcitrant material" (p. 18); or in other words, that in the central issue of the imaginary twin, "sparkling bits of material appear giving evidence of Bion's restiveness under the restraint of psycho-analytical theory" (*ibid.*). Bion's attitude about Klein's work on "symbol formation", "can easily be taken for, apostolic behavior" (p. 19); only after Klein death in 1960, did Bion manage to produce his major contributions (*ibid.*).

Inaccessible mental state: Bion refers very passingly to a mental state different from conscious or unconscious states and related to the ineffable, to the presence of the unknown, like primitive events that have taken place during very early in life or in the **intrauterine** stage. Other researchers, independently of Bion and some even

previous to his work, had also referred to this subject as "fetal psychic life" (Raskovsky, 1958; Aray, 1992); and also as the "schizoid
secret" (Lopez-Corvo, 1994). Bion states:

> I am suggesting that besides the conscious and unconscious states
> of mind, there can be another one. The nearest I can get to giving it
> a provisional title is the *inaccessible* state of mind. It may become
> inaccessible because the foetus gets rid of it as soon as it can.
> Whether it is an awareness of its heartbeat, or an awareness of feel-
> ings of terror, of sound, or of sight—the kind of sight experienced
> through the pressure on the optic pits by changes of pressure in the
> intra-uterine fluid—all that may never have been what we would
> call either conscious or unconscious. [1997, p. 50][33]

In *Attention and Interpretation* (1970), there is some allusion to the
subject, but in a rather implicit manner as compared with the previous statement, which, according to Francesca Bion, was written
previously (*see*: 1997, pp. vii–viii).

> Material may be pre-verbal because the individual who seeks to ver-
> balize it has not had sufficient experience of the material to observe
> a **constant conjunction**. He is in a state analogous to that seen in a
> number of similar configurations such as: having pain without
> suffering it; not understanding planetary movement because the
> differential calculus has not been invented; not being conscious of a
> mental phenomenon because it has been repressed; not knowing an
> event because the event has not occurred. [1970, p. 11]

Inanimate: *see*: **Animate and inanimate, difference between.**

Induction: From Latin *inducere*, meaning "to drive to". From the
point of view of logic, it means to extract general conclusions from
particular facts. Bion introduces a more complex situation, where
induction might represent a way to answer questions, although
some times unsuccessfully, that has been introduced by reality
(1992, pp. 190–191). For instance, a patient might feel guilty about
the death of X, but he might deal with it by the following hypothesis

---

[33] Although there is not a precise date when this was written, Francesca Bion
believed it could have been in 1963, at the time *Elements of Psycho-Analysis* was
published (*see* 1997, pp. vii–viii).

"All men are mortal", which helps him to establish a deductive system that make him conclude that X died because of his mortality.

Bion described several steps in the process of induction, for instance in the act of creating an **interpretation**: (a) awareness of the existence of incoherent elements: (b) capacity in the observer to tolerate such incoherence; (c) to formulate a correct question dictated by **common sense**; (d) what follows could be an inspiration on observation, or the creation of a **selected fact**, or the formulation of a **hypothesis**, or rather a chain sequence that would help create a **scientific deductive system**. Such an hypothesis would show that certain elements are in **constant conjunction** and not the other way around, that is, that elements in constant conjunction give place to a hypothesis. There should be a movement from high-level to low-level hypotheses, decreasing generalization until a particularization is reached, one that is open to validation by empirical testing; (e) the social aspect of the process, the **public-ation** (finally phrasing the interpretation) as something essential and not as an accident (1992, p. 195) (*see*; **psychoanalytic listening, interpretation**).

Inner reproductive system: Bion refers to this concept as the "mental counterpart" of: (a) "the reproductory system", analogous to an "inward eye", "visualizing", or "seeing in imagination", etc.; (b) representing also a counterpart of the "visual system" (1965, p. 91). It should not be confused with "**awareness** of reproductory activity" either; in much the same manner as visual images related with the mental counterpart of vision, should not be mixed up with visual objects. The mental counterpart of the reproductory system is related to **premonitions** of pain and pleasure. Although Bion has not mentioned it, it could be speculated that this concept might be akin to what has been referred to as "feminine intuition" (*ibid.*). *See*: **Intuit, O, Act of faith**.

Inquiry: Represents column 5 on the **horizontal axis** of the **Grid**, and is a word that precisely describes its purpose, that is, the increasing curiosity to understand the last "issue of the matter", of the unconscious; this perhaps explains why Bion originally decided to use the name of "**Oedipus**" to designate it. Parthenope Bion, in her introduction to *Taming Wild Thoughts*, a book posthumously edited by Francesca Bion, discusses this change:

> . . . the Grid itself has a slight change in it: in the paper printed here, Column 5 is indicated as Oedipus, whereas the Grid printed in *Elements of Psycho-Analysis* and onwards has this column labelled as Inquiry, as though the author had decided to opt for the more general category, of which "Oedipus" is simply a special case, as the discussion of this column in the book shows. [1997, pp. vii–viii]

Insanity, realization of: (*see*: "Notes on the theory of schizophrenia", 1967, pp. 33–34). If psychoanalytic treatment has been successful in helping a **psychotic** patient to solve processes of massive **splitting**, to improve their ego and their object integration, as well as to give them a greater awareness of reality and a proper articulation of **verbal thought**, the analyst, alerts Bion, should be prepared to face an even more difficult situation. He says:

> What takes place, if the analyst has been reasonably successful, is a realization by the patient of psychic reality; he realizes that he has **hallucinations** and delusions, may feel unable to take food, and have difficulty with sleep. [1967, pp. 33–34]

The patient feels hatred for the analyst, whom he blames for everything bad that is happening to him. The analyst, on the other hand, would have to reassure the family, now concerned about the patient's welfare, and to keep distant the surgeon and electroshock therapist who would like to profit from the situation. But the most important situation, according to Bion, would be to avoid the patient's rejection of the awareness he now has of being "crazy" and of the **transference** hatred against someone he feels was courageous enough finally to bring him to face all he had been trying to avoid throughout his life.

Instincts: The most important difference between what Freud and Klein said about instincts is based on the separation between drives as independent forces and drives as object representations. Bion, on the other hand, emphasizes as "a more fruitful division", a polarization between **narcissism** and what he refers to as "**social-ism**":

> By these two terms I wish to indicate the two poles of all instincts. This bi-polarity of the instincts refers to their operation as elements in the fulfilment of the individual's life as an individual, and as

elements in his life as a social or, as Aristotle would describe it, as a "political" animal. [1992, p. 105]

The problem, he states, is not around the dichotomy between ego and sexual instincts, but in relation to their tendencies, if love (**L**) impulses are narcissistic, then hate (**H**) would be aimed at the **group** and *vice versa*; if hate is directed against the individual, the group would be loved socially (*ibid.*, p. 122). The ego is involved in this conflict, because it is the ego that establishes a link between internal and external realities, between narcissism and social-ism.

It is possible that Bion's experience during War World I might have had some influence on the conception of this form of polarization:

The exclusive mention of sexuality ignores the striking fact that the individual has an even more dangerous problem to solve in the operation of his aggressive impulses, which, thanks to this bi-polarity, may impose on him the need to fight for his group with the essential possibility of his death, while it also imposes on him the need for action in the interests of his survival. [*ibid.*, pp. 105–106]

Nebbiosi and Petrini (2000) suggest that what defines this polarization between self and group is "**common sense**", because exactly what provides cohesion to the senses inside is also what provides a sense to the relation with the group (pp. 174–177). If, by any chance, the individual feels attacked by the group and is not able to reach a consensus between both criteria, the interest towards the self could create a rejection of the group (hate), turning his attention to what he believes or does (love), because his common sense might help him to see how unfair the reaction of the group is. An example taken from Bion's work, could be the relationship between the **mystic** and the **establishment**.

Integrative reticulum: Described by Elliot Jaques (1960) as part of a mental mechanism necessary, according to him, to conceive a total object. He defines it as follows. The integrative reticulum is the mental schema of the completed object and the means of creating it, organized in such a manner that the gaps both in the mental picture of the object and in the methods of creating it are established. Consciously, it is a combination of any or all of concepts, theories,

hypotheses, and working notions or hunches. Unconsciously, it is a constellation of ideas-in-feeling, **memories**-in-feeling, phantasies, and internal objects—brought together and synthesized to the extent necessary to direct behaviour, even if not sufficiently to become conscious (p. 360).

Interference: When questioned about this **concept**, Bion said:

> When you are talking to your patient you can sometimes see and feel that he is not attending to you. At the same time you can feel that he is attending to *something*; the conversation between the patient and the analyst is being interfered with. That is what I mean by interference. Are you going to pay **attention** to what he tells you, or what your books have told you, or are you going to pay attention to the interference? . . . What you have to listen to then is psycho-analytic 'interference', just as somebody had to listen to radio interference. [1974a, pp. 72–73]

Interpretation: Psychoanalytic interpretations, says Bion, could be understood as theories sustained by the analyst in relation to **models** and theories the patient feels about the analyst, and if correct in expression as well as in content, they might be able to exercise a therapeutic effect (1963, p. 17). Also, from the point of view of metatheory, that is, beyond theory, Bion synthesizes interpretations as "those words, or collection of words, which indicate a **constant conjunction** of **elements**" (1992, p. 257).

"An interpretation should not be given on a single association; a single association is open to an enormous **number** of interpretations" (*ibid.*, p. 210). Just as two different **points** might determine the direction of a **line** in **Euclidian geometry**, two different associations (or more) might also provide the direction that the interpretation would eventually trail. Usually, the choice about when and how to interpret is determined by the analyst's personality and historical development (1965, p. 166). There are also other variables capable of affecting the **form** in which an interpretation is made, and they should be avoided: (a) to make it just because it is available, an attitude that would correspond to column 2 in the **Grid**; (b) to avoid **turbulences** in the analyst; (c) recondite interpretations related to distant "desires" in the analyst belonging to the area of the **hyperbole** (*ibid.*, p. 167). The interpretation represents the product of a relation based on **K** and not on **L** or **H** (1963, p. 70). In relation to **O**, Bion said: "The interpretation is an actual event in an evolution of O that is common to analyst and analysand" (1970, p. 27).

Bion researches the interpretation from several perspectives:

(A) According to **functions** theory, α-**function** changes sense impressions related to **emotional** experiences into α-**elements** that will cohere as they proliferate, would be able to **agglomerate**, to order sequentially and give the appearance of a **narrative**; something Bion has referred to as the **contact barrier**. In this sense, α-function is indispensable for the **transformation** of emotions into something meaningful like α-elements, and this is precisely what the interpretation attempts to achieve, to help patients provide a meaning to their emotions in such a way that they could learn from them, a process that necessarily requires the presence of α-function (1962, pp. 17–18).

(B) From the **point of view** of container–contained ($♀ ♂$) theory, where contents ($♂$) represent doubts, questions or variables bound by emotional experiences that sequentially add to each other in a series that could be represented as: $♂n + ♀n$; a process that will eventually guarantee the **growth** of the **apparatus for thinking** and the possibility of **learning from experience**. Such learning would depend on the capacity of $♂n$ to integrate while at the same time remaining open, free from rigidities and ready for successive and future **assimilations**. An individual who uses this mechanism, will show that he is capable of withholding experience, learning from the interpretation, and also, associate it with past experiences. The level of K will depend on the capacity to sustain container–contained relations of a "**commensal**" kind, where the three elements involved: patient ($+♂$), analyst ($+♀$) and the interpretation ($+K$) would benefit from each other. However, if the interaction is dominated by strong feelings of **envy**, the relationship might become destructive, something Bion represents as $-(♂♀)$ and the link between them as $-K$. In contrast with $♂n + ♀n$, the relation would be: $-♂n - ♀n$, where + is replaced by envy, and the contained, subdued by the container, is stripped from its **meaning** leaving only worthless remnants. This is exactly what happens to any interpretation when it is contained by a mind dominated by envy that will convert it into $-\male$, or something insignificant like a simple noise; different from the relation $+(\male\ \female)$ dominated by K, where the interpretation under a process of **abstraction** promotes growth and learning (1962, pp. 96–99). Bion believes that a "sense of achievement of a correct interpretation will be commonly found to be followed almost immediately by a sense of depression" (1970, p. 124).

(C) From the point of view of the theory of transformation, Bion states that from the **vertex** of any specific psychoanalytical theory, all interpretations are transformations of representations embodying **invariants**, thus all interpretations can be meaningful depending on the invariants that they contain, for instance the **Oedipus** situation.

> Just as impressionism can be regarded as a method of transforming landscape into a painting, so the grouped analytic techniques are part of transformation of analytic experiences into interpretation. As the painter's transformations vary according to the understanding his painting is to convey, so the analyst's transformation will vary according to the understanding he wishes to convey. [1965, p. 5]

When the patient and the analyst agree upon a certain interpretation, this can be symbolized by the signs Tp and Taβ[34], and since it has been shared by two persons, it is not a private but a public **communication**. In **psychoses** the interpretation should illuminate the condition of the apparatus for thinking, the nature of its deficiencies and associated drives, for instance, that an impulse might induce a defect in a particular form of **thinking**, or the opposite, that frustration, induced by failure to solve a problem, brings about a destructive attack on the analytic situation (*ibid.*, p. 60).

The interpretation should also facilitate the transition from knowing about **O** to becoming O. Bion describes a particular form of perversion where the patient induces growth of K in order to obstruct a growth to O. He said:

> By agreeing with the interpretation it is hoped that the analyst will be inveigled into a collusive relationship to preserve K without

---

[34] See "abbreviations" at the beginning of this dictionary.

being aware that he is doing so. If the manoeuvre is successful transformations in K fulfil an F2[35] role preventing the inception of $T\alpha \rightarrow T\beta = K \rightarrow O$. [*ibid.*, p. 160]

Interpretations that imply becoming O can produce apprehension, because they might be experienced as related to megalomania, or what the psychiatrist calls delusions of grandeur (to be like God) (*ibid.*, p. 164).

(D) Referring to the scope of the interpretation, Bion suggested that if he was correct in assuming that **phenomenon** is known but reality becomes, the interpretation should be able to provide something more than just increasing knowledge. It could be argued that this "something" should not really be a concern of the analyst, for he can only "increase knowledge"; the rest, the more advanced steps to reduce the gap should come from the analysand, most of all from his **"Godhead"**, or the capacity of O to "incarnate" in the person of the analysand. Bion uses the Godhead, as a concept taken from religion to signify the capacity of **at-one-ment** with God, something Bion uses as a simile to explain the capacity to become O or the ultimate **truth**. *See*: **Godhead, Meister Eckhart, O, Psychoanalytic listening, Pure and absolute interpretation, Transferential interpretation**.

Interpretation, pure and absolute: *see*: **Pure and absolute interpretation**.

Intra-uterine life:[36] In "Inhibition, symptoms and anxiety" Freud (1926) said: "There is much more continuity between intra-uterine life and earliest infancy than the impressive **caesura** of the act of birth would have us believe" (p. 138). Based on this statement Bion questioned:

> After all, if anatomists can say that they detect a vestigial tail, if surgeons likewise can say that they detect tumours which derive from

---

[35] See the Grid.
[36] There is a wide Latin-American psychoanalytic literature about "foetus' psychics" or intra-uterine life, such as the works of Aray (1992) and Raskovky (1958).

the branchial cleft, then why should there not be what we would call mental vestiges, or archaic elements, which are operative in a way that is alarming and disturbing because it breaks through the beautiful, calm surface we ordinarily think of as rational, sane behaviour? [1987, p. 308]

Bion presupposed that the foetus, at the end of gestation, could be aware of unpleasant oscillations in the amniotic fluid as a consequence to conflicts between the parents, or something similar, or hear voices or loud noises coming from the mother's digestive system, etc. Bion thinks that at this level of nearly full-term, the personality might develop to experience feelings of hostility towards these disturbing things: "proto-ideas" or "proto-feelings", that would **split** them up, fragment them and try to **evacuate** them. He also suggested the existence of certain conditions that could appear at a given moment to be so ephemeral, so imperceptible that we might not even be aware of them, but that could later on become so real that they might even destroy us without our being **conscious** of them (*ibid.*, p. 318). *See*: **Caesura, Proto-thoughts, Ideogram.**

Intuit: It means intuition by means of perception. Bion proposes that this concept be used in the psychoanalytic domain in the same way a physician will use "see", "touch", "smell", and "hear", because **anxiety**, for instance, has no smell or taste.[37] (1970, p. 7). He argues about the existence of a psychoanalytic domain with its particular "intuitable" realities:

> I am supposing that there is a psychoanalytic domain with its own reality—unquestionable, constant, subject to change only in accordance with its own rules even if those rules are not known. These realities are "intuitable" if the proper apparatus is available in the condition proper to its functioning . . . The conditions in which the intuition operates (intuits) are pellucid and opaque. [1992, p. 315]

The **opacities** that obstruct such aptitude to intuit psychoanalytic reality, are revealed by Bion as "understanding, **memory** and

---

[37] Communicating with patients presents similar limitations; how do we know what patients are talking about if their anxiety has no physical qualities, like odour or taste? The only reference we have in these cases, is our own.

desire"; conditions that can be avoided only through permanent and continuous discipline.

Invariants: Specific characteristics of an object that, by remaining unaltered regardless of any **transformation** experienced by that object, will allow the identity of that object. An interpretation, for instance, carries invariants that belong to some particular psycho-analytic theory, like the **Oedipus** situation (1965, p. 4).

The relationship between invariant and constant, on one hand, and variable or **non-saturated** element, on the other, is represented by Bion with the formula $K(\zeta)$, representing an **ideogram** where both, the latent content, the invariant or **unconscious phantasy**, coexist with the manifest content and variable or non-saturated element (1974, p. 25).

Invisible–visual hallucination: Bion describes this kind of **hallucination** in relation to a patient who suddenly sat on the couch and stared attentively into **space**. When interpreted that it seemed that he was looking at something, he answered that he "could not see what he saw". Bion concludes that the patient is dealing with an invisible object, a kind of hallucination related with **dreams** in **psychotic** patients, which are usually mentioned but never described because the images of which they are made of had suffered a process of **splitting** that makes it impossible to recognize the existence of real objects and to be able to refer to them. In these patients dreams are used as a process of discharge of the mental apparatus, a condition that reaches the extreme in the case of invisible–visible hallucinations. Bion states:

> . . . this **evacuatory** process may not reach the extremes that are represented by invisible visual hallucinations that are the outcome of **transformation** into pictorial images, extremely minute fragmentation, and ejection by the eyes to a great distance. Some degree of pictorialization and other transformations take place to form the (from the analyst's point of view) **bizarre**, hallucinatory objects. [1992, p. 79]

J

Judgement: According to Freud (1911), one of the functions used by the ego to achieve awareness of reality, together with **attention**, **notation**, **action** and **thought**, is judgement; a condition that allows the ego to discriminate between a **true** and a **false idea**, or to know if it could develop to take the place of the repressed. In psychotic patients, not capable of discriminating between reality and phantasy—Bion states—judgement as a **function** of the mind has been repressed and expelled inside some external object to become part of a **bizarre object** that will then contain the patient's "capacity to judge" (1967, p. 81).

K

K(ζ): Represents a formula used by Bion, where **K** signifies a constant, for example the repetitive aspects of the **Oedipus myth**: triangulation, exclusion, **envy**, incest, etc.; and ζ is a sign that stands for a **non-saturated element** that could be represented by those particular or latent aspects of the myth, such as the specific courses the tragedy might have pursued in each individual. It can also represent an "**ideogram**" containing "what is not spoken (constant) but is articulated (variable)" (1974, pp. 23–25).

−**K**: *see*: **Minus K**

Keats, John, *see*: Negative capability, Language of achievement. (*See* references.)

K link: Bion uses the initial of the word "knowledge" to designate the capacity to "know" something; not about what is already known, but about the propensity to know or to contain:

> "Knowledge" has no meaning unless it means that someone knows
> something, and this . . . is an assertion of relationship, or of some

part of a relationship. The term, "knowledge" I propose provisionally to employ to describe a state of mind indissolubly associated
with a relationship between communicable awareness on the one
hand, and the object of which the person feels thus aware, on the
other. [1992, p. 271]

K represents, together with **L** (love) and **H** (hate), a **hypothesis** that
expresses a **constant conjunction**. These **links**, L and H, remain sub-
ordinated to K in a fashion similar to the subordination that exists
between a **basic assumption** and a **work group** (W). L and H are
respectively related to the classical conceptions of sexual and aggressive instincts made by Freud (1917), whereas K appears to follow
a line similar to Klein's (1931) notion of the epistemophilic instinct
or drive to knowledge. However, Bion has provided knowledge
with such a level of relevance and independence, as was never
previously emphasized (*see* Green, 2000, p. 122).

From a **container–contained** ($\female$ $\male$) theory perspective, the level
of K will depend on the capacity to sustain container–contained
relationships of a "**commensal**" type, where the three elements
involved, for instance: baby (+$\male$), mother (+$\female$) and mental growth
(+K), would benefit from each other (1962, p. 91); or the relationship
between a thinker who contains an idea or invention, and a purpose
that is beneficial for both the thinker and the invention. Contents
($\male$) represent doubts, questions or variables bound by **emotional**
experiences that sequentially add to each other in a series that can
be represented as: $\male n + \female n$; a process that will eventually guarantee **growth** of the **apparatus for thinking** and of K, as well as the
possibility of **learning from experience**. Such learning would
depend on the capacity of $\male n$ to integrate while at the same time
remaining open, free from rigidities and ready for successive and
future **assimilations**. An individual who contains this mechanism,
will show that he is capable of withholding experience, learning
from **interpretation** and, also, associating it with past experiences.
There is a successive increment in degrees of sophistication, for
instance, to create new hypotheses that will then form systems and
afterwards **scientific deductive systems** that can recombine again
and again (*ibid.*, pp. 92–94).

However, when the interaction is dominated by strong feelings
of **envy**, the relationship might become destructive, something Bion

represents as $-(\sigma^{\!?}\ \varphi)$ and the link between them as $-\mathbf{K}$. In contrast with $\sigma^{\!?}n + \varphi n$, the relation would be: $-\sigma^{\!?}n - \varphi n$, where $+$ is replaced by envy, and the contained subdued by the container, is stripped from its **meaning** leaving only worthless remnants. If K represents growth and α-function, $-K$ stands for absence of α-**function** and presence of **thing-in-itself** equal to β-**elements**. K should be represented as something open in continuous **transformation**, always **unsaturated** like a state of "being knowing", because the level of knowledge, as can be seen for instance when comparing Freud with Bion, is always changing as it moves closer to the **truth**.

From notes, written perhaps in 1960, Bion states that he has reserved the term "knowledge" for the total sum of alpha and beta elements:

> It is a term that therefore covers everything the individual knows and does not know. As I use it, the term must not be supposed to imply the existence of a thing in itself called "knowledge"; it is a name for a postulate that has no actuality. [1992 p. 182]

Later on Bion would discriminate between K and $-\mathbf{K}$.

Grinberg *et al.* (1972, p. 101) states that a process of **abstraction** is essential to K link emotional experience, because those elements that have been abstracted are useful for the understanding and learning of that experience.

Knowledge: *see*: **K**.

L

−**L:** *see:* **Minus L.**

Language of achievement: An expression Bion has borrowed from a letter written by John Keats[38] to his brother, referring to a "Man of Achievement". It was used together with another expression: "**Negative capability**" or the capacity to tolerate uncertainty. It is equivalent to the expression: "action speaks louder than words", that is, language is a prelude to action but also its substitute. Although "Language of Achievement" is present during the analytic session; it should not be a place for the analyst to react, instead he should remain sensible to it. It is a concept related to the envy produced by the consensus that decides who is the one who knows or who is the one that chooses what is and what is not, etc. There is a subtle difference between the exact significance of "Language of Achievement", on one hand, and the exact meaning of an envious and destructive attack that would obstruct growth, on the other. It would be a consequence of the incapacity to build a mental space

---

[38] The fragment of this letter that inspired Bion to describe "**Language of Achievement**" and "**Negative Capability**", can be found in the description of this last concept, in the last chapter of Bion's book *Attention and Interpretation.*

in which to contain uncertainty, ignorance or Negative Capability. It is possible that the obscurity in the explanation of this concept, considered in the last chapter of *Attention and Interpretation*, might have been a consequence of Bion's sentiments about the rejection some of his ideas had produced within the British Psychoanalytical Society:[39]

> Who or what is to exercise the power and what voice is to utter the Language of Achievement is a matter of consequence and has been accepted as such whether the field in which the struggle is carried on is the individual or agglomerations of individuals. [1970, p. 127]

Leaderless groups: The main philosophy in this technique was introduced by Bion, and it consists in applying mechanisms of individual psychoanalytic therapy to **group** dynamics as a whole, such as maintaining the "abstinence law", or the therapist's intervention remaining always on an interpretative level and directed to the totality of the group's unconscious phantasy, depending on the predominant **basic assumption**. **Interpretations** directed to one person, as a form of individual therapy taking place in public, should always be avoided. "The endeavour that I myself make", says Bion, "is to illuminate the obscurities of the situation in the group by clear thinking clearly expressed" (1948b, p. 84).

One of Bion's innovations in this form of treatment, in order to follow a parallelism with individual analysis, was his capacity to deal with the anxieties of the "**dependent group**", always trying to establish and to profit from the *status quo* of a relationship based on a "doctor–patient" model. He tried, despite the difficulties that such an attitude represented within the group culture, to remain neutral, as another member and in the position of observer.

> As I said, the doctor–patient foundation for a sophisticated structure soon shows its inadequacy, and one reason for this is that it is only a thin disguise for the dependent group, so that emotional reactions proper to this kind of basic group are immediately evoked, and the structure of sophistication sags badly. [*ibid.*, p. 79]

---

[39] See, for instance, Donald Meltzer's ambivalence in "The Kleinian Development, Part III", in *The Clinical Significance of the Work of Bion* (1978).

The dependent group can have the following disadvantages: (a) it promotes rivalry for the leader's attention; (b) the benefit experienced does not come from the group but from the leader and is only possible when he speaks, something that induces the belief that the treatment is something simple that requires little effort; (c) the "dependency game" generates feelings of deceit and hunger for affection, because members always feel that they are not receiving enough from the leader; (d) the belief that the therapist looks after everyone equally is never possible and never convincing.

Learning from Experience: Bion used this expression as a title for one of his books, which summarizes some of the clinical experience he had acquired during his previous psychoanalytical research. He emphasizes the danger of failing to communicate accurately what he wishes to say, or not being truthfully understood by others.

He discriminates between a form of "learning from experience", that changes the learner, and "learning something" that might increase information, but does not change the individual. He refers to the hatred of "learning from the experience", which represents the feeling that "experience" is not necessary for learning, because it can be achieved suddenly, as it were by magic. Such an attitude is often observed when patients in analysis ask about the length of treatment, as if knowledge was only the analyst's privilege. In relation to **groups**, Bion states that this difficulty to learn can be a consequence of feeling that the "**Dependence Basic Assumption**" (Dba) is insufficient and thus searching for other **basic assumptions** will be needed.

Lie: The difficulty to research lies, said Bion, hinges, among other things, on the issue that the same language required to search for the **truth** is also used to fabricate lies. Lies are **thoughts** that require a "thinker" to formulate them; truth, however, does not require any. To say for instance, "the sky is blue", does not need anyone to think or formulate it, it is a truth that stands by itself. When a "thinker" feels he is indispensable to some thought, he might feel very **envious** of someone else who might also feel indispensable to the same thought. What Descartes implicitly felt, that thoughts presupposed a thinker, is valid only for the lies (1970, pp. 102–103).

Can a liar be psychoanalysed? Although Klein, according to Bion, felt at a given moment that it was not possible, he thought that, usually, the analyst as well as the patient suddenly stumbles into lies without expecting them and frequently after the treatment has began. Also, the possibilities that lies could put themselves forth as **unsaturated** elements associated with −**L** and −**K**, might leave them open to a possible saturation or **realization**. For instance, dealing with a patient who is always late and repeats the same excuses, the analyst has several possibilities: (1) to accept the excuses as if truth was of no importance to him and become its host; (2) to turn into the patient's conscience, representing an unthought thought; (3) or to wait for a proper moment to appear, when he can provide the precise **interpretation** that might saturate the lie with truth (1970, p. 98). On the other hand, lies can represent a reaction against change, similar to what happens in "**catastrophic change**" (*ibid.*, p. 99).

Lies can correspond to category 2 of the **Grid**; however, when they became evocative or provocative of accusations and defences, they can then correspond to category 6, because they might be capable of inducing **emotional** disturbances related to **action**. If they change into fabrication of idealizations, resembling a **myth**, they could then be placed in C category. Many liars in history have defended the world threatened by the truth of science: "It is not too much to say that the human race owes its salvation to that small band of gifted liars who were prepared even in the face of indubitable **facts** to maintain the truth of their **falsehoods**" (*ibid.*, 100). The nature of a lie might be suggested by the use of −L or −K, which enter into conflict, in theory, with the analyst's interest for the truth; furthermore, the intelligence and degree of sophistication of some patients allow them continuously to make use of their resources to convince themselves of the efficacy and superiority of lies (*ibid.*, p. 99).

Access to the truth might be equivalent to a step taken from the **paranoid–schizoid** to the **depressive position**. The domination of **O** can change into a paranoid system and a threat for the liar, or in other words, the impact of becoming O within the territory of a "thinker" who "thinks" the lie, is marked by persecutory feelings like those present in the paranoid–schizoid position: O and lies are incompatible by definition.

Meltzer (1973), using the **concept** of "idealization of the bad object", as well as Rosenfeld (1971) with his notion of the "narcissistic gang", have emphasized the idealization of lies and the systematic attack of truth represented by the "object's goodness". In this case, following Bion, the relationship between thinker and lie is equivalent to a **parasitic** form of **container–contained** interaction where both destroy each other (*ibid.*, p. 103). In this sense, Bion has suggested the creation of a **"negative Grid"**, some kind of a mirror image of the regular Grid capable of representing concepts such as lies, equivalent to category 2 as well as −L, −H and −K.

Bianchedi *et al.* (2000) discriminate between: (a) the lie as a kind of defence; and (b) another form representing a **projective identification** destined to denude the receptor of any contact with the truth (pp. 220–235). For Bléandonu (1994) lies represent an attack on free association making analysis an impossible task. Grotstein (1996) states that **psychotic** patients, because of their closeness with O, will confuse O with K, while neurotics and normal persons will do the opposite, confuse K with O.

Line, the (___): Could be conceptualized in a manner similar to the **point** (.) and the **circle** (O), corresponding to visual images that remain invariable in the face of many situations, and are used by Bion as geometric representations of symbols. Different from the point that has been used to represent the "place where the breast was", or the circle signifying the "no-inside-or-outside" (O), the line, because of its shape, represents the absent penis or the place where the penis was, or no-penis. It would correspond in the **Grid** to category A1, the same as "no-breast" or β-**elements**. The line can be annihilated and changed into a series of points, or into a single point, to the place where the point was. "The point" concludes Bion, "is thus indestructible" (1965, p. 95). Bion also questions whether line and point should not be considered together, like "different manifestations of one entity" (*ibid.*, p. 89). He considers the existence of a minus line: − ___ , similar to a minus point: −., capable of holding meaning similar to the **"no-thing"**, not only because they represent the footprint of something that once was but no longer is, but mainly because while they are capable of retaining a notion of time, while they keep their duration, they will not be empty of past and future. *See*: **point, circle, no-thing, no-breast, complex conjugates**.

Link (linking): *see:* **Emotional link, Attacks on linking.**

Listening: *see:* **Psychoanalytic listening.**

L (love) link: Represents a **psychoanalytic element** taken from the initial of the word Love, and used by Bion to denote, together with **H** and **K**, one of the passions or **feelings**, as well as a dynamic **link** that, following mechanisms of **container–contained**, bound different elements in the **Grid** (1963, pp. 34–35). Bion also considers the existence of –H, –L and –K, although he says little about –L and –H. In relation to love, Bion says so precisely:

> A term like "love" cannot describe something even as well as the term, "the love of God"—that at least makes an attempt to introduce an element that shows that it is not a discussion about something that is so simple as physical love known to the human animal. A lioness nuzzles and shows every sign of feelings of love and affection—if interpreted in human terms—for prey it has destroyed; but it is murderous love, the love that destroys the loved object. Such visual images may be used to talk about love, even what we imagine to be mature love, but there is some other love that is mature from an absolute standard. This other love, vaguely adumbrated, vaguely foreshadowed in human speech, is of an entirely different character; it is not simply a quantitative difference in the kind of love one animal has for another or which the baby has for the breast. It is the further extension to "absolute love", which cannot be described in the terms of sensuous reality or experience. For that there has to be a language of infra-sensuous and ultra-sensuous, something that lies outside the spectrum of sensuous experience and articulate language. [1992, pp. 371–372]

Love: *see:* **L.**

M

Magic: Bion defines magic as an attempt to control the physical environment, and "ritual", as a part of magic concerned with the control of the spiritual world. There are two areas of importance in magic that eventually developed into scientific research: one is Astrology, that gave place to astronomy based on mathematical calculation; the other is alchemy that produced experimental chemistry. This can make one think that the existence of a universal spirit or principle animating the world could be "a psychoanalytic **fact**". Bion adds: "The gap between theories of psychoanalysis on one side and invocation and prayer on the other is narrow. Sometimes it becomes narrower; sometimes it widens" (1992, p. 298).

Marbles: *see*: **Transformations**.

Maternal reverie[40] Concept based on Kleinian **projective identification** theory (1962, p. 90) and mentioned by Bion in his **"Theory of thinking"** (1967, p.116). It refers to the mother's capacity to develop a psychological receptor organ capable of metabolizing

---

[40] According to the Symingtons (1966), *reverie* derives from Latin *radix*, meaning *root*; "through *rabere, to be furiously angry*, presumably uprooted in the mind, to the Old French *reverie, rejoicing, wildness*, thence to *resverie, a state of delight, violent or rude language, delirium*, to *rever*, to dream" (p. 67n).

167

the baby's conscious sensuous information and transform it into α-**elements**, which are in turn necessary to develop α-**function** (*See*: **factor** and **function**) and a **thinking apparatus**. "Reverie", says Bion, "is a factor of the mother's alpha-function" . . . her love is expressed by reverie (1962, p. 36).

According to him, a normal development takes place if the relationship between the baby and the breast enables the baby to project inside the mother a feeling such as, for instance, that he is dying, and then re-introject it after its permanence in the breast has made it more tolerable for the baby's mind. If the projection is not accepted by the mother the baby feels his death to be real and instead of re-introjecting a more tolerable fear of dying, he will re-introject a **nameless terror**. The baby benefits from the mother's daydreaming or capacity for reverie, just in the same way he benefits from the milk he consumes that is digested in the digestive canal. If the α-function is the one that makes available to the baby that which in other circumstances would be unavailable for any purpose except for evacuation as β-**elements**, ". . . what are the *factors* of this function that relate directly to the mother's capacity for reverie?" (*ibid.*, p. 36). If the mother's reverie is not associated with love for the baby, this fact will be communicated to him although in an incomprehensible way.[41] Bion associates reverie only with feelings of love and hate from the child, and believes it to be a factor of the mother's α-function, which permits a total disclosure towards the reception of any projective identification coming from the baby regardless of being felt as a good or bad object (1962, p. 36; 1974, pp. 83–85). *See*: **Projective identification, Alpha-function, Alpha element, Tropism, Nameless terror.**

Mathematical objects: *see*: **Psychoanalytic objects**.

---

[41] I have previously referred to these "incomprehensible feelings", as the "schizoid secret", that is, patients who have suffered tragedies at such an early age that later on such memories became inaccessible. I used as a paradigm the situation that took place at the Eleusinian Mysteries in ancient Greece, where the initiates took LSD (*Kykeon*) without knowing it, during special offerings to Persephone, and afterwards were incapable of communicating the experience, because their delusions were so private, so schizoid, that they were never able to reach a consensus, a "**common sense**" to share it, fabricating through history a "secret" impossible to make public, to disclose (Lopez-Corvo, 1993, 1994).

Mathematical symbols: Bion considers that symbols, such as addition, subtraction, multiplication and division (+, −, × and ÷), can represent different forms of interaction:

This and this and this and this = a table (*addition*);

A table without legs or a top or hardness or softness = a hallucination (*subtraction*);

A table *multiplied* by today and tomorrow and the next day and the next day = lots of tables;

But if it is the same table? And if two people have to share it, is the table *divided* by two? [1992, p. 274]

Meaning: Represents the relationship between the opinion one might have of oneself (narcissism)—or self-esteem or meaning—and the opinion others have (social-ism). Bion states that the importance in psychoanalysis of the **"narcissism-social-ism"** extension can be better understood, if the relationship between meaning and narcissism is considered. The breast is an essential source from where to gather meaning—or even more, it is meaning itself—or narcissistic relevance, which later will be translated into love, understanding, and meaning, as well as incrementing the capacity to learn. This last skill is observed in the response towards the **interpretation**, which can be considered either as a criticism or as a source of knowledge and insight. The loss of the breast, regardless of the reason, is translated into a fear of losing everything, as well as a fear of losing all meaning, as if the person were "a material thing" that had ceased to exist (1965, p. 81).

Meaning is a function of the kind of love (**L**), **hate** (**H**) and knowledge (**K**) we might feel about ourselves. The criticism of a universe without meaning, said Bion, regardless of how big or small that might be, derives from the fear that such lack of significance could be a sign that it has been completely destroyed, something that might change into a threat to the person's own narcissism. When this happens, that is, when the universe cannot provide meaning, a belief that meaning could be obtained from some powerful beings or objects might develop. Incapacity to experience love of oneself can translate into intolerance towards meaning or its absence (*ibid.*, p. 73). It could be thought in this sense, that significance is associated with hope, depending on whether the opinion

given by someone else is positive or negative, like the patient who
demands the analyst's interpretation regardless of what has been
said, just for the comforting sound of the voice, as an attempt to
deny an internal (narcissistic) lack of meaning (*ibid.*, pp. 81, 101).
There is the danger in these cases that analysis could halt, because
the patient's need to project "insignificance" could be acted out by
minimizing the interpretation, coming late, missing sessions,
reversing perspective or eventually discontinuing altogether. *See*:
Dreams, Dream-work, Dream thought.

Mechanical links: *see*: **Dynamic links**

Medical model, the: In relation to medicine, Bion said:

> The parallel with medicine was, and still is, useful. But as psycho-
> analysis has grown so it has been seen to differ from physical med-
> icine until the gap between them has passed from the obvious to
> the unbridgeable. [1970, p. 6]

An important difference between physical and mental categories is
based on the quality of **realizations**, while the former depends on
sensuous experiences, such as touch, vision, smell, etc., the latter
lacks these kind of realizations: **anxiety** for instance, has no taste or
smell. Bion recommends that psychoanalysts make use of the term
"**intuit**" in the same way smell, touch or test, etc., is used within
the medical domain. While the **model** of realizations is linked to
the presence of objects, the mind has to deal with absences, with
"**no-things**" or nothingness. Communicating with patients presents
similar limitations: how do we know what patients are talking
about if their anxiety has no physical qualities? The only reference
we depend on in these cases is our own, because there is no odour
or taste to compare.

Eigen, trying to explain Bion, said, "To treat the mind as a thing,
would mean to murder it" (1995). To avoid the difficulty of **containing** the no-thing, not only do we fill no-thing with things, but
we also relate to no-things as if they were things. Intolerance to
mental pain induces the need to free the mind from such pain with
the use of β-**elements**—since they are good only for evacuation—
by means of **projective identifications** and **acting-out** (corresponding to category 2 of the Grid). The capacity to tolerate pain induced

by the absence of the "thing" or the "no-thing", on the other hand, is a good protection for psychic life, to guard it from being changed into a thing like the body, or from being reduced to the condition of a thing.

Viewed from a different perspective, somatic language displaces speech–unconscious scotomas that have been suppressed, filling them with soma, while the symptoms, often conditioned by culture, determine the profile of neurosis. Animism or **magic** is the product of the incapacity to conceive a notion of totality, to conceive those dimensions that form the architecture of total objects, instead magic or animism creates the paradox of denuding life from live objects and projects it into **inanimate** things, this in turn represents, as is often observed, the culture of potential violence, for life becomes worthless. It represents a flat or bi-dimensional perception of the world, where there is no sense of selfness, of identity, and analysis would not be different from a mechanical intervention as if the patient perceived him/herself as a machine. The body can be experienced as alien, even as someone else's affair, but the mind represents the place of "selfhood", of **at-one-ment** with oneself and thus the only path through which to achieve autonomy.

Medicine: *see:* **Medical model.**

Meister Eckhart or Eckehart: German Dominican monk and mystic philosopher, born in Hochheim in 1260 and dying probably by 1328 in Avignon, France. His real name was Johannes (Johann) Eckhart von Hochheim, but after obtaining a master's degree in theology in Paris, he became known as Meister Eckehart. Accused of heresy, some of his sermons and writings were posthumously condemned and were almost forgotten until more recently when interest has revived, both inside and outside of religion, the latter mostly from **Zen Buddhism**. A review of a number of his sermons reveals some of this connection; for instance, when referring to God, Eckhart said: "He is He because He is not He" or "Separate yourself from all **two-ness**, Be one on one, one with one, one from one". The sense of universality sensed in this and many other quotations, made some scholars consider him a Pantheist as well as a follower of Plotinus' Neoplatonism.

Bion has chosen Eckhart, as well as Saint John of the Cross, because of their mystic experience and sense of inner illumination in what they have described as an union or **at-one-ment** with God. Bion uses these experiences as a paradigm of what he wished to portray in his description of the meaning of **O**. This is why some have judged O to have a "metaphysical and religious meaning" (Symington and Symington, 1966, p. 10). Bion described O as:

> that which is the ultimate reality represented by terms such as ultimate reality, absolute truth, the **godhead**, the infinite, the **thing-in-itself** . . . does not fall in the domain of knowledge or learning save incidentally . . . It is darkness and formlessness but it enters the domain **K** when it has evolved to a point where it can be known, through knowledge gained by experience, and formulated in terms derived from sensuous experience; its existence is conjectured phenomenologically. [1970, p. 26]

Bion's interest in Eckhart's Godhead, is not so much on the "**contained**" (♂), on what is contained as a proof of God's existence or any other religious concern; his interest is directed towards the phenomenology of the experience itself, towards the "container" (♀) that experiences such union with something unknown, unthinkable, the ineffable, the truth itself or ultimate reality. For Bion, the revelation of the mystic with his God, whatever this God might be, is similar to the revelation experienced by the psychoanalyst while **listening** with "floating attention", without "**memory or desire**", with O, with the **ineffable**, the unknown, unthinkable, the **truth** itself or ultimate reality, of what the patient might be expressing in that particular moment.

A Memoir of the Future: Trilogy written by Bion in the seventies, during the time he spent in California. He refers to this book as a "science fiction" story, possibly modelled around the three songs of Dante or Milton (Bléandonu, 1994), and perhaps inspired by the literary style of Joyce and Ezra Pound, according to professor Meotti (2000). It consists of three parts sequentially published: *The Dream* (1975), *The Past Presented* (1977b) and *The Dawn of Oblivion* (1979). In 1979 they were all published in one book with the title *A Memoir of the Future* (1991).

According to Bion Talamo (1997) in the first place, this book represents some kind of theatre script, and its reading was "intended to be interactive . . . in the sense that the reader is supposed to react emotionally: **emotions** first and reasoning afterward". In the second place, its reading also entails some kind of **attention** similar to the one required by the analyst during **psychoanalytic listening,** which could be validated by **common sense** obtained from him and from the psychoanalytic community. In the third place, she feels that Bion demands from his readers, **patience** in order to tolerate:

> The **paranoid–schizoid position**, induced by the fragmentary, non-linear, non-**narrative** presentation of the text, long enough for a **selected fact**, α-**element**, to emerge and convey the reader to a temporary island of "**security**". "Oh, so *that's* what he's getting at!" But this is precisely what Bion thinks happens in an analytic session at its best, so that the reading of *A Memoir of the Future*, on one level, is an exercise in the **PS⟷D** shifts and oscillations, a sort of practical demonstration of them—so it is hardly surprising that it is tough going. [p. 238]

Francesca Bion (1995), on the other hand, referring to this volume depicts it as a:

> "magnum opus" (it is certainly a hefty tome of almost seven hundred pages) is a fictionalized, dramatized presentation of a lifetime's experiences, filled with a crowd of characters voicing the many facets of his own personality and **thought**; at the same time we recognize ourselves among the "dramatis personae." Had he remained in England he would certainly not have felt able to express himself in this frank and revelatory way. [p. 12]

And Bion himself made the following warning in the epilogue:

> "All my life I have been imprisoned, frustrated, dogged by common-sense, reason, **memories, desires** and—greatest bug-bear of all—understanding and being understood. This is an attempt to express my rebellion, to say "Good-bye" to all that. It is my wish, I now realize doomed to failure, to write a book unspoiled by any tincture of common sense, reason, etc. So although I would write, "Abandon Hope all ye who expect to find any **facts**, scientific, aesthetic or religious—in this book" I cannot claim to have succeeded. All of these will, I fear, be seen to have left their traces, vestiges, ghosts

hidden within these words; even sanity, like "cheerfulness," will creep in." [Bion, F., 1995, p. 13]

It is possible that this trilogy represents a sort of "Biography of his unconscious life", just as the *The Long Week-end* (1982) and *All my Sins Remembered* (1985) represent a "Biography of his conscious life".

Memory: For Bion memory is related to **K**, it relies on the senses and it represents a **container** that contains the past—which might try to **evacuate** by means of **projective identification**—but does not contain the future because this does not exist, unless it has been changed into a past. Memories are possessions, similar to **desires**, although the latter can possess the memory and the mind, when they change, under certain circumstances, into a container that imprisons memory. The analyst who knows and remembers everything is not able to learn, instead he would appear as a **saturated** element unable to absorb anything else. It is important for the analyst, while **listening** to his patient, to discriminate between memories that saturate and the capacity to remember (1970, p. 107). Memory cannot be trusted because its origins are either retentive or evacuative, dominated by the pleasure principle and with a tendency to remember what is pleasant and to forget what is not.

As a recompilation of past events, memory is usually distorted due to the presence of unconscious forces, such as "desires" for instance, which can act as a resistance to remembering, something delineated by Freud in his description of 'screen-memories'. Memories deal with the past, while desires deal with the future, but psychoanalysis depends on the present, on what is happening now:

> Every session attended by the psychoanalyst must have no history and no future. What is "known" about the patient is of no further consequence: it is either **false** or irrelevant. . . . If it is "known" by the one but not the other, a defence or **grid** category 2 element (1,2) (*see* Grid, p. 295) is operating. . . . Nothing must be allowed to distract from **intuiting** that. [1992, p. 381]

Bion distinguished between **evolution** and memory. He defines the first as the "experience where some **idea** or pictorial impression floats into the mind . . ." and is regarded as "based on experience that has no sensuous background but is expressed in terms that are derived from the language of sensuous experience" (*ibid.*, p. 383); for instance, to say "I see", meaning a form of intuiting through a visual impression. Memory, on the other hand, implies the conscious and deliberate attempt to recall something (*ibid.*). *See*: **Desire, Evolution, Act of faith, Psychoanalytic listening.**

Mental counterpart: Bion uses this expression to describe the inner representation of a given situation, for instance to visualize an internal figure without any outside representation: it is similar to the use of "the inward eye", "seen in imagination", etc. "I consider this activity", says Bion, "to depend on a 'mental counterpart of the sense of sight'. Similarly the 'bitterness' of a **memory** is dependent on a mental counterpart of the alimentary system similarly with others including the reproductory system" (1965, p. 91). *See*: **vertex, internal reproductory system.**

Mental development: *see*: **Growth.**

Mental disaster: *see*: **Psychological disaster.**

Mental pain: Considered by Bion as a **"psychoanalytical element"** and an essential part of the whole analysis, not because it is indispensable as a sort of achievement, but because if there is no pain it means the analysis is leaving out a "central reason for the patient's presence" (1963, p. 62). Many patients feel analysis should implicitly carry a decrease of pain, however, it is not necessarily so; what analysis does accomplish is an increase in the capacity to tolerate suffering. The **analogy** with physical **medicine** is noteworthy, in the sense that to destroy the capacity to feel pain can be very dangerous, unless you are dealing with death. For instance, posture can be a form of avoiding physical pain; in a similar way, patients can resort to **reversible perspective** as a means of avoiding pain, by changing something dynamic into something static (*ibid.*, pp. 60–63).

Using these contributions from Bion, Joseph (1981) has presented an article: "Toward the experiencing of psychic pain", where she compares tolerance of mental suffering with Keats' expression **"negative capability"**, used by Bion.

Mental space: Described by Bion as a synonym of **O**, as a **thing-in-itself**, or the unknowable, although capable of **thought** representation (1963, p. 22). "In thought", said Bion, "I include all that is primitive, including **alpha-elements** . . . I exclude, arbitrarily by definition, **beta-elements**" (1970, p. 11). **Psychotic** patients or the **psychotic part of the personality**, on the other hand, lack the equipment, such as α-**function**, that would help them map the **realization** of a mental space. Their position would be "analogous to that of the geometer who had to await the invention of Cartesian co-ordinates before he could elaborate algebraic geometry (*ibid.*, p. 12). They lack the conception of a **container** into which the **projective identification** can take place, something equivalent to the absence of a coordinate system such as α-function capable of producing α-elements and thought representations. In psychotic patients the mental realization of space is "felt as an immensity so great that it cannot be represented even by astronomical space because it cannot be represented at all" (*ibid.*). Therefore, capacity to experience **emotions**, use **verbal thoughts** or to be aware of **time** and **space**, are all destroyed, leaving only debris that float and get dispersed in the immensity. It is accompanied by feelings of panic, or "psychotic panic"[42] that the patient often expresses "by sudden and complete silence", equivalent to moving to "an extreme as far from a devastating explosion as possible" (*ibid.*). Bion makes comparisons with the condition seen in some patients during a "post-surgical shock", where the dilatation of the capillaries throughout the body increases so much that the blood escapes inside them creating a situation similar to bleeding to death inside their own body (*ibid.*).

Bion associates the theory of the "expansion of the universe" with the tendency of the individual to escape from the **Oedipal** situation, something he refers to as "a kind of expansive mental universe from primary scene to the nebulae." Later on he writes:

> The attempt to escape will tend to betray the corresponding attempt to discover that from which escape is sought in the expanding concepts of space as the individual travels from infancy to

---

[42] Bion has previously refer to this kind of panic as "**nameless terror**" (*see* 1967, p. 116).

adulthood. The psychotic shows a desire to occupy a very small space. [1992, p. 204]

He also tries to differentiate between "physical limits" and "mental realities", where the former is considered to be limited and concrete, whereas the latter is conceived as infinite and unknown, "because we do not know where the boundaries of the mind are, or where the impulses commence" (*ibid.*, pp. 372–373). *See*: **beta-space, no-breast, nameless terror.**

Mental suffering: *see*: **Mental pain.**

Messiah: *see*: **Mystic.**

Messianic idea: In **group** dynamics it represents the "**idea**" produced by the couple in the '**pairing group**' (baP), although also considered by Bion as the counterpart of the **mystic** or genius. When idea and mystic are fused, the former can consider himself as messiah, or in other words, the mystic may contain the idea, or the idea may contain the mystic and thus become an "idol", as observed in **psychotic delusions** of grandeur (1970, p. 110). "The messianic idea may be supposed to have a counterpart, the absolute **truth, O**, for which a thinker is not necessary" (*ibid.*, p. 117). The messianic idea represents the point where the **evolution** of O and that of a thinker intersect, like the analyst at the moment of grasping the **unconscious phantasy** during **psychoanalytic listening**, or when the religious man feels in communion with God as in the **Godhead**. The messianic idea appears also to be similar to an idealized phantasy, for instance the "wish to cure" or the idealization of **transference** (*ibid.*, p. 119).

The messianic idea could be unknown and would then be hated or feared. People deal with it by projection or materialization in a thing or a person, which will make it less persecutory because it can be controlled either by idealization, and thus proved to be real, or by **realization** and in turn proved not to be ideal (1992, p. 318). Scientific curiosity (representing the conscious) characterizes a threat for the messianic idea within magic or religious beliefs (representing the unconscious), although an important break could still remain between the two preventing the **correlation**, as it can be observed in psychoanalysis (*ibid.*, pp. 319–320).

Minus −(♂♀): Represents a relationship where the **container–contained** interaction is linked to −**K**. This situation is dominated by the presence of powerful feelings of **envy**, which Bion has referred to as "**without-ness**", which would prevent the possibility for a **commensal** kind of relationship to take place. Commensal represents a kind of relationship where the three elements involved: +♂, +♀ and K (like baby, breast and thinking; or scientist, idea and invention) benefit from each other. In contrast, when the condition is represented as: −♂, −♀, it means that a content, subdued by a container will be denuded of every **meaning**, until useless remains are the only thing left, a situation that would take place when the mind is dominated by envy (−♀). In relation to the **interpretation**, for instance, it would be transformed into an insignificant noise; a condition very different from the interaction based on a +(♂♀) dominated by K, where the interpretation under a process of **abstraction**, will promote **growth** (1962, pp. 96–99). "Successful operation of −(♂♀)" would be translated into an increment of −♀ power that will convert ♂ into −♂ **elements**. "In other words **alpha-elements**, however obtained, are acquired for conversion to **beta-elements**", which means that the patient feels surrounded not by real objects, but by **things-in themselves, bizarre objects**, representing residues of **thoughts** "and conceptions that have been stripped of their meaning and ejected" (*ibid.*, pp. 98–99).

Minus H (−H): *see*: **Minus L (−L)**

Minus K (−K): Normal growth can be achieved when a mother–child relationship is established as a **container–contained** interaction dominated by a **commensal link**. In this condition the baby projects his feelings inside the mother, for instance, that he is dying, and then re-introjects it after the mother has changed it into something more bearable to the baby's mind. This condition represents a basic model where the **apparatus for thinking thoughts** can be structured as well as the **growth** of **K**. But if the situation were dominated by **envy**, the baby would **split** and project his feelings inside the breast together with envy and hatred, which will hinder the possibility of establishing a ♂+♀relation of a commensal type. Under these circumstances, the breast is felt enviously to **denude** all good and valuable **elements** capable of metabolizing the baby's fear of death, and in its place it will force back denigrated residues that will determine the manifestation of a **nameless terror**, or a container–contained interaction between the baby and the breast, represented by Bion as −**K**. Such a condition is serious indeed because the breast not only does not mitigate the fear of death, but also takes away the **desire** to live (1962, pp. 97–99). Bion represents this state as −($\male \female$) and qualifies it as a **"without-ness"**, which he describes as:

> . . . an internal object without an exterior. It is an alimentary canal without a body. It is a super-ego that has hardly any of the charac-teristics of the super-ego as understood in psycho-analysis: it is "super" ego. It is an envious assertion of moral superiority without any morals . . .The process of denudation continues till −$\male$ −$\female$ represent hardly more than an empty superiority–inferiority that in turn degenerates to nullity. [*ibid.*, p. 97]

If we draw two straight **lines** crossing each other, O will be the **point** where they cross and whatever is on the left we name −**K**, and K what is on the right. O can be replaced by a word like "breast" or "penis" or any other sign representing a **constant con-junction**, it would be equivalent to the knowledge of the "breast" or the "penis" or K, and should be placed on the right. For the left side it could be used a point (.) or a line (___), representing the absent breast and the absent penis respectively equivalent to −**K** (1965, p 77). They could also, according to Bion, be equivalent to an absence of **space** or the place where a space once was, occupied by **no-things** or objects that have been violently filled with envious greed towards any object showing existence. For instance, referring to the abstract painter, Bion said:

> . . . that −**K** "space", is the material in which, with which, on which (etc.) the "artist" in **projective transformation** works. As an **anal-ogy** with space may easily distort I propose to drop the term and speak of **transformation** in −**K**. [*ibid.*, p. 115]

Bion describes the dynamics seen in **reversible perspective**, as a clinical example of the interaction between −**K** and K. Other examples could be used, like the case of a patient, the last of three brothers, who remembered being sent away when very small to a summer camp. Although he remembers little about the event, feelings appearing in the **transference** showed that it was a very traumatic experience. He only remembered two situations: that he was always carrying a camera with him, to the point that he was nicknamed "little camera", and that he had a dream in which he saw a car with someone inside, that was pushed away by the powerful stream of a nearby river, which in reality was a dry water bed. Motivated by the memory of the camera he searched family albums for pictures and felt rather bewildered after finding nothing. It was then interpreted that the camera he carried had just that purpose, to make sure he would remember nothing, it was a "minus camera", to photograph absences and forgetfulness (−K) as the only means to make sure something was completely forgotten in order to avoid a terrible mental pain. He wished not to photograph the absent breast, or what Bion would refer to as a "minus point": (−.) It was the presence of an absence. He pursued his investigation further and decided to go back to the summer campsite he had not visited since. He found the place very different, invaded by "delinquents" and when he called at the door two "murderous dogs" appeared. He was then told that perhaps the picture he did not wish to take was the invasion of his memories with "murderous violence" because of the impotence he then experienced when sent away; the only picture taken that *remained*, was the car with someone inside (his parents? brothers who stayed at home?), which was being carried away, *but not ever to be carried away*.

Minus L (−L): Together with −H and −K, it represents a negative form of **link**, not equivalent to H, as −H is not equivalent to **L** either. Bion provided little illustration of the meaning of −L and −H, as he did with −**K**. They are related to the "absence of something" but it is not clear what exactly was that something for Bion. "The first problem", he says, "is to see what can be done to increase scientific rigour by establishing the nature of −**K**, −L and −H." Later he questions:

> Is it possible to glean from the mechanisms involved in this behaviour any material that will throw light on *minus phenomena* . . . and incidentally on the problem of establishing the elements of psychoanalysis? [1963, pp. 51, 53, my italics]

Perhaps –L could be represented by **emotions** observed in the transference, as in " transference love", or the difference between "need" and "unconditional love". –H, on the other hand, might be equivalent to emotions present in autistic patients, where repudiation of the object is achieved by means of mechanisms different from **splitting** and direct aggression, which Meltzer has described as **dismantling**.

Minus Ps ←→D (–Ps ←→D): Different from the positive form of Ps←→D, that could represent "interaction involving dispersal of particle with feelings of persecution [related to the **paranoid–schizoid position**] and integration with feelings of depression" [related to depressive position] we have according to Bion, in (minus) –Ps←→D, the following clinical characteristics: "disintegration, total loss and depressive stupor; *or* intense impaction and degenerate stuporose violence." He adds: "Although these descriptions . . . are incomplete they may serve until further experience is forthcoming" (1963, p. 52).

Model, the: A "model" represents for Bion a construction that conjugates observations related to each other, following a non-fortuitous logic of cause–effect produced by the experience, where the **links** that bound them are secondary and are expressed in the form of a **narrative**. A model can be made of any observation or series of observations that would acquire coherence or would be precipitated by a **selected fact**. Bion makes a difference between models made to provide understanding of some kind of observation, and the person who creates the model. An **interpretation** is a model used to provide an illumination of the latent content from a given manifest discourse. It is precipitated by a "selected fact", it is ephemeral and it differs from theory in this respect: it will also require the analyst's α-**function** to produce α-**elements** in order to abstract the necessary elements to construct the interpretation. "The model", says Bion, "may be regarded as an **abstraction** from an **emotional** experience or as a concretization of an abstraction . . . The model was made to illuminate the experience I had with a particular patient and is used for comparison with the **realization**" (1962, p. 79). The interpretation has to be matched against its realization to prove its degree of success or failure.

I have no compunction in discarding a model as soon as it has served or failed to serve my purpose. If a model proves useful on a **number** of different occasions the time has come to consider its **transformation** into a theory. . . . A psychoanalyst may make as many models as he chooses out of any material available to him. [*ibid.*, p. 80]

It is important not to confuse a model with a realization, because the latter is a consequence of the model, it is its main purpose, but it is different from the model. Abstraction might follow a realization and from there proceed to make a model and then to elaborate a **scientific deductive system**. The model, however, advises Bion, should not be confused with the realization, because then the model would lose its purpose: "I ignore the contingency that arises when the realization is mistakenly matched with the model; that failure is dealt with by the creation of a new model" (*ibid.*, p. 80). The transformation that a model has to suffer in order to allow generalization is similar to the process by which sense data is transformed into α-elements.

Bion discriminates between models made with inanimate objects and models related to living organisms, for instance the characteristics of growth, as is the case with psychoanalysis: "The term mechanism implies the model of a machine which is precisely what the realization is not" (*ibid.*, p. 81). *See*: **Medical model**, **Psychoanalytic elements**.

Money: Following contributions made by Eizing (1949), Bion attempts to use **group** dynamics to connect money with **basic assumptions**. For instance, if originally money appeared as a need to provide the bride with a dowry—a 'bride-price'—it would then be related with the **pairing group (baP)**; but if linked with the payment made to the kindred of someone murdered or *wergild*, it could then be considered as expression of a **flight–fight basic assumption (baF)**. The dominant "ba" in a given group, for instance the political situation of a country, will psychologically determine the value of money (1948a, pp. 109–112).

In a note made some years later, Bion explains how money can be used to measure the position of an individual, such as the dowry, the papal bull, etc. It could represent the **thing-in-itself**, determining someone's value, like the fee paid to the analyst, which can be used either to exalt or debase, like hiding his/her devaluation behind a high fee (1992, p. 307).

Moral System: Bion refers very briefly and defines this system as similar to the sense of morality induced by a **myth**, or as its **narrative** cause; that is, the way elements in the myth associate with each other. For instance, the myth of the sphinx in **Oedipus**, showing how men's curiosity turns against themselves, or the **tower of Babel**, trying to reach heaven; they represent different ways in which curiosity towards knowledge changes into a sin (1963, p. 46). *See*: **Myth, Narrative, Oedipus, Tower of Babel, myth of**.

Mystic (Genius or Messiah): They could be creative or destructive and might establish themselves in religion as well as in science. The creative one fulfils the demands of his **group**, whereas the destructive or the "mystic nihilistic" destroys his own creations: "I mean the terms to be used only when there is outstanding creativeness or destructiveness, and the terms 'mystic', 'genius', 'messiah' could be interchangeable" (1970, p. 74). It is also the person who contains or is contained by the **messianic idea**, in a similar form as a container contains a content, or a **meaning** contains the word that expresses it (*ibid.*, pp. 87, 110). The mystic could be a thinker who confesses having a direct access to the **truth**, to God if he is religious, or to O if he is a psychoanalyst. On the contrary, if it were the **idea** that contained the mystic, then he would be transformed into an idol. The degree of **falsehood** between the mystic and O varies depending on whether the **container–contained** relationship between them is **commensal, symbiotic** or **parasitic**. The mystic appears in the analyst when he is capable of grasping the patient's unconscious, or becoming O, corresponding from the vertex of religion to the messianic idea.

Myth: Corresponds to a primitive form of **pre-conception**, as well as a stage in the **publication** or **communication** of individual private knowledge to the **group** (1963, p. 92). "Myths", says Bion, "must be defined; they must be communicable and have some of the qualities of **common sense**—one might call them 'common nonsense'" (1992, p. 186). They could be represented by the formula

K(ζ), where **K** represents the constant in a myth, what is always repeated, whereas ζ means what is variable, what is individual and **unsaturated** (1974, p. 23).

Myths correspond to category C of the **Grid**. Bion refers mostly to the myth of the Garden of Eden, the **Tower of Babel** and the Sphinx in **Oedipus**, as **concepts** representing evolutions of **O** (1970, pp. 84–85) The common **fact** in all of these myths is the attitude of the deity that punishes men for their wish to satisfy their curiosity towards knowledge (*ibid.*, p. 92). *See*: **Ur**, **Xi**, also Abbreviations.

N

Name: (For instance the name of a person.) Stands for something invented with the purpose of binding together in **constant conjunction**, a series of **phenomena** of unknown **meaning** is unknown. The binding performed by the "name" not only provides cohesion to a **pre-conception** and prevent its components from getting dispersed and lost, but it also allows the possibility of finding a meaning for it. When we say, for instance, "dog", we presume we know what we are speaking about, because the penumbra of associations related to the constant conjunction bound by the "name" dog, represent the pre-conception. We will require the presence of a true dog, as a **realization**, to reach its real meaning or **concept**. (1963, pp. 88–90). The name, says Bion, is capable of accumulating meaning with the use of operations of **container-contained** (♀♂).

Nameless terror:[43] Mentioned for the first time in 1962, in Bion's **"theory of thinking"** (1967, p. 116), when he refers to feelings experimented with by the baby when the mother is unable to

---

[43] Grotstein (1993) suggests that concepts such as **"nameless terror"**, **"catastrophic change"**, **"thalamic terror"**, etc., are closely related to Bion's life

metabolize the sensory information of **anxiety** she has received from her baby; or in other words, when the mother's capacity for **reverie** does not exist. A normal development between the baby and the breast is established when such a relation allows the baby to project feelings inside his mother, for example that he is dying, and then re-introject it after its permanence in the breast has changed it into a more bearable feeling for his mind. If such projection is not accepted by the mother, the baby might feel that his fear of death is real, and its re-introjection would be, not just a more tolerable fear of death, but a "nameless terror". The baby's **rudimentary conscious** cannot deal with the demand placed on it (1967, p. 117). Another way to say it, would be that if reverie prevails the **container–contained** relationship would be of a **commensal** kind, because all the elements involved will benefit from this relationship and the end result will be an **apparatus for thinking** and **K**. But if **envy** dominates the relationship, the product would be $-K$ and a nameless terror (1962, pp. 96–99), a **container–contained** condition represented by Bion as $-(\female \male)$. This condition is really serious because the breast not only does not obstruct the wish to die, but subtracts the wish to live (*ibid.*, pp. 97–99).

Narcissism: *see*: **Social-ism**.

Narrative: Represents a form of public and well known kind of cause–effect interaction, for instance the narration of a renowned story. It would be different from what happens in the **selected fact**, the **constant conjunction** or the move from **paranoid–schizoid** to the **depressive position**, where the **realization** or association of **elements** is absolutely private, it begins by chance but repeats itself by compulsion, tied by a constant conjunction. The **Oedipus myth** represents a public narrative related to the theory of **causality**, equivalent to the maxim: "who live by the sword die by the sword". However, at the same time there is a personal side to the Oedipus complex, the product of a constant conjunction, of how everyone has carried out their own history, their own private travelling to build their own myth. Narrative and causality represent the

experience during World War I, when he became the only survivor of his company on the 8th August 1918 (Bion 1985, *see* also the Introduction to this dictionary).

memory, of how **facts** once did relate—or in relation to the Oedipus myth—as Bion stated: "where the penis once was"—and its relation to the future-"where the penis will be". It could be placed in category 3, or **notation**, of the **Grid**. What happened at the **crossroads** in Thebes, says Bion, is something public or well known to everyone and would correspond to column 3.

On the other hand, a word like "cat", for example, where obviously there is not narrative, could reunite a series of private events to a certain individual, provide a sort of personal meaning representing a constant conjunction, or a **definitory hypothesis** belonging to category C1 (1965, pp. 96–97).

Negative Capability: Represents a mental state capable of tolerating "ignorance", uncertainty, mystery and doubt, a condition that, according to Bion, psychoanalysts must promote. He associates it with the **depressive position** and the concept of **"security"**. The concept is based on an expression invented by poet John Keats in a letter written to his brother, to describe his concept of creative receptivity:

> I had not a dispute but a disquisition with Dilke on various subjects; several things dove-tailed in my mind, and at once it struck me what quality went to form a Man of Achievement, especially in Literature, and which Shakespeare possessed so enormously—I mean Negative Capability, that is, when a man is capable of being in uncertainties, mysteries, doubts, without any irritable reaching after fact and reason. [1970, p. 125]

The incapacity to build a mental space that tolerates ignorance or uncertainty, induces the creation of a language of **action** or **Language Achievement**, from where power can be exercised arbitrarily. In a note written in 1969, Bion said:

> The capacity of the mind depends on the capacity of the unconscious–negative capability. Inability to tolerate empty space limits the amount of space available. Curiosity should be part of the **dependent group**, but it can share **fight–flight** qualities when the wish is to avoid impending discovery (category 2). [1992, p. 304]

Reading between the lines, it could be conjectured that Bion was also referring to the reactions he was observing in many colleagues towards his innovative ideas; such as his emphasis on listening without memory, desire or understanding. In other words, the "negative incapability" to tolerate spaces of ignorance and allow new discoveries to take place: instead of a dependent group, a fight–flight **basic assumption** was induced.

Negative Grid: Bion has introduced the idea of the possibility of a "negative grid", a sort of mirror image of the Grid, a table to represent lies corresponding to column 2. He considers the possibility of adding a "negative" extension to the standard table by expanding the **horizontal axis** from–n and continuing it with –5, –4, –3, –2 and –1. He concludes that in this way the negative use could serve as a barrier against the unknown or against what is known but disliked. According to the theory of **transformation**, the "negative Grid" represents the possibility of a movement contrary to the movement ordinarily followed by the Grid's axes: from H to A in the genetic axis, and . . .n to 1 in the axis of uses. Bion represents this negative movement geometrically with arrows: ↑←. If they were to represent an object, this object would have the following characteristics: "violent, greedy and envious, ruthless, murderous and predatory, without respect for the truth, persons or thing" (1965, p. 102).

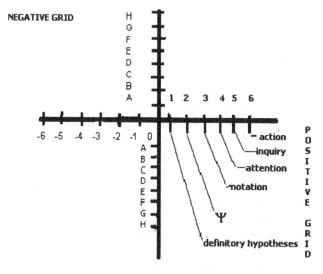

Figure 1.   Negative grid.

But if presented like this: ←.↑ it would then mean geometrically, a "no-breast"; or in this way: ← _→, a "no-penis", carrying the characteristics described above. Such representation implies a contradiction, because "a thing can never be unless it both is and is not" (1965, pp. 102–103).

Meltzer (1973), through his concept of the "idealization of the bad object", and Rosenfeld (1971) with his notion of the "narcissistic gang", have emphasized the "idealization of lying" and the systematic attack on the truth and represented the latter as the "goodness" of the object. In a similar way, Bion refers to the relationship between the thinker and the lie, corresponding to a container–contained parasitic relationship, where they destroy each other.

Negative growth: *see*: **Growth**.

Negro, dream of the: *see*: **Significant dreams**.

Newton, Sir Isaac: *see*: **"Ghosts of departed quantities"**.

No-breast: For Klein this represents a kind of presence–absence, that is, a negative **realization**, in the sense that the absence of the breast is translated into a series of **emotions** that would later consolidate as the presence of a "bad breast", as a psychic entity opposed to the presence of the breast or "good breast." According to Freud, **thinking**, originating from ideation, acquired special qualities of **action**; something that allows the **mental apparatus**, if motor discharge is obstructed, to free itself from accretion of stimuli. When satisfaction is not possible (no-breast) the future will depend on how the ego would or would not tolerate **frustration**. Following Bion, the ego could: (a) use **evacuative** forms of **thoughts** or β-**elements**, which are projected into internal or external objects; (b) modify the situation; (c) establish a **splitting** between physical (materialistic) and mental aspects; or (d) create a thought by mating a **pre-conception** with a **conception** or negative realization of the absent object. *See* **projective identification, thought.**

The no-breast differs from the breast and can be represented using **geometric** similes such as the **point** (.), a mark or a stigma (στιγμή), an ephemeral spot analogous to a *staccato* mark in a musical score. It would correspond to a breast that has been reduced to a simple position, to the place where the breast was, but disappeared consumed by greed or because **splitting** has destroyed it leaving only its position, its στιγμη (1965, p. 54). Regarding the relationship between the psychological concept and the geometric representation, Bion wonders: "Why then, to revert to the point and **line**, do these visual images lead in one case to the efflorescence of mathematics [when absence of the breast is translated into mathematical thoughts] and in the other to mental sterility [**psychosis**]?" (*ibid.*, pp. 56–57).

Bion describes the case of a psychotic patient who continuously repeated for almost three years that he had not been able to find ice-cream: "no **ice-cream**", something Bion interpreted as representing the expression "no I-scream"; he explains:

> I now know that a violent attack had been delivered on a relationship in which the **link** between the two personalities had been "I scream". This had been destroyed and the place of the link "I scream" had been taken by a "no—I scream". The "I scream" link had itself previously been food, "ice-cream", a "breast", until **envy** and destructiveness had turned the good breast into an "I scream". In **narrative** form: he had been linked to his object by a good breast (he liked ice-cream). This he had attacked, possibly bitten it in actuality. The place of the breast as link was then taken by an "I scream". Further attacks made it a "no—I scream". [*ibid.*, p. 13]

The patient's complaint recurred over many years, something Bion did not realize until the end, representing the immensity of time and space within the psychotic's mind:

> **Mental space** is so vast compared with any realization of three-dimensional space that the patient's capacity for **emotion** is felt to be lost because emotion itself is felt to drain away and be lost in the immensity. [*ibid.* p. 12]

Non-existence: Bion states:

> The patient feels the pain of an absence of fulfilment of his **desires**. The absent fulfilment is experienced as a **"no-thing"**. The emotion aroused by the "no-thing" is felt as indistinguishable from the "no-thing". The emotion is replaced by a "no-emotion". In practice this

can mean no feeling at all, or an **emotion**, such as rage, which is a column 2 emotion, that is, an emotion of which the fundamental **function** is denial of another emotion. . . . As a column 2 element [*see*: definitory hypothesis and Grid] all felt emotion is a "no-emotion". In this respect it is analogous to "past" or "future" as representing the "place where the present used to be" before all **time** was annihilated . . . "Non-existence" immediately becomes an object that is immensely hostile and filled with murderous **envy** towards the quality or function of "existence" wherever it is to be found. [1970, pp. 19–20]

Bion uses the signs ←↑ to symbolize the movements opposite to the direction followed by the Grid's axes, that normally move from left to right and from top to bottom. Such opposite movements represent what Bion calls a state of "awareness", alertness or **Cs**, different from the concept of consciousness used by Freud. It is similar to the awareness of an insect, that driven by phototropism, searches for the light:

This "consciousness", is an awareness of a lack of existence that demands an existence, a **thought** in search of a meaning, a **definitory hypothesis** in search of a **realization** approximating to it, a psyche seeking for a physical habitation to give it existence, ♀ seeking ♂. [1965, p. 109]

But if preceded by a minus sign: – ←↑, it would then imply a C3 category in the Grid, and may be personified by a non-existent "person":

whose hatred and envy is such that "it" is determined to remove and destroy every scrap of "existence" from any object which might be considered to "have" any existence to remove. Such a non-existent object can be so terrifying that its "existence" is denied, leaving only the "place where it was". [*ibid.*, p. 111]

X is the third of four brothers who consulted because of intense **anxiety** attacks, insomnia and all sorts of hypochondriacal complaints. He is the son of a very successful Italian immigrant, "a rather ruthless businessman", and a very dependent, phobic and hypochondriacal mother. Together with his three brothers he worked for his father until three years ago when, with the help of his wife, he started his own business, a courier company that lately has been performing very well. Leaving his father was not easy because the father demanded absolute commitment, was very demeaning with everybody, including his mother and disapproved of his departure assuring him that he was going to fail. X states that he had always tried to please his father; he went to university to study architecture because it suited him for his construction business, but he has never practised it, even now when he is working on his own. He had suffered from panic attacks in the past and sporadically looked for professional help with rather poor results; however, lately there has been an increment of his symptoms apparently related to "stress" because of the success of his own business, something that could be understood according to the **crossroads** or **Oedipus** murder mechanisms. In the sessions, X continuously repeats the same complaints about his anxiety attacks, body ailments, bad luck, poor achievement, etc., giving the impression of a "negative therapeutic reaction" and bringing to mind the **countertransference** image of a child threatened by a castrating father, and hopelessly screaming in distress for help to an unmindful mother. He complains in order to make others—like his wife and the analyst—feel useless, a total failure; because of very intense envious feelings against sentiments of well being that he feels others are experiencing but he is not. Nullified by his father's envious castrating need and rather abandoned by his dependent mother, he feels as "non-existent" and attacks others whom he experiences as comfortable with their own life. First of all he destroys his α-**function, memory** and capacity to **learn from experience**; his mind then fills up with β-**elements** in the form of narcissistic rage, hopelessness, body ailments (language) he projects as **projective identifications** inside others endlessly. Every session is a carbon copy of the previous one and all **interpretations** attempting to clarify the reason of his permanent suffering are also continuously forgotten. As Bion has described it, he "is determined to remove and destroy every scrap of 'existence' from any object which might be considered to 'have' any existence to remove", regardless that by doing so, he pays such a high price. He attempts to induce feelings of non-existence in other persons, as a way of freeing himself from feelings of non-existence, but in so doing he creates more feelings of non-existence. It is precisely this feeling of non-existence which is the main reason for his terror, which he paradoxically continuously induces in himself, while trying inefficiently to free himself from them.

See: **Cs, no-breast, no-thing,** −**K.**

Non-saturated: *see*: **Saturated–non saturated, elements**.

Noösphere: From Greek *noos* (νουσ) = "mind" and *sfaira* (σφαιρα) = "sphere". A word used by Father Pierre Teilhard de Chardin (1959) in 1925 to explain the notion of a "sphere of reflection, of conscious invention, of conscious souls" or "collective mind or conscious", some kind of global trade network, **communication**, accumulation, and exchange of **knowledge**, related to fields such as economy, "psychic affiliations" and so on, which knits itself at increasing speed, penetrating and engulfing each of the individuals within the media who, as **time** evolves, find it much more difficult to think or act in any other non–collective way. For many, Chardin had predicted what we know today as Cyberspace or the Internet.

Bion uses the concept of "noösphere" to explain what he refers to as α-**space**. He explains that the concept of "noos" is more useful than that of "sphere", because the latter carries a penumbra of associations that could complicate instead of facilitating understanding, therefore he prefers the use of Greek letter Σ (S), sigma, something he explains: "I shall employ a sign that is as devoid of meaning as I can make it", capable of carrying the communication expected, identified as sigma (1992, p. 313).

Later on he contrasts sphere with "amorph", because the former entails a limit, a contention, different from the latter that has no **form**. However, there should be no conflict between the two, similar to the situation portrayed by **quantum** theory of light which sometimes behaves as a wave (amorph) and other times as a corpuscle (sphere) (1992, p. 319). Bion also creates the neologism "psycho-sphere", similar to the Cartesian **definitory hypothesis** of "a **thought** without a thinker", equivalent to "a psycho-sphere without a noösphere" (*ibid.*, p. 326).

No-penis: *see* **no-breast**.

Notation: Bion takes the concept from Freud (1911) together with **attention, judgement, action** and **thought**, as **functions** used by the ego to reach **awareness** of reality. Its purpose would be, as an ingredient of **memory**, to secure results from the continuous search for attention. Afterwards Bion uses notation as one of the elements of the **horizontal axis** of the **Grid**, together with the other functions already enumerated above.

"No-thing": A concept Bion relates to **space** in the same manner that "no-present" would be related to **time**. "Words", for instance, symbolize "no-things" or representation of absent things, different from nothing or, as Bion states, "a thing can never be unless it both is and is not". He also presents this rule in a different way: "a thing cannot exist in the mind alone: nor can a thing exist unless at the same time there is a corresponding no-thing" (1965, p. 103), meaning that −. (minus **point**) and +. (plus point) coincide, like Shakespeare's Falstaff, if there is no-thing the thing must exist. The "no-thing" has taken the vacant space of the thing, or of that space that should have been occupied by it, it is a **saturated(ζ)** space with "no-thing".

The "no-thing" represents a space linked to **mental suffering** due to absence of the object and it could be, depending on the condition of the mind, either **contained** and suffered, or if there is intolerance to pain, changed into a **thing-in-itself** or **β-element** and **evacuated** by means of **projective identifications**. The no-thing also represents the breast, or the place where the breast was or **no-breast**: (−.), or no-penis (− ___). The no-thing is indispensable to **symbolize** or represent the absent thing, something that does not exist in **psychotic** patients, where things and no-things are the same, following mechanisms of **symbolic equation**, that is, the no-thing will always exist in a state of no-thing, because there is no difference between one state and the other.

From a geometric point of view, Bion represents three different positions of the no-thing in relation to the mind: (i) *Conscious, real and coincident*: symbolized by a straight **line** between two points and tangential to a **circle** (representing the mind), meaning that there is no distinction between a thing and a no-thing or that they both coincide, representing a thought disturbance as observed in psychotic patients. (ii) *Conscious of an external reality, real and separated*: represented by a straight line inside the circle, meaning something real and external represented internally; (iii) **conjugate complex** *or straight line completely outside the circle*: representing the narcissistic relationship of something staying in a mirror like fashion, inside and outside (1965, p. 83).

Bion also distinguishes three other possibilities between the presence of the no-thing and the **realization** that is felt to approximate to it: (a) the no-thing and no corresponding realization, like hunger without a breast; (b) the realization but no corresponding no-thing, like the presence of the breast without hunger; (c) the co-incidence of the no-thing and the thing, when they are both present (*ibid.*, p. 107).

Noumena: Concept used by Kant to describe what is intuited, what cannot be conceived and is beyond **phenomena**. Represents the **thing-in-itself**, the absolute reality for which we have no empirical or sensible knowledge, and can be grasped by **intuition** only. Bion uses it to explain the notion of instinct, what we are born with but have no knowledge of; for instance the need to suck the breast, sexual intercourse, curiosity, epistemophilia, etc., whatever guides the initial relationship with the object or **realization**, that later on acquires structure as we **learn from experience**.

Number: All numbers but one represent signs denoting a **constant conjunction** that keeps a **group** together and provides them with a **meaning**. Number 1 would symbolize the negation of the group. The numbers constitute an **element** in category 1 of the **Grid**, or a **definitory hypothesis**, that is, an object that contains the potentialities of all undeveloped distinctions in a group: the attempt to bind and then to understand or find a meaning for the group; or as Bion states: "to bind the 'groupishness' of the group by a name, a column 1 element" (1965, p. 150).

O

O, ultimate reality: Letter taken from the word "Origin", probably related to the same term used to designate the centre of the Cartesian coordinates that correspond to the point where the X and Y axes intercept; however it could have also been taken from the **concept** of "Origin" in **Zen Buddhism**. Bion defines O as the **thing-in-itself**, or that which is immeasurable, the "absolute fact" taking place in a session (1965, p. 17, 40), in an artistic creation or in a state of "illumination", and because of its own nature, it cannot be known (**K**) (*ibid.*, p. 17). There is a possibility for O to become known only if the transformation of O is capable of combining the **invariants** present, in such a way that its **communication** to others becomes feasible. In order for this to happen two things must take place: **memory** and **desire** must be abandoned, and a state of union with O which—Bion calls it a state of **at-one-ment**—must be allowed to take place (*ibid.*, p. 102). O is continuously becoming, O from this moment—just like the present time—would not be the O of later on, this is why it cannot be known because if you know it, it is not O any longer, or in other words, just when it is, it is no longer, it can only be when it is not. It is not a "position" or a condition, O is just a possibility that could be or could not be. In classical theory O would be equivalent—although different—to the concept of "insight" as a sudden revelation of the truth, either in the analyst, the patient or—ideally—both.

He also refers to the existence of some kind of a function that permits the precipitation of a **"constant conjunction"**, which is identified as a **constellation** that would act as some sort of catalyst to enhance fusion or at-one-ment with O (1970, p. 33). This fusion can become public in several circumstances; by means of interpretation during the analytic session, or through the feeling experienced by some artists, when faced with their own O, who are able to transmit their work to the audience that listens to (music) or watches (painting) their piece of work (1965, p. 97). It is as if O will become visible through the invariant that results from the thing's transformation, something that can be observed in Descartes' (1641) communication about the transformation of a piece of wax from the honeycomb.[44] In religion, for instance, Meister Eckhart expresses that the **Godhead** evolves to a point where it becomes apprehensible by man as the Trinity. O could be interpreted as the unconscious continuous becoming; for instance, no matter how dense our experience might be, we will always face unknown dilemmas about some of our dreams.

There cannot be a genuine becoming of O based on **falsehood**, O is the absolute **truth** of any object. The analyst cannot identify himself with O, instead he must be it (at-one-ment) and in this way he will be able to know the events from the **evolution** of O (1970, p. 30). Perhaps O could be better understood if one thinks that it represents the ultimate reality, be it good or bad. Bion makes a distinction between the patient's O (Op) and the analyst's O (Oa). To ask in a session, for instance, "what is Op?", implies asking what

---

[44] A piece of wax taken fresh from the honeycomb has not yet lost its taste of honey, the smell of flowers, its colour, shape, malleability, it is hard and cold, and when struck with a finger emits a sound. But if you put it near a fire, all these qualities disappear, the taste goes away, the aroma evaporates, the colour changes, the shape is destroyed, the size increases, becomes liquid and it is impossible to manipulate it and if struck no sound is produced. Is that the same wax after all of those changes? We shall confess that it remains, and nobody could judge differently . . . Certainly, we could have known absolutely nothing about it, about what my senses make me notice [because all the things contained in them had changed] . . . however, the wax remains (Descartes, R., 1641).

the patient is talking about (1965, p. 17). "I therefore postulate," says Bion, "that O in any analytic situation is available for transformation by analyst and analysand equally" and hence, concludes, in psychoanalysis any O that is not at the same time common to both patient and analyst, and therefore is not available for the transformation of both of them, must be ignored and considered irrelevant, for it would not be feasible to investigate it in any way (*ibid.*, p. 48).

The *reaction* of some patients to O can be primitive, with material belonging at the same time to rows A and B of the **Grid**: for example, a patient who comes to analysis with the unconscious purpose of denying the existence of the analyst, trying in this way to deal with the dread of the analyst's absence (TpO). The patient's presence in the session is evidence that the patient knows that the analyst is present (sensuous level or β-elements, row A of the Grid: A2); but at the same time, the patient acts as if the analyst is not there, corresponding to row B, column 2: B2 (*ibid.*, p. 53). Bion has considered O as different from the patient's *reaction*, conceiving it as a definitory hypothesis, belonging to column 1, that could be defined as containing the following negative characteristics: its existence as a dweller or inhabitant within a person is irrelevant, regardless of the individual being God or the Devil, because O is neither good or bad, it cannot be known, loved or hated, can be represented by terms such as "**ultimate reality**" or truth. The most or the least one could be is to be it, but to identify with it is a way of getting away from it and is often an expression of psychopathology in the form of delusions of grandeur. In classical psychoanalysis inaccessibility to O is an expression of **resistance**. There is, as Bion states, a penumbra of associations related to O: Truth, **form**, and those **phenomena** distinguished as ζ[45], **distance**, **Godhead**, etc. (*ibid.*, p. 162).

He also points out the existence of a bipolar condition in O, especially within the analyst, for there could be a conjunction of: (a) an aspect of O dependent on the *analytic experience*; together with (b) another *intuitive* aspect of O (*ibid.*, p. 49). He refers to the first one as Taβ of O1 and to the second as Taβ O2 (*ibid.*, p. 50) (*See* **transformations**).

---

[45] *See* "Abbreviations" at the beginning of this dictionary.

The **space** into which **psychotic** patients project can have infinite dimensions, where the total analysis can be seen as a transformation in which a catastrophic intense emotional explosion of O has taken place: "elements of personality, link, and second personality having been instantaneously expelled to vast distances from their point of origin and from each other" (1970, p. 14), a mechanism Bion described as "**hyperbole**". Such an explosive event in O is then transformed, by virtue of the β-elements, into some sort of **action** or **acting-out** (contortions, changes of mien, grimaces, etc.) in the patient, which corresponds to Tpβ (1970, p. 14), and may be registered in column 6 of the Grid.

Even though Bion does not state it this way, I believe that capturing O at a given moment, or the transformation of O into K, can somehow be equivalent to the **concept** of **unconscious phantasy** described by Klein, but going even further and touching an intuitive deepness and generalization, something Bion compares with what mystics have described as an act of illumination. On the other hand, I believe O has been mistakenly described as "zero" (Grinberg *et al.* 1972, Bion, 1974, p. 107). Transformation of O into K (O →K) represents the act of structuring the interpretation, but this act will require from the analyst a special stance in order previously to allow transformation of K into O, a condition already present in Freud's "free floating attention", although observing in Bion's notion a greater density that perhaps indicates a connection with **Zen Buddhism**. In order to apprehend O one must accept and believe whatever comes up intuitively during analytic **listening**, something Bion describes as an **Act of Faith.**

Bion has referred to **Eckhart** as well as Saint John of the Cross, because of their mystic experience and sense of inner illumination in what they have described as a union or **at-one-ment** with God. Bion used these experiences as a paradigm of what he wished to portray in his description of the meaning of **O**. This is why some have judged O to have a "metaphysical and religious meaning" (Symington and Symington, 1966, p. 10). However, Bion's interest with Eckhart's **Godhead**, is not so much with the "**contained**" (♂) or with what is contained as a proof of God's existence or any other religious concern; instead his interest is directed to the phenomenology of the experience itself, with the "**container**" (♀) that experiences such union with something unknown, unthinkable, the ineffable, the truth itself or ultimate reality. For Bion, the revelation of the mystic with his God, whatever this God might be, is similar to the revelation experienced by the psychoanalyst while listening with "floating attention" and without "memory or desire", to O, to the ineffable, the unknown, unthinkable, the truth itself or ultimate reality, to what the patient might be expressing in that particular moment.

In summary, it could be said that as a proof for his theory about O, Bion used several hypotheses: (a) Kant's concept of noumenon or the unknown (or the pre-conception, the thing-in-itself, the ineffable, etc.) that can only be **intuited**, and the phenomenon (conception, object, breast, etc.), as the end result of a mating or realization between the noumenon and a particular object; (b) Aristotle's theory of form, which can be considered as the opposite, because now the phenomenon acts as a reminder of an abstract concept considered as the "form". Bion also presents some strophes from Milton's *Paradise Lost* as a paradigm of Aristotle's theory; (c) the Godhead, as can be inferred from descriptions made by Meister Eckhart, Blessed John Ruysbroeck, as well as the description of St. John of the Cross of his union with God in "The Ascent of Mount Carmel".

See: **Godhead, Transformations of O, Transformation in O, K, Transformation of K, Act of faith, At-one-ment, Thing-in-itself, Noumenon, Phenomenon, Form, Meister Eckhart, Zen Buddhism, Memory, Desire, Truth, Lie.**

Oedipus complex: There are two sides to the Oedipus **myth**: one is private, the other public. The first one represents the person's own reading of the tragedy, what each individual has experienced in private; the other side represents the account communicable to the public. The private version corresponds to an α-**element** or **pre-conception**, used by the baby to establish a contact with his parents just as they exist in the external world. The mating of this α-element or pre-conception with a realization of the real parents provides a **conception** of them. At the same time, the envious attack towards the parental couple carries destruction of α-elements or pre-conceptions, in such a way that not being able to conceive his parents it is impossible for the baby to "resolve" the complex because, paradoxically, he has never been able to structure it. Bion believes that behind this myth, just like in the Tower of Babel, the Garden of Eden and the Sphinx myths, there is a hostile attitude from God to humans acquiring knowledge (–K), because this is felt as a threat to supremacy. It represents the myth's moral characteristics.

Bion discriminates between an "Oedipus theory" (psychoanalytical understanding) corresponding to categories F4, G4, F5 and G5 of the **Grid**, and an "Oedipus myth" (narrative of the story) pertaining to C area (1963, p. 58). He describes three parameters in the theory: (1) the realization of the relation between Father, Mother, and child; (2) an emotional pre-conception that mates with awareness of a realization to produce a conception; (3) a psychological reaction stimulated in an individual by the members of the triad.

From the point of view of the myth and by virtue of its narrative, its elements would combine with each other in a fashion similar to the way in which letters come together to create words, or the way different hypotheses combine within a **scientific deductive system**. All elements in the myth, such as sex for instance, acquire meaning due to the manner in which they are arranged in the narrative of the myth. Bion emphasizes two aspects: (a) the insistence of Oedipus to know the truth even after Tiresias had alerted him to the danger (*ibid.*, p. 45), something Bion has referred to as Oedipus' **arrogance, curiosity, and stupidity**; (b) the enigma, traditionally credited to the Sphinx, could represent an expression of men's curiosity.

Bion attempts an exercise to evaluate the myth—although incomplete—using the **horizontal axis** of the Grid. He admits the possibility of trying to force the facts by making up pre-conceptions (1963, p. 49), and apologizes: "It is not my object to establish an exact correspondence . . . Therefore to make the correspondence between the horizontal axis and the elements of the myth appear to be exact would be a falsification that obscured the nature of the myth" (*ibid.*, pp. 65–66). Bion considers, in relation to the horizontal axis, the following elements:

(1) (Category 1) The Oracle's account of the story of the myth cn be considered as a **definitory hypothesis**, similar to a pre-conception or an unsaturated element, that progressively **saturates** as the story unfolds.

(2) (Category 2) The warning given by Tiresias, who was blinded because of his attack on the snakes he had seen mating, can represent a false **hypothesis** as a defence against the **anxiety** generated by incidents in the myth.

(3) (Category 3) The Sphinx's riddle can signify at the same time, a menace and a stimulation to curiosity; representing the Freudian **concept** of **attention**.

(4) (Category 5) Because Oedipus pursues the investigation with arrogance, he can be guilty of hubris or exaggerated pride, a behaviour that could be considered as a **symbol** of scientific integrity or instrument of investigation or **inquiry**.

(5) (Category 6) The unfolding of the myth itself might stand for **action** of column 6, represented either by Oedipus' exile or the dispersion of the characters, or both. To these elements could be added a series of disasters: the plague that attacked Thebes, the suicides of the Sphinx and Jocasta, Oedipus' blindness, the slaying of king Laius, the original riddle introduced by the monster, or an object made by a number of characteristics that are incongruent with each other (*ibid.*, pp. 46–47).

Following Plutarch, Bion attempts an association between the triangulation of the complex and the triangle rectangle as presented by **Euclid**'s theorem of the "**Bride's chair**". He also uses the theorem of "**Pons Ansinorum**" about the isosceles triangle, and an ancient description of this triangle as "**the three-kneed thing** with equal legs". Plutarch had stated that the triangle rectangle can be equated to the triangulation made by both parents represented by the sides of the right angle and the child by the hypotenuse. Onians (1951) also stated that the Greeks considered the term "knee" equally to represent the angles of the triangle as well as the genitals.

Omniscience: Incapacity to tolerate **frustration** can obstruct the foundation of an **apparatus to think thoughts**. But if frustration is tolerated the mating between a **conception** and its **realization** is feasible, making it possible to **learn from experience**. Between these two extremes there can be an intermediary stage, in which frustration intolerance is not so great as to activate mechanisms of evasion, but important enough to determine a control of reality. In this case, omnipotence is stimulated as a substitute for mating the **preconception** with the conception. Bion states that omniscience will take the place of both the capacity to learn from experience with the use of **thinking**, as well as the mental ability that enables discrimination between **true** and **false**. In this sense, omniscience will represent a dictatorial and capricious intention, outside of every scientific logic, to discriminate between true and false, as can be observed in **magic** or religion (1967, pp. 114–118).

Opacity: A concept that contrasts with **transparence**, representing a **saturated** mental state due to opacities such as **memory**, **desire** and understanding, capable of generating states of **turbulence**, that may interfere with the capacity to intuit **O** during **analytic listening**.

Organs of perception: *see*: **Perception, organs of.**

Origin: *see* **O.**

Oscillations of Dependent basic assumption: **Emotional** oscillations present in a **group** dominated by a **dependent basic assumption** (Dba), between the therapist leader of a **working group** (W) and the accidental leader chosen in a given Dba, the latter usually being represented by a disturbed individual. Emotional oscillations produced between both situations can generate high levels of **anxiety** that if not properly **contained** by the therapist, get extended to other larger groups. For example, the need of a small therapeutic group (or any other kind), to write to hospital authorities, the press, the Congress or even the President. *See*: **basic assumptions, Dba, Fba, Pba, group, valence, schism.**

P

Pairing basic assumption (Pba): It is based on the creation of a couple, whose union would produce an **idea** or a **messianic** leader, who will finally put an end, in a future not too far off, to all suffering produced by feelings of hopelessness, **hate**, and destruction. However, in order for this to be feasible, there is the ineluctable paradox that the leader would never be born, that is, the hope must stay in suspense, and it should always remain as such: "pure hope". At the very moment when it is felt that the idea or leader can become a reality, feelings of anger and destruction will again predominate (1948b, pp. 151–152). Under the dominance of this kind of ba, feelings of messianic hope will prevail. These feelings can also be observed outside the therapeutic **group**, for example in religious beliefs or in the aristocracy, and in some sense, assures Bion, in the analytic couple (*ibid.*, p. 176). A good example is given by Bion in presentation No. 4 of his Brazilian seminars (1987, pp. 19–24). *See*: **Basic assumptions, Work group (W), Dependent ba, Fight–flight ba, Group, Valence.**

Palinurus, death of: Bion uses the death of Palinurus narrated by Virgil at the end of the *Aeneid*'s 5th book, as a metaphor to explain the danger faced by the analyst when he is not ready to give up **memory, desire**, and understanding during **analytical listening**.

> After the storm, Aeneas had ordered all the sails to be raised and Palinurus to steer the pilot vessel ahead of the fleet. The sailors exhausted lay on the benches to rest. As Palinurus sat watching the stars, Somnus (Hypnos or Dream) sent by Neptune approached in the guise of Phorbas and said: "Palinurus, the breeze is fair, the water smooth and the ship sails steadily on her course. Lie down awhile and take needful rest. I will stand at the helm in your place." Palinurus replied: "Tell me not of smooth seas or favouring winds, I who have seen so much of their treachery". And continues holding tied the helm and watching the stars. But Somnus waves over him a branch moistened with Lethaean dew, and his eyes closed in spite of all his efforts. Then Somnus pushed him overboard and he fell. When Aeneas discovered his loss he weeps with sorrow for the fate of his loved steersman.[46]

The metaphor is used to explain the danger of remaining stubbornly harnessed to **memory** and **desire** as Palinurus did with the helm. Perhaps, argues Bion, this attitude might be contrary to the

> . . . conventions of ordinary medical practice to be unaware of so many and such apparently important items in the family and individual history, and it would leave the psychoanalyst open to attack on the grounds of negligence should something go wrong. [1977a, p. 15]

At another moment he stated:

> I do not make notes in a session or afterwards so that it is open to anyone to object that the account cannot be true. [*ibid.*, p. 14]

He argues, however, that it would be even:

> . . . less true if mechanisms had been devised which seemed to record and repeat whatever was to be thus preserved (*ibid.* p. 14) . . . Naturally psychoanalytic colleagues would like to have evidence; naturally I would like to give evidence. But with the passage of time I am convinced that there is no substitute for psychoanalysis. [*ibid.*, p. 22]

---

[46] Publius Vergilius Maro, *The Aeneid*, Book V, pp. 826–871.

More important than to provide evidence is to psychoanalyse without memory or desire, an exercise that will leave no more evidence than what privately takes place between the analyst and the patient. It is obvious that Bion is also referring to the mechanism of **at-one-ment** with **O, transformation** of O into **K** and **act of faith**.

Paranoid–schizoid and depressive position: Bion refers to both of Klein's positions very similarly to the way she has described them. D is regarded as an integrated object or "**agglomeration** produced by the convergence of elementary particles" (1963, pp. 42–43), on β-elements, "or as a special instance of integrated objects" (*ibid.*, p. 42) like either ♀ or ♂. In this form Bion connects **PS ←→D** with the **theory of thinking,** meaning a **transformation** from an "uncertainty cloud"[47] of primary particles representing the paranoid–schizoid position, to β-elements, and then into ♀ or ♂. The movement is also reversible and the object thus formed could "become fragmented and disperse" (*ibid.*). PS←→D could assume a form of operation similar to ♀♂ and *vice versa*; while the former provides a "delineation" of the whole object, the latter provides meaning (1963, p.90):

> ... I have tried to show that PS←→D and ♀♂ are not to be regarded as representing a **realization** of two separate activities but as mechanisms each of which can at need assume the characteristics of the other. [*ibid.*, p. 44]

Such a **correlation** is easy to follow in relation to D, but if applied to PS, it would then present a certain difficulty, because it would be hard to conceive PS as conforming either with ♀or ♂, something Bion attempts to convey by the use of an imaginary clinical description. An incoherent discourse from a patient (= PS = ♂), states Bion, will induce a **countertransference** response from the analyst as a **container** (♀); however, what is important in this **communication** is not the patient's incoherence, but the capacity of the analyst to be exposed to such incoherence, meaning to take the place of the ♂. The movement from PS to D is negotiated

---

[47] It is quite possible that with the expression of "uncertainty cloud", Bion is borrowing from quantum theory, from Heisenberg's "uncertainty principle".

during **dreams**[48] (1992, p. 37) and will depend on the existence of a **selected fact** that may lead the process of integration from one position to the other (*ibid.*, p. 213).

Meltzer (1978) criticizes Bion for restricting the concept of positions PS$\leftrightarrow$D to the status of a mechanical condition related only to "disintegration–integration" interactions, rather than providing them with an economic sense—as Klein did—related to value attitudes (p. 75). *See*: **Progression and regression, thoughts; verbal thoughts; thinking, apparatus for.**

Parasitic relationship: A kind of interaction between "**container**" (♀) and "**contained**" (♂), where one **element** depends on the other to produce a third one that will destroy the three of them (1970, pp. 95–96). A man, for instance, wishes to communicate his anger, but ends up feeling so overtaken by the **emotion**, that he begins stuttering and becomes incoherent. In this case, the language will be the container, the anger the contained and the "incoherence"—which destroys **communication**—the third (*ibid.*, p. 104). The language, not being able to contain the emotion he intended to express only with words, ends up dispersing and abandoning the attempt to express what he originally wished to say. Or expressed in a different way, his attempt to use his tongue to express himself verbally, fails to contain his wish and he ends up stammering as an expression of masturbating inside his mouth (*ibid.*, pp. 93–94). **Envy**, jealousy and induced possession would be the mental equivalents of the toxic elements found in physical parasitism. Within this kind of parasitic relationship, **thoughts** contained by a thinker would be **false** by definition—for **truth** does not require a thinker—and would be used as a barrier against truth, which in turn is experienced as dangerous and destructive of the container.

Part objects: A kind of object relation that according to Klein (1946) rules the **paranoid–schizoid position**, and represents the form in which the mind arranges itself within this position, the way it relates to the outside world and with itself. Following Bion, this form of relation or **link** is established not so much on the corporeal

---

[48] *See*: López-Corvo, 1987.

aspect of things, but also in relation to the **functions**, not so much on the anatomy of the breast, but on the physiology of nutrition, loving, hating, poisoning, etc. (1967, p. 102). For a child, a word, for instance "dirty", can mean everything that he dislikes, or that bothers or threatens him. This helps us to understand what takes place when a patient says, for instance: "it seems" instead of saying "I think" or "I believe". "It seems" corresponds to a feeling, "an 'it seems' feeling" and not to the quality of "**thinking**" or "believing" as the expression of a "total object" capable of thinking or believing (*ibid.*, pp. 101–102). At this level of **communication**, to ask "why" makes no sense, for because of to guilt, it has been **split** off and expelled. For instance, patients seldom question themselves, for they have a tendency to believe that the analyst has created the problems they are dealing with. They lack the conception of totality and therefore are not capable of thinking about problems, not to mention solving them, when awareness of reality is needed. There is not, in other words, a conception of totality and those problems depending on **awareness** of **causality**, cannot be introduced and even less, resolved.

Another important aspect is related to the kind of link between part objects. Bion states that relationship between part objects, such as the baby (mouth) and the breast, is established by means of **projective identifications** and the capacity to introject them. A failure in this latter capacity could induce in the baby the feeling that the object is hostile to curiosity and might interfere with any disposition towards learning and **growth** (*ibid.*, p. 108). "The result is an object which, when installed in the patient, exercises the function of a severe and ego-destructive superego" (*ibid.*, p. 107). Bion states that this object is experienced as a total object that will obstruct the movement from paranoid–schizoid or part object relationships to depressive or total object relationships.

Passion: By passion or its absence, Bion describes an **emotion** experienced with intensity and warmth though without any insinuation of violence, unless it is associated with greed. He includes **L**, **H** and **K** as well as dimensions emanating from them. Although passion always links two minds, it must be differentiated from **countertransference**, because in this last case it would mean repression of a latent content. Passion cannot be evidenced by the senses, because often an emotion can really hide some other affect, as apparent hate can mask love or *vice versa*, or elation might conceal depression (1963, pp. 12–13).

Meltzer (1986) states that passion can induce **turbulence** or a **catastrophic change** because of the impact that novel emotions might have on already existing affects, such as the passionate love observed in adolescents (pp. 187–190)

Patience: Term used by Bion to describe a state analogous to Klein's notion of the **paranoid–schizoid position**, although free from its pathological components but retaining "its association with suffering and tolerance of **frustration**." He immediately quotes Keats:[49] "Patience should be retained without 'irritable reaching after fact and reason' until a pattern evolves" (1970, p. 124). The "pattern" will evolve towards the **depressive position**, and for this state, says Bion, "I use the term **security**. This I mean to leave with its associations of safety and diminished **anxiety**." (*ibid.*) The move between patience and security should be very brief, as in the final stages of analysis, although it could also be very long. Bion does not believe it is possible for an analyst to believe that he or she has done the necessary work to provide an **interpretation**, unless he has passed through both phases. I think Bion is referring to the patience and capacity to tolerate frustration, for an analyst must deal with uncertainties induced in analysis by object relations of the kind experienced in the paranoid–schizoid position, in contrast with the feeling of certitude, stimulated by the security provided by object relations that takes place during the depressive position. *See*: **Paranoid–schizoid position, Security.**

Pba: *see*: **Pairing (group) basic assumption.**

Pellucidity: Represents an **unsaturated** mental state, which allows perception or **intuition** of reality, for instance, during analytic **listening**. It is opposite to states of "**opacity**" that are induced by **memory**, **desire** or understanding and are capable of inducing **turbulence** (1992, pp. 315–316).

---

[49] The fragment of Keats' letter from which Bion has quoted, can be found in the description of "**Negative Capability**", in the last chapter of Bion's book, *Attention and Interpretation* (1970).

When the **noumena**, the **things themselves**, push forward so far that they meet an object [a **realization**] which we can call a human mind [for instance] . . . The religious man would say, "There is, in reality, God". What Freud and psychoanalysts have investigated is **phenomena**. [1974, p. 41]

Through realization we meet the unknown, the thing-in-itself, representing what Bion, on the other hand has referred to as turbulence, that is, the capacity to produce opacity in order to make visible what has been so far invisible. *See*: **Turbulence, Opacity, Memory, Desire, Thing-in-itself, Noumena, Phenomena, Fraunhofer lines**.

Perception, apparatus of: Originally Bion identifies "apparatus of perception" with "**conscious awareness**". In 1956 he stated:

> . . . attacks are directed against the apparatus of perception from the beginning of life. This part of his personality is cut up, split into minute fragments, and then, using the **projective identification**, expelled from the personality. Having thus rid himself of the apparatus of conscious awareness of internal and external reality, the patient achieves a state which is felt to be neither alive nor dead. [1967, p. 38]

Freud had described the apparatus of perception as a set of activities produced by demands from the **reality principle**. For Bion this apparatus is connected with **verbal thoughts** and with whatever it might have produced since the time of its inchoation (1967, p. 38). In **psychotic** patients, or in the **psychotic part of the personality**, there is an Id attack against sense organs and against consciousness attached to them; there is also a great hatred towards reality, something already pointed out by Freud (1924). In these patients, the reality principle is never achieved, because all attempts towards the integration of the **conception** of a total object cannot be reached because **consciousness** of reality induces guilt feelings and depression associated to the process of reparation present in the **depressive position** (*See*: **Verbal thoughts**). Psychotic patients directed their attacks against those ego aspects (apparatus of perception) necessary to link internal and external realities. *See*: **Link, attack on**, and **Cs**.

Perception in reverse: Mechanism that, according to Bion, is used to perceive backwardly from outside objects, whatever had already been projected into them that will come back by the same path, but in the opposite direction. Bion has used this mechanism to explain the dynamic present in **hallucinations, delusions** and the creation of bizarre objects. *See*: **projective identification in reverse**.

Perception, organs of: Bion uses contributions from Adrian (1947), who states that the first sensations perceived are from light rays and sound vibrations, both considered perception from a **distance** and linked to development of intelligence. They differ from touch and other corporal sensations, which are considered close- and middle-range receptors related to immediate transformation into **action**. All of these perceptions operate automatically without any intervention of **consciousness**. Receptors of distance, such as sight, sound, smell, intuition, etc, are associated with the development of intelligence and wisdom, while middle-range receptors, such as bowel and bladder senses, or immediate-range like touch or sex, are to do with action (1992, pp. 321–322). Bion also considered the successive steps in which an original visual perception changes into a sense of taste, for instance, or the way in which the vision of an object is progressively transformed into a mental representation, like the visual perception of a horse, which is primarily changed into an **ideogram**, then into a word, a **thought** or α-**element** until it reaches the ineffable, the **thing-in-itself** and **O** (*ibid.*, p. 325).

Personification:[50] Concept originally used by Klein (1929) to describe a form of identification observed in children, who provided objects of play with characteristics of real or imaginary persons. "Personification, ubiquitous in all plays", said Hinshelwood (1989) "led Klein to the view that all mental activity is conceived with relationships between personified objects" (p. 389). Bion used the term in the "Imaginary twin" when he referred to "personification" given by his patients to a **split**-off part of the personality conceived as a phantasied twin. He explains that personification can be considered as an expression of improvement in the capacity to

---

[50] I am grateful to Dr Paolo Polito (2001) for his suggestions in relation to the concept of "personification".

symbolize (*ibid.*, p. 20) and as a consequence, it represents "hopeful-ness about the outcome of the analysis" (1967, p. 16). *See*: **Imaginary twin**, **Splitting**.

Phenomenon: Kant defines phenomenon as everything that pre-sents itself to the senses; it contains two aspects: (a) what belongs to the external object which he called "sensation"; and (b) what belongs to our apparatus of perception capable of ordering what-ever is perceived, which he called "form". Noumena, on the other hand, are objects of which we have no sensible intuition and hence no knowledge at all, they are **things-in-themselves**, and in a posi-tive sense, can be conceived as objects of intellectual **intuition**, a mode of knowledge which man does not possess. **Platonic Ideas** and **Forms** are "**noumena**", while phenomena represent the result of an *aprioristic* conception of the noumena, meaning the capacity to know about the unknown. For Bion, the "phenomenon" is trans-formed into a representation such as Tβ, which could also be con-ceived of as a representation of O in individual experience, or **transformation** of **O** into **K** in psychoanalytic listening, or from noumenon to phenomenon by means of a realization, or God into **Godhead** in mystical terms. Bion states:

> As I understand the term, various phenomena, such as the appear-ance of a beautiful object, are significant not because they are beau-tiful or good but because they serve to "remind" the beholder of the beauty or the good which was once, but no longer is, known. This object, of which the phenomenon serves as a reminder, is a Form. [1965, p. 138]

The Form or the noumenon, says Bion, can also be presented in **mystical** terms like God in the Godhead (or O in K), considered as a "spiritual substance, so elemental that we can say nothing about it" (1965, p. 139). "In this view", continues Bion, "God is regarded as a Person independent of the human mind . . . the phenomenon does not 'remind' the individual of the Form but enables the per-son to achieve union with an incarnation of the Godhead, or the thing-in-it self." Forms and Incarnation give the:

> . . . suggestion that there is an ultimate reality with which it is pos-sible to have direct contact although in both it appears that each

direct contact is possible only after submission to an exacting discipline of relationships with phenomena, in one configuration, and
incarnate Godhead in the other. (*ibid.*)

Bion presents a similar mechanism in relation to the concept of O.
See: **O, Form, Godhead, Meister Eckhart, thing-in-itself.**

Place where something was: *see*: **Awareness; Space; Geometric
space; Euclid, geometry of; line, point, no-thing, no-breast.**

Platonic forms: *see*: **Forms, theory of.**

Point (.): **Euclid** defined the point as something indivisible that contains no parts, while others subsequently described it as "a place
without extension", "a geometric entity without dimensions", "a
line's limit", "infinite **elements**", etc. The word στιγμη (*stigma*) with
which Plato originally labelled it means "instant" or "point".[51] Bion
used it to represent the "absence of the breast", perhaps because in
its Greek conception the word "point" conjugates both dimensions
of **time** and **space**: instant, moment, stigma or trail (1965, p. 53). If
the point represents the absence of the object, "**no-breast**" or "no-
penis", etc., and if we were to use the **theory of thinking**, then the
point would represent a **pre-conception** related to **K** (row D in the
Grid) (*ibid.*, p. 77). But if we regard the "point" as a spot, it can then
be conceived of as a conjunction of **part objects** representing an
absence–presence, such as breast, penis, faeces or a cruel and
malignant persecutor (*ibid.*, p. 78). It could mean "the place where",
"the time when", or a "stage of **growth**" (*ibid.*, p. 119).

Words stand for **thoughts**, they are the void of the thing, or the
"**no-thing**" and can be represented by a (.), which can signify the
place or trail where the breast used to be, or the "no-breast" (*ibid.*,
p. 82). In relation to time, it could then mean "where the present
was" (*ibid.*, p. 86). In the Grid it would correspond to category A1.
Similar to the "line", the point represents a visual image that
remains invariable in spite of many situations. Minus point (–.)
is equivalent to the place where the object "that is not" (absent), is;

---

[51] In English both meanings are condensed in the word "period", besides
"dot" and "spot" (Bion, 1965, p. 78).

which for not been, is; or the place where "not being" would always be. It is exactly the situation that takes place in the **transference**. *See*: **Circle, Line, no-thing, no-breast**.

Point of view: *see*: **Vertex**.

Point-pair: Would correspond to two different **points** located on a **line** in a system of coordinates. Bion uses this **concept** in relation to the **theory** of **transformation**, together with other mathematical concepts such as "**number** and "**conjugate complex**", to establish a "geometrical" relationship between points corresponding to internal and external realities, or between unconscious and **conscious** contents or present and absent objects (1965, pp. 86, 103). *See*: **Complex conjugates, number, Circle**.

Pons Asinorum: Name given to **Euclid**'s theorem 1.5 depicting the demonstration of an isosceles triangle, according to which the base angles are equal to each other because they are congruent with their mirror image. Epicurus gave this theorem the name of "Pons Asinorum", which means "The Asses' bridge", because the complex picture drawn by Euclid during its demonstration resembles a bridge, which contrasts with its simplicity, to the point that Epicurus stated that anybody who tried to "cross it", meaning to solve it, was an ass.

Bion attempts a relationship between the **Oedipus myth** and Pythagoras' theorem as well as **Euclid's geometry** and **paranoid–schizoid** and **depressive positions**. These comparisons are proposed in his book "**Cogitations**" in an extremely dense and cryptic style, as if he were emulating the Sphinx itself. In relation to Pythagoras, for instance, he stated:

> The side subtending the right angle: the sides containing the right angle. How much can be obtained by ignoring the figure, the diagram, except in so far as it serves a function—like that of the material of a sculpture by Henry Moore—in framing the place where there is *no* material? To act as a boundary to the open **space**, that is to say the part where the figure is *not*. Then the squares on the sides containing, and the squares on the side subtending, the right angle serve to enclose the triangle—the "three-kneed thing", but also the right angle. The construction is a trap for light. [1992, p. 206]

In this rather enigmatic communication, Bion invites us to ignore
the diagram, that is, the mathematical aspect of the theorem, and concentrate on what is enclosed, for instance, the Oedipus myth: in a
right-angled triangle there are the two sides forming the right angle,
that would represent both parents (e.g. vertical = father, and horizontal = mother), while the opposite side or hypotenuse would represent the son. The **"three-kneed thing"** refers to the interpretation
apparently given by the Greeks to the triangle, when they considered
that the angles that put together all the sides, that is, father, mother,
and son, were equivalent to the genitals. Bion says something similar when he states that "Euclid 1.5 marks the point at which the 'elements' of geometry are left behind when the student crosses the
Pons" (*ibid.*). In other words, in order to avoid being an ass, the content of the figure must be ignored and attention must be directed to
its meaning; only then would the trapped light escape, and thus the
Pons would finally be crossed—or the theorem properly understood—without having, as Epicurus announced, to be an ass.

Bion also refers to Pythagoras' theorem known as the **"Bride's
Chair"**, because its demonstration resembles, according to the
Arabs, a horse riding chair used to carry the bride. It has also been
said that the French referred to this theorem by the name of Pons
Asinorum, something questioned by Bion who assures us that this
last one corresponds to No. 5 of Book 1 and represents the theorem
of the isosceles triangle, while the Bride's theorem represents a
right-angled triangle, which corresponds to Book 13, No. 47 (*ibid.*,
p. 207).

Positions, the: Concept used by Bion to refer not to both positions
as described by Klein: **PS←→D**, (1992, p. 207), but to something in
between:

> For convenience I propose to call this state, which is neither the
> paranoid–schizoid position nor yet the **depressive position** but
> something of each, the Positions. [*ibid.*, p. 215]

Positive growth: *see*: **Growth**

Pre-conception: Bion discriminates between pre-conception and
preconception. The former he describes as part of the **Grid**'s **vertical axis**, corresponding to row D, that is, to the existence of a **desire**

in demand of a **realization**. The latter, on the other hand, refers to **premonition** and represents a **theory** belonging to Grid columns 3 and 4; for instance, when an analyst has the presentiment that something is taking place in the session that he is not completely aware of (1963, p. 75). **Thoughts**, says Bion, can be classified according to the nature of their developmental history, as pre-conceptions, **conceptions** and **concepts** (1967, p. 111). Pre-conception would be analogous to Kant's notion of "empty thoughts", a state of expectation (1962, p. 91) comparable with the supposition that the baby has an innate or **a priori disposition** towards the breast; in other words, when the baby (pre-concept) gets in touch with the breast, a realization takes place, that is translated into a concept and represents for Bion a kind of **container–contained** relationship. "Conceptions therefore will be expected to be constantly conjoined with an emotional experience of satisfaction" (1967, p. 111) The classical concept of "instinct" could be intuited behind Bion's notion of pre-conception. *See*: **Conceptions, Concepts, Realization, Thoughts**.

Precursors: Used by Bion to refer to feelings that can act as precursors of other emotions, like for instance "if the hate that a patient is experiencing is a precursor of love its virtue as an element resides in its quality as a precursor of love and not in its being hate. And so for all other emotions" (1963, p. 74). *See*: "**Premotions, Premonitions**".

Premonition: Represents an "emotional state rather than an ideational content", because the latter would be better characterized by a **pre-conception**. "I do not dissociate 'pre-monition'", said Bion, "from its association with a sense of warning and **anxiety**"; meaning that premonitions could be interpreted as **precursors** of the **emotions**. Directly observed, emotional states are meaningful only if they can be conceived as premonitions; for instance **countertransference** anxiety can be interpreted as a premonition capable of guiding the analyst in his/her investigation and finally help to structure the **interpretation**: "If premonitions cannot be experienced", states Bion, " correct interpretation becomes difficult for the analyst to give and difficult for the analysand to grasp". In this sense premonition appears to be related to other important **concepts** such as **O** or **hallucinosis**. Bion also interchanges premonition with "**premotion**".

As a **"psychoanalytic element"** premonition could be represented as follows: (Anxiety (ζ)), where ζ stands for an **unsaturated** element.

Premotion: Bion uses this word without giving any definition. He mentioned it twice in Chapter Sixteen of *Elements of Psycho-Analysis* (1963, pp. 75–76), where he says: ". . . when a patient comes for a first consultation his *premotions* (my italics) give information about him that cannot be obtained from other factors" (*ibid.*, p. 75). Perhaps he was referring to feelings that can be intuitively grasped by the analyst. A few lines later, he says:

> I do not dissociate "pre-monition" from its association with a sense of warning and **anxiety**. The feeling of anxiety is of value in guiding the analyst to recognize the *premotion* in the material. The premonition can therefore be represented by (Anxiety (ζ)) where (ζ) is an **unsaturated element**. [1963, p. 76]

There are doubts whether "premotion" is a printing misspelling for "premonition" or a neologism implying a condition previous to an **emotional** state. However, there still remains the question of why he did not use something like *"pre-emotions"* instead. Bianchedi (2001, personal communication) has expressed a similar opinion. Meotti (2001, personal communication), had called attention to the meaning given by followers of St Thomas Aquinas ("Thomists") who used the term "premotion" to refer to some kind of "motion" emanating from God's omniscience, as a form of causality and used upon people to move them through their apparent freedom. They have referred to it as a "physical premotion" (*proemotio physica*). Based on this definition, Gooch (2001) put forward an interesting hypothesis:

> I think the premotion of the analysand stimulates the premotion of the analyst or parent. The premotion may be the **beta element** and the premonition the dawning of the corresponding **alpha-function** or element that is required for psychic **awareness** (secondary process, reality principle, signal affect, ego function) to develop, in contradistinction to discharge (pleasure principle, primary process, evacuation, somatization, **acting-out**, symptom formation). [Personal communication]

Primary and secondary splitting: Klein described as "primary splitting" a process present during the **paranoid–schizoid position**. Bion on the other hand, refers to "secondary splitting" as the one that takes place when **psychotic** patients, during analysis, regress to the paranoid–schizoid position after having reached the **depressive-position**. When this happen, says Bion, the patient turns with great anger and **anxiety** against those fragments that were capable of fusing together to create total objects during the depressive position, and splits them again with such strength and violence, that any possibilities of ego reparation become inaccessible and therefore the prospect of recovering is impossible (1967, pp. 80–81). The consequence of this condition is an attack against the **pre-conceptions**, or against the **thinking apparatus** that would allow the **conception** of the relationship between both parents as well as the understanding of the **Oedipus** complex (1965, p. 60).

Primary qualities: *see*: **Qualities, primary and secondary**.

Prisoner: Similarly to the way in which the baby feels he has sadistically attacked and destroyed the breast, **psychotic** patients, or within the **psychotic part of the personality**, sense impressions can also be attacked and mutilated. As a consequence, the person feels a "prisoner" inside such a mental state and believes he is not able to free himself from it, because the mind, which represents the means and ends of escape, has become impoverished and lacks the capacity to be **conscious** of reality (1967, p. 51). The feeling of being a prisoner increases under the threat from those projected elements, that are part of the **constellation** by which the patient feels **contained**.

Some time later Bion (1970) stated that when analysts do not free themselves from **memory** and **desire**, they face the danger of inducing in the patient the phantasy of being prisoner inside the analyst's desire, something that can be observed in patients in whom "false self" pathology predominates, that is, when the other person's wish is privileged over the analysand's own desire.

Progression and regression: Represents a form of **oscillation** between the paranoid–schizoid and the **depressive position** and *vice versa*, which can be observed between the **psychotic and the**

non-psychotic parts of the personality. Progression would face the danger of depression and guilt from reparation of destroyed objects. Regression, on the other hand, can imply danger of suicide, **secondary fragmentation**, and total deterioration (1967, p. 81).

> The Positions are not to be regarded simply as features of infancy, and the transition from paranoid-schizoid to depressive position as something that is achieved once for all during infancy, but as a continuously active process once its mechanism has been successfully established in the early months. [1992, pp. 199–200]

When this movement between both directions is not established early, growth can be defective and deprive individuals of the healthy capacity to have progressions and regressions at their disposition (*ibid.*, p. 200). This mechanism could also be considered to be related to formation and use of thoughts, similar to the relationship between container–contained ($\male\female$) where their functions can be interchanged (1963, p. 44). It could also be understood as an interaction between a dispersion of particles with feelings of persecution (PS), on the one hand, and integration of particles with feelings of depression (D) on the other (*ibid.*, p. 52). Bion states that PS$\leftrightarrow$D organizes the object while $\male\female$ provides meaning (*ibid.*, p. 90). *See:* **Depressive position**.

Projective identification: Bion used this concept following closely on from what Klein had previously stated, adding that it could also have represented a very primitive **form** of **thinking** and **communication**, phylogenetic as well as ontogenetic (1962, p. 37; 1963, p. 37). He emphasizes the importance of this mechanism in **psychotic** patients and in the **psychotic part of the personality**, where it is used to **evacuate** ego aspects, such as the **apparatus of perception** or **verbal thoughts**. In these kind of patients, projective identification takes the place of repression (1967, p. 52), because as we shall see next, these patients have the need to split and evacuate the apparatus on which the psyche depends to carry out repression, and the unconscious seems to be replaced by a world similar to **dream furniture** (*ibid.*). In his theory of thinking, Bion established that thoughts result from the experience between the **pre-conception** of the breast the baby brings with him at birth, and its **realization** after he begins to feed. When the breast is available and the need satisfied, it will give place to a **conception** of the present breast or "good breast". But if there is the need and the breast is absent (no-breast) it would give place to a "negative realization" and then two possibilities can follow: (a) **frustration** is tolerated and will promote the commencement of thinking about the absent breast; (b) frustration is not tolerated, inducing the need to expel to avoid frustration—which is experienced as the presence of bad objects—by means of mechanisms of projective identification. Such **evacuation**, proposes Bion, is experienced as the "substance of a good object", because it alleviates tension, something that will stimulate further evacuation with the use of more projective identifications. At the end, concludes Bion, it is felt that:

> the appropriate machinery is . . . not an apparatus for thinking the thoughts, but an apparatus for ridding the psyche of accumulations of bad internal objects. The crux lies in the decision between modification or evasion of frustration. [*ibid.*, p. 112]

Bion believed that when Klein referred to "**excessive projective identifications**", she was not only talking about frequency, but also about an excess of omnipotence in its use (*ibid.*, p. 114).

Projective identification in reverse: A mechanism described by Bion to explain how **psychotic** patients are capable of introjecting or incorporating concepts or mental content coming from outside, similar to the way in which **interpretations** attempt to help understand the nature of their **delusions**, if they lack an apparatus for **thinking thoughts**. "These objects", he said, "are brought back by the same route as that by which they were expelled" (1967, p. 61).

Because the **apparatus for thinking** has been **split**, mutilated, and projected inside the external objects, patients lack an apparatus for introjection, making them perceived interpretations given equality with **projective identifications** that assault and split them, perhaps as revenge coming from those objects where they feel they have placed their own projections. Also, because those re-incorporated particles have the character of "things", it makes it difficult for them to figure them out (*ibid.*, p. 62). Bion illustrates this mechanism with a patient who said that he used his "intestine as a brain", and when

Bion told him that "he had swallowed something", the patient answered that "The intestine doesn't swallow". Because the patient cannot synthesize his objects to re-introject them, he would have to **agglomerate** and compress them, and as a consequence, perceive them as concrete things, as **bizarre objects** or **ideograms,** that he will use in order to **communicate** with others (*ibid.*, pp. 40–41, 61). *See*: **Psychosis, Psychotic and non-psychotic part of the personality, Ideogram.**

Projective transformations: Concept borrowed from projective geometry and used by Bion to describe a kind of **transformation** opposite to **"transformations in rigid movement"**, because the deformations that result in the transformation (Tα) of the original object are so immense, that it makes it difficult or impossible to recognize the original **elements** in the end results (Tβ). In relation to the patient it would mean that the material presented is so distorted, that an identification of the end products of **projective identifications**, present in the **transference** as well as in Op (patient's O), are almost impossible to recognize, and as a consequence, the **interpretation** would be highly speculative (1965, p. 19). This kind of transformation is observed in **psychotic** patients and corresponds to categories in file A of the **Grid** (*ibid.*, pp. 36, 114). Meltzer (1978) associates this kind of transformation with Klein's concepts about "early transference", based on **part objects**, internal objects, **splitting,** and projective identification (p. 73). *See*: **Transformation in rigid movement, Transformations, Transformations in hallucinosis, Projective identification.**

Proto-mental system: Initially Bion used this concept in relation to **group** dynamics, in order to describe the existence of "undifferentiated feelings" or a "potential state" preceding the emergence of a **basic assumption** (ba) (1948b, pp. 101–102). It can be considered as the system or matrix where differentiation of physical and mental states began. It contains precursors for **emotions** present in all basic assumptions, including those that remain latent. When any of the basic assumptions becomes manifest and its feelings predominate in the group, the others that remain latent stay contained within the proto-mental system; for instance, if fight–flight is manifest, dependent and pairing emotions will be latent (*ibid.*, p. 105).

Bion attempts to explain, with the use of this system, the appearance of diseases, regardless of their aetiology. Diseases are manifested in the individual depending on the group to which they belong (city, family, work, etc); that is, they are the product of the relationship between the proto-mental system, the dominating basic assumption and the latent basic assumption. In all diseases there are three dimensions: (a) the "matrix", corresponding to the undifferentiated or proto-mental system, (b) a determined "affiliation" to the latent basic assumption, and (c) a "cause" determined by the dominant basic assumption. Usually there will be psychosomatic pathology, although they could be infectious too. Tuberculosis, for instance, because of the need for the patient's care, would be associated (matrix) with a **dependent basic assumption** (baD), it will have an affiliation with a **pairing basic assumption** (baP) and will have as a cause a **flight–fight basic assumption** (baF). Clinical experience has shown me that exophthalmia present in hyperthyroidism, can be interpreted as the watchful monitoring (dependency) of a projected "internal murderer" and thus correspond to a flight–fight ba where baD and baA remain latent.

> This evocation of primitive, perhaps tribal, life in the depths of the mind, which can surface as group behaviour or, conversely, express itself through bodily processes, has a frightening, even haunting impact. [Meltzer, 1986, p. 38]

Meltzer (1978) has also established a parallel between the notion of a "proto-mental system" and Freud's concept of primary narcissism: "as a level at which object relation and identification are undifferentiated and where the ego is still purely a body-ego" (p. 9). Some time later Meltzer (1986) interpreted that the distinction made by Bion between the proto-mental system, as an extreme representation of what is "non-symbolic, nominative, externally factual, quantitative"; from what at the other extreme would be considered as "mental or emotional, symbolic, internally oriented, qualitative and aesthetic", would be extremely clarifying. "At the boundary between the proto-mental and the mental", continues Meltzer, "he has placed a hypothetical, "empty" concept, **alpha-function**, the mysterious, perhaps essentially mysterious, process of **symbol** formation" (p. 10). The Symingtons (1966) suggested that the proto-mental system foreshadowed Bion's more mature conceptualization of β-**elements** (pp. xvi, 35).

Proto-real objects: According to Bion, they are primitive objects that surround the baby, conforming a world dominated by reality and pleasure principles, where objects will be alive if they satisfy or dead if they frustrate. Later Bion referred to them as α- and β-**elements** respectively. If intolerance to **frustration** increases, either because the level of tolerance decreases or because the aggression from the objects increases or both, the need to be free from the displeasure induces the baby to attack the apparatus responsible for the **transformation** of sense impressions into material used for the creation of **dream-thoughts**. As a consequence, if there is no **apparatus that can think** or process **thoughts**, they might change into things. The excess of these "dead proto-objects", besides the call for placating them, induces the need to idealize and to change them in the future into objects of adoration that possess super-human attributes; a mechanism that according to Bion is implemented exactly because they *are dead*.

> Contrary to common observation, the essential feature of the adored or worshipped object is that it should be dead so that crime may be expiated by the patient's dutiful adherence to animation of what is known to be **inanimate** and impossible to **animate**. This attitude contributes to the complex of feelings associated with fetishism. [1992, p. 134]

In other words, the crime would be paid for by the useless dependency on those objects that being inanimate (dead) are believed to be animate, but exactly because of this they are not capable of providing anything; for example, the belief that statues can produce miracles. **Fetishism** and religious faith could be explained with these mechanisms. *See*: **Animate–inanimate, difference between**.

Proto-thoughts: Kind of primitive **thoughts** or **ideograms**, which appear when the ego has to deal with the absence of the breast or **no-breast**, which is considered to be bad exactly because it is needed. Such an absence would induce the formation of primitive forms of **thinking** or proto-thoughts, that take the place of the absent or bad object. These "bad objects" are dealt with in two possible ways: they can be evacuated through **projective identification** mechanisms or the absence can be modified through the use of **verbal thoughts** and the creation of an **apparatus for thinking thoughts**. *See*: **Verbal thoughts; Thinking, apparatus for**.

PS↔D: *see*: **Paranoid–schizoid and depressive positions**:

Pseudo-causation: Cause–effect interaction related to −**K**. *See*: **Causality, theory of** and −**K**.

Psi (Ψ): Bion used the Greek letter Ψ (psi) as an **element** or **psycho-analytic object** to represent several concepts: the mind in general, like the mind of the patient or the analyst; column 2 in the **horizontal axis** of the **Grid**. The use of Ψ to designate column 2 could be related to *"proton pseudos"* (πρῶτον ψευδος)[52], a concept Freud (1886) used, parodying Aristotle, to refer to the "first lie" present in hysterical patients. There is a certain discrepancy in the use of Ψ, between such a general representation of the patient or analyst's mind, on the one hand, and the narrow representation of lies in column 2 of the Grid, on the other. *See*: **Function, horizontal, axis, Grid**.

Psi + ksï = Ψ(ζ): Equation representing the union of Ψ as a constant meaning, for example, the condition of the analyst or patient's mind, with ζ as an **unsaturated element** that determines the value of the constant once it has been established (1962, pp. 69–70). In this case it would be equated with the patient's uncensored condition of free association, or the analyst's mind without **memory** or **desire**. The equation could be equivalent to a **pre-conception** waiting for a **realization** that would produce a **conception** and then a **concept** in the form of an **interpretation** (if it were the analyst) or an insight (if it were the patient). *See*: **Psychoanalytic element**.

---

[52] (πρῶτον (*proton*) = first, and ψευδος (*pseudos*) = false, to lie). The expression is from Aristotle's First analytics (book II, Chapter 18, 66a); possibly taken from Aristotle's Prior Analytics (Book II, Chapter 18, 66a) which deals with false premises and false conclusions, asserting that a false statement is the result of a proceeding falsity (*"proton pseudos"*) (Freud, 1886, p. 400).

Psychic mathematics: In **Cogitations**, in a note without a date, Bion asks why mathematicians do not "speak" mathematics:

> Is it that a string of mathematical formulas cannot be made to say, "It's a nice day"? Is the vocabulary not big enough? No: it must obviously be that its primary purpose is not conversational, although it is clear that one of the **functions** of mathematics is **pub-lic-ation**. [1992, p. 110]

In *Learning from Experience* (1962), Bion predicts that although there is no prospect yet for psychoanalysts to use mathematical formulations, there are "suggestive possibilities" that something like that might happen (p. 51). A first attempt to establish a relationship between mathematics and psychology can be observed in "A theory of thinking" (1967, p. 113) where he states that "**mathematical elements**, namely straight **lines**, **points**, **circles** and something corresponding to what later becomes known by the names of **numbers**, derive from **realizations** of **two-ness** as in breast and infant, two eyes, two feet and so on", or in other words, the empirical realization that there are things that come in pairs. On the other hand, he also suggested that the development of mathematical elements or "mathematical objects" as Aristotle calls them, is analogous to the development of **conceptions**; for instance, something like a **pre-conception** of the breast mates with a realization (breast feeding) to produce a conception or a two-ness, similar to 1+1=2. If a child, for example, has two marbles and later on finds two more, it will not be long before he concludes that he has four. In this sense, Kant said that all **propositions** of pure mathematics exist **a priori**, similar to Klein's and Bion's affirmation that there is an *aprioristic* preconception of the breast, or the expression that "integral numbers were created by God".

The excess of **projective identifications** in **psychotic** patients or by the **psychotic part of the personality**, implies an impossibility to distinguish self from the external object, something that can be translated as a difficulty to distinguish differences or two-ness. Bion seriously attempts to provide precision to the uncertain, as can be observed in his effort and enthusiasm to square the mind with the use of his **Grid**. This reminds us of a similar enthusiasm previously experienced by Descartes, although much less complex, when he used geometry to square the abstract notion of mathematics.

Bion states that objects belonging to external reality (R) and feelings belonging to psychic reality (Ψ), can be quantifiable, because they could increase or decrease. Numbers can be used to evoke curiosity in the observer (category 4 of the Grid); for instance: "the majority of people . . .", "thousands (millions) all over the world . . .", "the Trinity", "Four out of five people . . .", etc.. Or expressions can be used to produce **envy**: "you are not the only one, thousands can do it", etc. He attempts to distinguish between relativity in **Euclidian geometry** and the precision of axiomatic algebra; while the former represents approximations to **space**—because its exactitude is variable depending on whether the space is flat or curved—the latter represents absolute reality independent of the environment. Bion also used psychological meanings and symbolisms to make a distinction between geometric and mathematical developments. Geometry can be associated with presence–absence or existence–**non-existence** of an object, whereas mathematical developments are associated with the conditions of the object, whether it is whole or split, total or partial. Besides, while geometric space is associated with depression (absence–presence, separation), mathematics would be associated with persecutions as observed in the Kleinian **paranoid–schizoid position**. (1965, p. 151)

Meltzer (1978), making comparisons between Bion's books *Transformations* and *Elements of Psycho-Analysis*, relates the great difficulties the reader faces with mathematical signs as used by Bion:

> In the present work no such hope sustains us in the face of the proliferation of mathematics-like notations, pseudo-equations, followed by arrows, dots, lines, arrows over (or should it be under?) words and not just Greek letters but Greek words. How are we to bear such an assault on our mentality? Is Bion patient B in disguise? [p. 71][53]

While Grotstein (1981) emphasizes the election of mathematical objects, because as he said, they:

> had the advantage of being a language of signs and/or symbols which could conveniently represent objects in their absence and therefore facilitate a language useful for **abstraction** without the penumbra of associations typical of words. [p. 12]

---

[53] About patient "B", *see Transformations* pp. 19–23.

Bion also uses the term "emotional mathematics" or "mathematics of emotion", to refer to different combinations of numbers to represent situations. For example, number 1 could represent:

> "one is one and all alone and evermore shall be so". [or] 1/1 = a relationship with "the whole of an object that is a whole object, that is unrelated to any other objects and therefore has no properties; since properties are a dimension of relationships". With religion as vertex this sign can represent the O represented by the term "**Godhead**". [1965, p. 154]

Psychoanalysis: According to Bion psychoanalysis must be "regarded as a term binding a **constant conjunction**. Years must pass before we understand what are conjoined and what the conjunction means" (1970, p. 63). And later, in a rather pessimistic way, he states:

> What makes the venture of analysis difficult is that one constantly changing personality talks to another. But the personality does not seem to develop as it would if it were a piece of elastic being stretched out. It is as if it were something which developed many different skins as an onion does . . . The patient has a breakup, or breakdown, rather than a "breakthrough". Many a façade has been saved by the misfortune that has made it a successful ruin. [1977a, p. 47]

During his experience in **groups** Bion defined psychoanalysis as a "**group work**" (W) that stimulates the **pairing basic assumption** (baP), and where sexuality occupies a central position. Later on, in **Transformations** (1965) he states that the analyst's work can be interpreted "as transformation of a **realization** (the actual psychoanalytic experience) into an **interpretation** or series of interpretations" (1965, p. 6). He also adds that we could not speak of invariants in psychoanalysis because this is not a static condition:

> Since psychoanalysis will continue to develop we cannot speak of invariants under psychoanalysis as if psychoanalysis were a static condition. In practice it is undesirable to discard established theories because they seem to be inadequate to particular contingencies, such a procedure would exacerbate a tendency to the facile elaboration of *ad hoc* **theories** at **times** when it were better to adhere to established discipline. [*ibid.*, p. 4]

He also emphasized the feeling of isolation within the atmosphere of intimacy that characterizes psychoanalysis, a feeling that should always be present in the mind of the analyst when he speaks with the patient's family or other colleagues (1963, p. 15). In *Attention and Interpretation* Bion investigates the relationship between psychoanalysis and other sciences. It is not that the psychoanalytic method is unscientific, but that:

> ... the term "science", as it has been commonly used hitherto to describe an attitude to objects of sense, is not adequate to represent an approach to those realities with which "psychoanalytical science" has to deal. [1970, p. 88]

Nor can science represent the ineffable, the unknown, or in Bion's terms, **O**. Such criticism can also apply to other **vertexes** such as music, aesthetics, politics or religion. Science takes care of the sensuous aspects of things, such as symptoms, but not of depression or **anxiety**, for instance, that lack weight or colour. What is needed is a science that does not restrict knowledge (**K**), some kind of mathematics of **at-one-ment**, of unification with the other. Bion attempts to introduce the hypothesis of **psychic mathematics**, he attempts, for instance, a relationship between O and mathematics based on the simple fact that the object being observed and the feelings of those who observe, can increase (+) or decrease (−).

Bion distinguished between a "psychoanalytic theory" and a "theory of observation". The former corresponds to specific formulations and determinations of the theoretical body of psychoanalysis that allows unification of criterion, corresponding to **conception's** row F of the **Grid**. An example is the theory implicit in the **concept** of **projective identification**. The "theory of observation", on the other hand, refers to the realization of theories in practice, something Bion exemplifies through the concept of "**hyperbole**", which corresponds to the realization of the theory of projective identification. (1965, p. 160). *See*: **Psychic mathematics, Psychoanalytic elements**.

Psychoanalytic elements: Initially, "**psychoanalytic elements**" and "psychoanalytic objects" were used interchangeably; for instance, in *Elements of Psycho-Analysis*, when Bion, referring to the relationship with emotional links (**L**, **H**, and **K**) (1963, p. 3), affirms that psychoanalytic objects *derive* from psychoanalytic elements (*ibid.*, p. 11). The opposite is said when referring to "**idea**": he states that psychoanalytical objects *are made* of elements, like α-**elements** (*ibid.*, p. 4). Later on, when referring to **passion**, he makes no difference between them: ". . . one of the dimensions of a psycho-analytic object *and therefore* of a psychoanalytic element . . ." (*ibid.*, p. 13, my italics).

Meltzer (1978) referring to this confusion states:

> It therefore becomes extremely confusing when he begins to describe ♀♂ as an element, along with **Ps←→D**, LHK, R (reason) and I (idea, or psycho-analytic object) when he later calls them mechanisms (♀♂) and Ps←→D or earlier had called them **factors** in a **function** (LKH). This is made even more confusing when he seems to discard ♀♂ as an element in favour of a "central **abstraction**" which it must contain or imply, to which the term "element" should be applied and reaches the conclusion that elements are essentially unobservable. [p. 56]

In the last chapter of *Elements of Psycho-Analysis*, however, Bion finally established a clear difference between psychoanalytic objects and elements. He states that the psychoanalytic object has three dimensions: analytic theory, mythology, and feeling.

> An analytic object is not the same as an element but may be regarded as having a relationship with an element analogous to that of a molecule to an atom. The analytic object is not necessarily an **interpretation** though an interpretation is an analytic object . . . [which] emerges as a result of the operation . . . of Ps←→D and ♀♂. (1963, p. 101–102)

He concludes:

> The *elements* of psychoanalysis are ideas and feelings as represented by their setting in a *single* grid-category; psychoanalytic objects are associations and interpretations with extensions in the domain of sense, myth and passion, requiring three **grid** categories for their representation. [*ibid.*, p. 103–104]

Referring to these dimensions, but before he made clear the difference between object and psychoanalytic element, he had said:

Psychoanalytic elements and the objects derived from them have the following dimensions:

1. Extension in the domain of sense.
2. Extension in the domain of **myth**.
3. Extension in the domain of passion.

An interpretation cannot be regarded as satisfactory unless it illuminates a psychoanalytic object and that object must at the time of interpretation possess these dimensions . . . Extension in the domain of sense . . . means that what is interpreted must . . . be an object of sense. It must, for example, be visible or audible . . . [*ibid.*, p. 11]

It must also have a common sense to allow a consensus.

The extension in the domain of myth refers to personal myths that the analyst can use at a given moment in order to understand the patient's latent content; to say for instance in the face of the patient's aggression that his anger is like that of a "child that wanted to hit his nanny because he has been told he is naughty" (*ibid.*, p. 12). These represent **statements** of the analyst's personal myths and not statements of observed fact, or formulations of a theory intended to represent a **realization**. About the extension of passion, Bion says that it represents, "an emotion experienced with intensity and warmth though without any suggestion of violence . . . unless it is associated with the term 'greed'". Different from sense and myth, passion implies the presence of two minds linked (*ibid.*, pp. 12–13). It could correspond perhaps to what others call "empathy".

It is quite possible that the selection of the term "element" could have been encouraged by the "**Euclidian elements**" as well as by the relevance that such a concept has in chemistry. According to Bion, "psychoanalytic elements" represent abstractions, similar to letters in the alphabet, that if combined with each other form words; when combined they represent almost all the necessary theories for the analytical work. All elements must be functions of personality conceived as having dimensions which, in the analyst's mind, represents sense impressions, myths or passions. Bion says:

The combination in which certain elements are held is essential to the meaning to be conveyed by those elements. A mechanism supposed to be typical of melancholia can only be typical of melancholia because it is held in a particular combination. [1963, p. 2]

All elements must have the following characteristics: (a) they must be capable of representing the same realization that they originally described; (b) they must be capable of articulating with similar elements; and (c) when articulated they must form a **scientific deductive system** capable of representing a realization if it happens to exist. Among these elements are: (i) $♀♂$ representing the dynamic relationship between container and contained, similar to Klein's notion of **projective identification**; (ii) $Ps \leftarrow \rightarrow D$, representing approximation to a combination between Kleinian **paranoid–schizoid** and **depressive positions** with Poincaré's **selected fact**; (iii) L (Love); (iv) H (Hate); and (v) K (Knowledge), representing the last three links between psychoanalytic objects. All elements without exception are considered functions.

Grotstein (1981) stated that the election of mathematical objects:

> Had the advantage of being a language of signs and/or symbols which could conveniently represent objects in their absence and therefore facilitate a language useful for abstraction without the penumbra of associations typical of words. [p. 12]

Psychoanalytic listening: In a letter to Andreas-Salomé dated May 25, 1916, Freud suggested a method to reach a mental state that would bestow him with advantages to compensate for the "obscurity" that usually surrounded any object of investigation.[54] The method consisted in "blinding himself artificially", or in his own words: "I know that I have artificially blinded myself at my work in order to concentrate all the light on the one dark passage". Bion implicitly described "listening" as a situation in which the analyst should rid himself of any **pre-conception**, approximating to a state of pure naivete, which if translated into words, would mean: "*not* knowing [unsaturated] to make room for a pre-conception that will illuminate a problem that excites my curiosity" (1965, p. 47). Later on Bion adds the concept of "**patience**", something similar to Klein's **paranoid–schizoid position**, but free from any form of pathology, and referring only to feelings of suffering and **frustration** tolerance (1970, p. 124). (*See*: **countertransference**).

---

[54] In his obituary of Charcot, Freud (1893) mentioned having heard about this method from his French teacher (SE 3, p. 12; also in SE 14, p. 22).

Listening should be accomplished free from any understanding, **memory** or **desire**, and very often, especially with **psychotic** patients, in a state of **hallucinosis**. This preparation will allow for **O**, as the ultimate truth, to "evolve", a concept Bion described as "**evolution**" , which in classical psychoanalysis might be equivalent to the notion of "**unconscious phantasy**". Such evolution to illumination will allow, with the help of an **act of faith**, the construction of the **interpretation** (*ibid.*, p. 43).

In a note written in October 1959 (1992, p. 82), Bion made the following confession while listening to a patient:

> Drowsiness is coming to me; it is part of the relaxation I have to achieve if my ideas are to be accessible. I must *dream* along, but then I risk going fast asleep. I have had to shut my eyes because they sting. Then I nearly went to sleep . . . I must not know anything about. A wrapping up and packing of the goods I wish to remove from the environment. Does this mean that α is to *hide* things from the conscious? [*ibid.*]

And elsewhere:

> Since it is essential that the creative worker should keep his α-function unimpaired, it is clear that the analyst must be able to dream the session. But if he is to do this without sleeping, he must have plenty of sleep. [*ibid.*, p. 120]

Bion also explains that the suppression of understanding, memory, and desire, can result in the undesired complication of inducing in the analyst a state of stupor or sleepiness. Although there is a difference between this last condition and a state of normal listening, the difference is difficult to explain. The analyst could react against the sacrifice of his own desires (pain–pleasure), because it is something difficult to tolerate for both, the patient and the analyst. Bion gives certain rules:

> 1. *Memory*: Do not remember past sessions. The greater the impulse to remember what has been said or done, the more the need to resist it. This impulse can present itself as a wish to remember something that has happened because it appears to have precipitated an emotional crisis: *no* crisis should be allowed to breach this rule. The supposed events must not be allowed to occupy the mind.

234   DICTIONARY OF THE WORK OF W. R. BION

Otherwise the evolution of the session will not be observed at the
only time when it can be observed -while it is taking place.
2. *Desires*: The psychoanalyst can start by avoiding any desires for
the approaching end of the session (or week, or term). Desires for
results, "cure" or even understanding must not be allowed to proliferate. [*ibid.*, pp. 381–382]

Psychoanalytic objects: Similar to how philosophers of science and
psychotic patients (or the **psychotic part of the personality**) attempt
to change **abstractions** into concrete things (*see*: **symbolical equation**), Bion tries, imitating Aristotle's *mathematical objects*, to build
"psychoanalytical objects" in order to deal with **spaces**, such as
those experienced between "things" and "**no-things**". Bion states:

It is convenient to postulate the existence of a mind represented
entirely by **points**, positions of objects, places where something
used to be, or would be at some future date. [1965, p. 106]

And later on:

In mathematics, **calculations** can be made without the presence of
the objects about which calculation is necessary, but in psychoanalytic practice it is essential for the psychoanalyst to be able to
demonstrate as he formulates. [1970, p. 1]

The notion of **number** can be the consequence of the **realization**
of **two-ness**, like two ears, two eyes, two hands, etc., or deci-mals
(ten-ness): ten fingers, ten toes. The development of mathematical
objects can correspond to a **conception**: the mating of the **a priori**
notion of number with its realization.

The identification of such an object depends on (*a*) the possibility of
finding a means by which the nature of the object can be communicated. This involves the employment of the very methods that are
the object of this investigation, and (*b*) the mental equipment that
the observer can bring to bear. [1962, p. 68]

Using an example from Bion we can presume that a constant Ψ
represents, for instance, a **desire**: that a breast capable of satisfying
its own incomplete nature, exists. The realization of this desire, on
the other hand, symbolized as (ζ), would provide an "emotional

experience" of great pleasure (**conception**). Such an experience is equivalent to the **concept** of **phenomenon**, as explained by Kant, meaning the existence of an experimental or **empirical** object. The representation of this realization using "mathematical objects" would correspond to $\Psi(\zeta)$, equal to a conception. If an "inborn character" of personality, symbolized as σψμβολ, is added, we will have the following formula: $\Psi(\zeta)(\sigma\psi\mu\beta o\lambda)$. Bion produced other examples related to **growth** and knowledge or **K** (1962, pp. 69–70). A series of psychoanalytical objects could acquire coherence with the presence of a **selected fact** and this would eventually allow the formulation of a **scientific deductive system** (*ibid.*, pp. 72–73). This process implicitly carries a tendency towards concretization, something that brings it close to the **thing-in-itself**.

The notion of "psychoanalytic object" appears initially undistinguishable from "psychoanalytic elements", an idea Bion broadens later on in his book *Elements of Psycho-Analysis* (1963): for instance, when, referring to the relationship between emotional **links** (**L, H,** and **K**) (1963, p. 3), he affirms that psychoanalytic objects *derive* from **psychoanalytic elements** (*ibid.*, p. 11). The opposite is said when referring to **"idea"**, when he states that psychoanalytical objects *are made* of elements, like α-**elements** (*ibid.*, p. 4). Later on, when referring to **passion**, he makes no difference between them: ". . . one of the dimensions of a psychoanalytic object *and therefore* of a psychoanalytic element . . ." (*ibid.*, p. 13, my italics).

Meltzer (1978) referring to this confusion states:

> It therefore becomes extremely confusing when he begins to describe ♀♂ as an element, along with **Ps←→D**, LHK, R (reason) and I (idea, or psycho-analytic object) when he later calls them mechanisms (♀♂) and Ps←→D or earlier had called them **factors** in a **function** (LKH). This is made even more confusing when he seems to discard ♀♂ as an element in favour of a "central **abstraction**" which it must contain or imply, to which the term "element" should be applied and reaches the conclusion that elements are essentially unobservable. [p. 56]

In the last chapter of *Elements of Psycho-Analysis* Bion finally established a clear difference between psychoanalytic objects and elements. He states that the psychoanalytic object has three dimensions: analytic **theory**, mythology and feeling.

An analytic object is not the same as an element but may be regarded as having a relationship with an element analogous to that of a molecule to an atom. The analytic object is not necessarily an **interpretation** though an interpretation is an analytic object . . . [which] emerges as a result of the operation . . . of Ps$\leftarrow$$\rightarrow$D and ♀♂. (1963, p. 101–102)

He concludes:

The *elements* of psychoanalysis are ideas and feelings as represented by their setting in a *single* **grid**-category; psychoanalytic objects are associations and interpretations with extensions in the domain of sense, **myth** and passion requiring three grid categories for their representation. [*ibid.*, p. 103]

Meltzer (1978) also defined the psychoanalytic objects as "tri-partite molecules" compounded of sensa, myth, and passion (p. 86). When he compares the books *Transformations* with *Elements of Psycho-Analysis*, he alerts the readers about the difficulties they will have with all the mathematical signs used by Bion:

In the present work no such hope sustains us in the face of the proliferation of mathematics-like **notations**, pseudo-equations, fol-lowed by arrows, dots, **lines**, arrows over (or should it be under?) words and not just Greek letters but Greek words. How are we to bear such an assault on our mentality? Is Bion patient B in disguise? [p. 71]

Grotstein (1981), on the other hand, states that the election of mathematical objects,

. . . had the advantage of being a language of signs and/or symbols which could conveniently represent objects in their absence and therefore facilitate a language useful for **abstraction** without the penumbra of associations typical of words. [p. 12]

Psychological (or mental) disaster: *see*: **Arrogance, curiosity and stupidity**.

Psychological turbulence: Bion defines it as a state of resistance or mental disturbance associated with change, in relation to **commu-nication** with others, and most of all, with what might be considered as a psychological **growth** of great importance (1970, p. 34). It is similar to the way in which a stream of transparent water remains unnoticed, until the moment it finds an obstacle that generates turbulence. The **noumenon** or **thing-in-itself** remains invisible, unknowable—like the transparent stream of water—that can only be **intuited**, although it could be known through a **realization**—or turbulence—with an object, then giving place to a **phenomenon**:

> When the noumena, the things themselves, push forward so far that they meet an object [a realization] which we can call [for instance] a human mind, there then comes into being the domain of phenomena . . . The religious man would say, "There is, in reality, God". What Freud and psychoanalysts have investigated is phenomena. [1974, p. 41]

Through realization we get to know the unknown, the thing-in-itself, that Bion has referred to as turbulence, the capacity to produce a disturbance in something invisible to make it visible. Leonardo da Vinci—an extraordinary mind—"drew pictures of turbulence reminiscent of hair and water". He could translate this "turbulence and transform it by making marks on paper and canvas which are clearly visible to us." Also, from a religious vertex, Bion quotes St John of the Cross in "The Ascent of Mount Carmel", when he states, in a rather exaggerated fashion, ". . . the pain which is involved in achieving the state of naivety inseparable from binding", with God or the **Godhead** implying a state of deprivation from any desire of "worldly things which it possessed, by denying them to itself; the which denial and deprivation are, as it were, night to all the senses of man", in order to achieve such state of "binding" with God (Bion, 1965, pp. 158–159). It would be this "denial" and "deprivation" in order to achieve a state of communion with God, that represented a state of turbulence in St John's life, which he expressed with an exaggeration of his pain, similar to what, in a biological model, would be observed when a tadpole becomes very upset because it is changing into a frog (1965, pp. 158–159; 1974a, pp. 14–15). The psychoanalytic consulting room might appear as a quiet and transparent stream, however, said Bion, there is only turbulence there (1987, p. 308). Crossing a **caesura**, for example, birth, adolescence, marriage, old age, death, etc., would always determine a state of turbulence. When placing it on the **Grid**, it would correspond to column 1 or to a **definitory hypothesis** (1965, pp. 158–159). *See*: **Thing-in-itself, Noumenon, Phenomenon, Caesura, Godhead** and **Realization**.

Psycho-mechanics (of thinking): Bion uses this concept to explain some psychic mechanisms; for instance, the way in which β-**elements** are capable of **transformations**, or opening towards **growth**, necessary to understand **progression and regression** movements present in **PS←→D** in relation to **K**, or the alternating of **container–contained** movements (♂♀). Bion states:

> A solution may be approached through investigation clinically of the destructive **splitting** attacks that transform ♂ into fragments which nevertheless retain in their fragmented form an association with each other sufficient to permit *penetration* of a problem. Similar fragmentation of ♀ leaves an association of fragments that still perform the function of ingesting or introjecting. [1963, p. 84]

This mechanism could explain the alternating movements of both PS←→D and ♂♀, as well as the change from β to α **elements**, meaning the growth of the genetic or **vertical axis** of the **Grid**. *See*: **Progression and regression, Vertical axis, Paranoid–schizoid position**.

Psychosis: A great amount of Bion's work has dealt with psychoses and psychotic ways of **thinking**, distributed in several original publications, present in almost all of his contributions. Asked, in 1973, about his analysis of psychotic patients, he answered:

> I have only analysed **schizophrenic** patients who were able to come to my consulting room. Although I still think that the best description of them was "schizophrenic", I do not suggest they were comparable to the kind of patients who have to be hospitalized. . . . I am amazed how often an analyst seems to think that he can hardly claim his title [of analyst] unless he has treated many schizophrenic patients . . . From the little I know I find it difficult to believe that so many analysts are treating schizophrenics. Such a claim belongs to the domain not of the science of psychoanalysis but of fashion. As it is sometimes the fashion to wear feathers in hats, so psychoanalysts wear "psychotics in their hair". [1974, pp. 92–93]

See: **Schizophrenia, Hallucination, Attacks on linking, Splitting, Bizarre object, β-element, α-function, α-element, Psychotic and non-psychotic personalities.** . . .

Psychosis, splitting in: *see*: **Splitting in psychosis.**

Psycho-sphere: *see*: **Noösphere.**

Psychotic and Non-psychotic Personalities, differentiation between:[55] This article depicts the difference between psychotic and non-psychotic parts of the personality within the same person. A duality perhaps deduced by Bion from the fact that contacts with reality established behind a psychotic patient's ego, must be a consequence of the presence of a non-psychotic part that remains hidden by the psychotic part. The interplay and control between both parts, summons up the relationship Bion had previously established between the **work group** (W) and the **basic assumptions** (ba).

The major difference between psychotic and non-psychotic parts would originate from the use of **splitting** and **projective identification**, aimed to unload ego aspects, such as the **perceptual apparatus** (consciousness) and **verbal thought**, which have been split very early in life. This division of both personality aspects progressively increases over time up to the point where any connection between them becomes impossible. Just as the baby feels he has attacked and sadistically destroyed the breast, psychotic patients attack and mutilate their sense impressions, feeling themselves to be **prisoners** inside such a mental state, from which there is no way out. Unloading the perceptual apparatus leaves the mind impoverished and incapable of being aware of reality, which would have represented the means and the end of any possible "escape". However, at the same time that they feel prisoners, they also experience that the expelled fragments, projected inside the external objects—that "contain" or are "contained"—have a "life" of their own, becoming what Bion calls "**bizarre objects.**

---

[55] This article, read to the British Psychoanalytical Society in October 1955 and published in 1957, (*International Journal of Psycho-Analysis*, **38**, parts 3–4), shows the best systematization of Bion's discoveries about psychosis up to that moment.

The introjective processes are also seriously obstructed, therefore, in order to understand an interpretation or to reincorporate projected elements; the only possible way is to use what Bion has called a **reverse projective identification** (1967, pp. 40–41). There also exists a difference in the defence format: while the non-psychotic part of the personality uses repression, the psychotic one uses projective identifications. Because there is no repression the unconscious is replaced by a world made of objects similar to **dream furniture**, in which these patients move around. Extension of mechanisms of splitting and projective identification, increments the breach between both parts of the personality to such a point, that any attempt to reunite them becomes impossible.

In **Transformations**, Bion says that one of the difficulties of psychotics has to do with their incapability to transform **O** into T, besides the fact that they are not able to work analytically without the presence of the real objects with which the work has to be done. Such a limitation, he continues, goes as far as making them unable to "think" about anything unless whatever it is in their mind also appears in their external reality (*see*: **sign-objects**). Since psychotics are able to express words and phrases, it is logical to suppose that they are able to think; however, to think in the sense of manipulating words and thoughts to work with the object's absence is exactly what they cannot do (*see*: **symbolic equation**). Psychotics have no **memory**, instead they have undigested facts (1965, pp. 40–41). Bion also points out that, due to **transformations in hallucinosis**, these patients use "magic" omnipotent aspects of hallucinations capable of satisfying any **desire**. They do so in order to compete with interpretations by making them useless like "mental faeces", feeling at the same time, that the analyst is trying to steal their "sanity" or the power implicit in their **hallucinations** (*ibid.*, p. 132).

Meltzer (1978) points out that Bion does not discriminate between the psychotic part of personality and clinical psychoses such as **schizophrenia**, which could be due to Klein's influence in conceiving the **paranoid–schizoid position** as representing the fixation point for the latter. He also adds that it is not clear whether Bion "thinks that this part of the personality is ubiquitous or only present in the person who actually presents a schizophrenic disorder" (p. 26).

Psychotic panic: *see*: **Nameless terror.**

Psychotic transference: Transference in **psychotic** patients "is premature, ephemeral, precipitated and intensely dependent" (1967, p. 37). The pressure induced by both life and death **instincts** has three main consequences: (a) a state of confusion with the analyst because of massive **projective identifications**; (b) mutual mutilations between both instincts; (c) in trying to escape from the **anxiety** resulting from extreme confusion and harassed by painful mutilations, the patient attempts to restore a "restricted relationship." Bion characterized this restricted relationship as "featureless", although it can alternate with a more expansive form of interaction. It can be deduced that the term "strict" might be similar with what others have described as schizoid or autistic (*ibid.*).

Public-ation:[56] Within the mind, it represents the way in which **thinking functions**, in that it is capable of making sense impressions available to **consciousness**, and can communicate to the **group** what was private to the person. Similar to the mechanism displayed in the **horizontal axis** of the **Grid**, information that has been changed into **action** could be communicated or publicized by means of **common sense** (column 6 like G6 or H6 in the Grid). The conflict, said Bion, could be technical and **emotional**:

> The emotional problems are associated with the **fact** that the human individual is a political animal and cannot find fulfilment outside a group and cannot satisfy any emotional drive without expression of its social component. His impulses, and I mean all impulses and not merely his sexual ones, are at the same time narcissistic. The problem is the resolution of the conflict between **narcissism** and **social-ism**. The technical problem is that concerned with expression of **thought** or **conception** in language, or its counterpart in signs. [1967, p. 118]

For Bion, this course of public-ation is not different from the process used by the individual to translate a preverbal thought into a verbal one, or to make explicit what is implicit, or to make conscious what is unconscious. **Abstraction** could also be thought of as a necessary

---

[56] Bion breaks the word perhaps to emphasize its content of **"public action."**

step towards publication, as well as the **interpretation**, which represents a form of publication in the analyst's attempt to make conscious what has been unconscious. *See*: **Growth, Correlation, Social-ism, Common sense, Narcissism, Horizontal axis.**

Pure and absolute interpretation: A form of **interpretation** Bion considers as "free from contaminations or **countertransference** noise" or absolute "on the analogy of absolute zero or absolute cold". He said:

> There are certain patients who can recognize that any interpretation I give is not absolute. I can describe it in terms of an actual experience in this way: The patient cannot listen to what I am saying because of the noise. Sometimes the "noise" is the way I speak, sometimes it is the distraction produced by a fly in the room, but in a sense all the noises that he can hear appear to have an equal value. He can say, "I know you are angry", and if I am honest about it, I realize that he is right. But he may not differentiate between whether I am annoyed by the buzzing of a fly, or by the noise of the traffic, or by what he is saying and doing. All these facts are of equal value. [1974, p. 77]

Pythagoras, theorem of: According to this theorem, the square of the hypotenuse of a right-angled triangle is equal to the square of the sum of the opposite sides. Bion attempts to establish a relationship between the **Oedipus myth** and this theorem on one hand, and **Euclidian geometry** and Klein's **paranoid–schizoid** and **depressive position**, on the other (1992, p. 207). He made these statements in his book **Cogitations**, in such an enigmatic style, that it could be assumed that perhaps he was emulating the sphinx itself. In relation to **Pythagoras' theorem** he had this to say:

> The side subtending the right angle: the sides containing the right angle. How much can be obtained by ignoring the figure, the diagram, except in so far as it serves a **function**—like that of the material of a sculpture by Henry Moore—in framing the place where there is *no* material? To act as a boundary to the open **space**, that is to say the part where the figure is *not*. Then the squares on the sides containing, and the squares on the side subtending, the right angle serve to enclose the triangle—the **"three-kneed thing"**, but also the right angle. The construction is a trap for light. [*ibid.*, p. 206]

In this rather enigmatic **communication**, Bion invites us to ignore the diagram, that is, the mathematical aspect of the theorem, and concentrate on what is enclosed, for instance, the Oedipus myth: in a right-angled triangle there are the two sides forming the right angle, that would represent both parents (vertical = father and horizontal = mother), while the opposite side or hypotenuse would represent the son. The "three-kneed thing" refers to the **interpretation** apparently given by the Greeks to the triangle, when they considered that the angles that put together all the sides, that is, father, mother and son, were equivalent to the genitals. Bion says something similar when he states immediately after that "Euclid 1.5 marks the point at which the 'elements' of geometry are left behind when the student crosses the Pons" (*ibid.*). In other words, in order to avoid being an ass, the figure must be ignored for its content and attention be placed on its meaning, only then would the trapped light escape, meaning that the Pons would be finally crossed—or the theorem properly understood—without having, as Epicurus announced, to be an ass.

Bion also refers to Pythagoras' theorem, known as the "**Bride's Chair**", because its demonstration resembles, according to the Arabs, a horse riding chair used to carry the bride. It has also been said that the French referred to this theorem with the name of Pons Asinorum, something questioned by Bion who assures that this last one corresponds to No. 5 of book 1 and represents the theorem of the isosceles triangle, while the Bride's theorem represents a right angle triangle which corresponds to Book 13, No. 47 (*ibid.*, p. 207) *See*: **Euclidian geometry, Theorem of the Bride's chair, Pons Asinorum.**

Q

Qualities, primary and secondary: From Latin *qualitas, qualis*, meaning which? what? Of what nature? Represents the properties that determine the nature of both primary and secondary. Primary qualities are those represented by: (1) what is essential to all material objects and consequently present in all; and (2) what are represented by perceptual experiences and independent of the subject who perceives them. Secondary qualities, on the other hand, like colour, taste, sound, etc.: (1) are not essential to material objects and do not participate in the correct explanation of such experiences; (2) are not in all objects and depend more on the subject who perceives them—they are subjective. Primary qualities are more related to the object, whereas secondary qualities are related to the subject. However, for Berkeley and later for Kant, all qualities are subjective, because regardless of what they might be, either primary or secondary, they are all perceived by the senses.

Quality of contact: According to Lipgar (1998), J. D. Sutherland, who had worked with Bion during the World War II on the task of selecting candidates for officer training, stated that he often commented about the "need to judge the 'quality contact' the candidate had with others" (p. 30). Lipgar continues:

> They felt that many different personalities could make good officers, but Bion sought that "crucial quality which (is) 'a man's capacity for maintaining personal relationships in a situation of strain that tempted him to disregard the interest of his fellows for the sake of his own." [*ibid.*]

Quantum theory: Discussing what Heisenberg (1958) said, Bion wonders if the **hypothesis** on the dual demeanour of light, sometimes behaving as "elementary particles" and other times as a "wave", could be matched with primitive phantasies parallel to the Ps ←→D theory, in the sense that the "particle" would correspond to Ps and the wave to D. He argues:

> Is it possible that the explanation fundamentally has to be in terms of primitive phantasies?—e.g. elementary particles (paranoid–schizoid), or wave theory (depressive)—because these are limitations in the human mind which cannot be transcended? [1992, p. 60]

Heisenberg's theory of the "uncertainty principle", which determines that a subatomic (photons) particle's momentum or location, can be measured only at the particular and specific moment when it is found, because the conditions needed for accuracy in observation of the particles, are in direct conflict with those needed for the observation of its position. A certain resemblance between this hypothesis and Bion's conception of **O**, could be considered.

R

R (=Reason): A **function** that serves **passions**, whichever they might be, and dominates them within the world of reality. By passions Bion understands all emotions located between **L** (love), **H** (hate) and **K** (knowledge). R is associated with idea (**I**) in as much as the latter is used to fill in the fault between an impulse and its satisfaction (1963, p. 4). "Reason" says Bion, "is emotion's slave and exists to rationalize emotional experience" (1970, p. 1). *See*: **I (Idea)**, **K, L, H**.

Reality principle: Bion uses in detail what Freud originally described in 1911, about psychic reality and its relation to the interaction between consciousness and the external world, in order to build his **theory of thinking**, to understand the relationship between the **psychotic and non-psychotic parts of the personality**, as well as to structure the **horizontal axis** of his **Grid**. **Psychotic** patients make destructive attacks on those ego aspects necessary to establish a **link** between **consciousness** and external reality. Following Freud these aspects are: (i) **attention**: consciousness ascribed to sense organs and used to search the external world; (ii) **notation**: as part of **memory**; (iii) **judgement**: an impartial view developed to take the place of repression; (iv) **action**: a new function destined to induce motor discharges; and (v) **thought**: a process from where ideation developed. In 1911, Freud stated:

> Thinking was endowed with characteristics which made it possible for the mental apparatus to tolerate an increased tension of stimulus while the process of discharge was postponed. It is essentially an experimental kind of acting, accompanied by displacement of relatively small quantities of cathexis together with less expenditure (discharge) of them. [p. 221]

For Bion all of these adaptations were also related to the establishment of verbal thought and with the emergence of the **depressive position**. *See*: **Horizontal axis, Attention, Notation, Judgement, Action, Verbal thoughts, Thoughts.**

Realization: It can be interpreted as an **action** to bring something into real or concrete existence. In his "**theory of thinking**" Bion refers to the "realization of **pre-conceptions**" (1967, pp. 111–119); in other words, when the baby sucks the breast, a realization takes place between the innate preconception of the breast and the breast as a real object, a situation that will generate a **conception**, that is, the satisfaction of a wish. When the need for the breast meets an absence of the breast or "**no-breast**", the realization of this absence, of this **frustration**, if well tolerated, will be translated into **thoughts**, as well as into an **apparatus to think** thoughts and into a capacity for **abstract** thinking. Later on Bion states that the **theory of functions** "makes it easier to match the realization with **the scientific deductive system** that represents it" (1962, p. 2), in a sense similar to the way in which three dimensional "**Euclidian geometry** has the structure of ordinary space as one of its realizations" (*ibid.*, p. 99). In other words, the theory of functions facilitates the knowledge of the exact purpose a given scientific deductive system might have, similar to the way in which Euclidian geometry has as its purpose, dimensioning the ordinary space. Writing a book would be, for instance, a realization of **K**.

Following the theory of **transformations**, an artist can transform a landscape (realization) into a picture (representation), something he achieves by means of a series of **invariants** which make his work something intelligible. Through the use of a realization we might be able to know about the unknown, the **thing-in-itself**, which represents what Bion referred to as **turbulence,** or the capacity to rouse a disturbance that will make the invisible visible, like introducing a stick in a clear and smooth stream of water. Realizations allow us to know about the ineffable, the **noumenon,** by changing it into a **phenomenon.** From a religious vertex, for instance, we could intuit the existence of the **Godhead,** which would correspond to the thing-in-itself, or to that of which we know nothing; however, when we believe we know something about God through a realization, for example a miracle, then a turbulence will appear and it will introduce us to the world of phenomena. Exactly this same mechanism is used by Bion to explain the enlightenment of **O** as a thing-in-itself, its change from the unknown or the noumenon, into the world of phenomenon (O → K), which will allow the construction of **interpretations** and the possible realization of the patient's unconscious meaning during the analytic session. *See*: **Pre-conception, Theory of functions, Euclidian geometry, Thing-in-itself, Turbulence, Noumenon, Phenomenon, O, Godhead.**

Receptors: *see*: **Perception, organs of.**

Regression: In 1976, during a conference in Los Angeles, Bion said:

> We talk about "getting back" to childhood or infancy. It is a useful phrase, but I think it is meaningless. Do any of us "get back" to infancy or childhood, or even tomorrow? It is clear that we don't. Why do we bother to talk about these things which, supposedly, have their origin very early in one's life? What if we do develop a character in infancy or childhood? What does it matter . . . We could say that these characteristics which are supposedly **split** off, or got rid of in some way, are forgotten—and after all, we do not continue to behave like infants; apparently these things *are* got rid of. Do you remember when you were at the breast? No, it's forgotten or got rid of. But having been forgotten these things persist in some archaic way in one's mind, so that they still continue to operate, to make themselves felt . . . Since they operate in this archaic way they go on affecting one's work. [1994, p. 244]

Regression and progression: *see*: **Progression and regression.**

Reparation: Bion did not use this **concept** often, but when he did, he generally followed the description used by Klein. In **Cogitations,**

at a time when he referred to α-**function** as simply α, he stated that attempts at reparation exercised by α, "were destroyed by sadistic attacks made by **psychotic** superego" using minute **split** and **projective identifications**. Attempts to recover and reunite fragments were continuously "hampered by coincidental destructive procedures" (1992, p. 97).

He describes **assimilation** as the aptitude to incorporate sense impressions capable of enhancing the self. In psychotic patients this possibility is destroyed due to the domination of the death instinct as well as to the increment of the superego's sadism. Destruction of assimilation does not encumber incorporation of sense impressions and their subsequent storage, it would just hamper its integration within the self, remaining inlaid as foreign objects or **things-in-themselves**, useful only to be discharged by means of projective identification. Fear of annihilation can increase dominance of live instincts, something that would revert the process and introduce *reparation* of the capacity to assimilate (*ibid.*, p. 164). According to Bion this process can be observed during analysis, in the patient's use of certain words which evidence the production of material suitable to be used in the formation of **dream thoughts** in **dreams**, which the patient can associate and **communicate**. Such verbal statements are then capable of articulating with each other to form complete wholes and subsequently are not suitable for projective identification. They are also **transformations** in process of further transformations according with future assimilations of sensory impressions (*ibid.*, pp. 157–165). *See*: **Assimilation, Progression and regression.**

Reproductive system: *see:* **Internal reproductive system.**

Resistance: It represents the inaccessibility of **O**, the struggle to maintain **thoughts** always unconscious, the fear of **truth** and of the object becoming real, "resistance operates because it is feared that reality of the object is imminent" (1965, p.147). It would never represent fear of **falseness**, perhaps because it is felt that instead of dealing with reality inaccessibility, it is better to ignore it: "There are occasions . . . when it is felt to be wise, not pathological, to turn a 'blind eye' " (*ibid.*, p. 149). It is difficult to know reality, to grasp the truth, "it is impossible to know reality for the same reason that makes it impossible to sing potatoes", you can plant them, peel them or eat them, but never sing them (*ibid.*, pp. 147–148). Resistance is closely related to transformations of **K** in O (TK→ O) and linked to column 2 of the **Grid**.

Bion also suggests that resistance in **dream work**, would also result—besides what is known from classical theory—from the patient's "**felt need**" to convert his/her **conscious** rational experience into a **dream**, and not the other way around, to convert a dream into a conscious rational experience, which usually represents the **desire** or "felt need" of the analyst. Bion concludes:

> The "felt need" is *very* important; if it is not given due significance and weight, the true dis-ease of the patient is being neglected; it is obscured by the analyst's insistence on **interpretation** of the dream. [1992, p. 184]

See: "**Felt need**", **Truth**, **False**, **Horizontal axis**.

Reversal of α-function: Represents a condition where α-**elements** function in reverse, self-digesting themselves and resulting as a consequence in the formation of β-**elements**, as well as **bizarre objects** and a dispersion of the "**contact barrier**". Such reversal characterizes a mechanism Bion has used to explain the formation of the "**β screen**": Instead of sense impressions being changed into α-elements to be used in **dream** and **conscious thoughts**, as observed in the **non-psychotic part of the personality**, the development of the contact barrier is hindered and destroyed. The contact barrier loses its texture, α-elements are denuded from the characteristics that separate them from beta-elements and then projected to form the β screen (1962, p. 25).

Meltzer (1978, pp. 119–126) has used a clinical presentation to explain in detail what Bion had elucidated theoretically. Its reading is recommended. *See*: α-**function**, α-**element**, β-**element**, **Contact barrier**, β **screen**.

Reversible perspective: Represents a form of **splitting** of **time** and **space**, which Bion illustrates with the use of the well-known Wecker's cube and Rubin's vase. Both pictures show changes of perspective depending on which aspect of the diagram is seen as "figure" and what is seen as "ground". In the cube, for instance, it depends on which side—either AB or CD—is seen as closer;

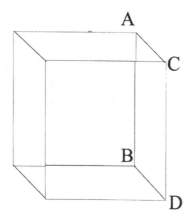

Figure 2. Reversible perspective.

whereas in the vase, it depends on whether the shape of a vase or two profiles looking at each other were chosen. With such double perspective, Bion attempts to illustrate, during his work with **groups**, the concept of **duality** observed between the **work group** (W) and one of the latent **basic assumption** groups. Then he stated:

> In the group the psychiatrist should consider from time to time what is the "dual" of any given **emotional** situation that he has observed. He should consider also whether the "dual" of the situation he has just described has not already been experienced and described at some previous sessions. [1948b, pp. 87–88]

Subsequently, Bion used a similar dynamic to explain the possible agreement or disagreement that might take place between the analyst and his/her patient, or within the patient himself, as a defence to deal with the pain of **growth**. He refers to a condition where the patient can use his own "**scientific deductive system**" to oppose and compete against the "scientific deductive system" provided by the **interpretation**. It can be summarized by the old maxim: "Sometimes the right hand doesn't know what the left is doing", or the Spanish one: "One thing thinks the mule and something else who is riding it."

The agreement can be quite obtrusive, like the patient who openly opposes the content of an interpretation. At other times it might not be so obvious, as in the case of reversible perspective. Seen from the particular **vertex** of **psychoanalytic elements**, such discrepancy takes place between **K** and **−K** (minus K), that is, between the analyst's knowledge and the patient's void of knowledge. The agreement implies how to change a dynamic condition that produces growth and advancement, for another one that is repetitious and static. As the analysis elapses in a "reversible" condition, an unconscious agreement between both analyst and patient might take place. Sometimes it is based on almost imperceptible sense impressions, such as gestures, attitudes, **silences**, etc., but giving the impression that the analysis is really "working", as Bion states, structured on a "**contact barrier**" between patient and analyst, when in reality this is not the case. This divergence is usually never talked about; it elapses between silences and agreements, although Bion strongly believes that if exposed to the **Grid**, it might be revealed (1963, p. 54n). Sometimes it might become evident, when the patient is caught unguarded; however, reversible perspective would be re-established immediately. Deep down, concludes Bion, this mechanism really represents a defence against mental pain induced by growth (*ibid.*, p. 63).

A young patient, who used phobic and avoidant defence mechanisms, after one month of initiating her analysis and almost at the end of the session, said that she "continuously repeated my interpretations in her mind in order not to forget them". I then told her that perhaps we could consider the opposite, that she repeated them to be certain she could free herself from them and leave nothing inside. After a long silence, she stood up looking in the opposite direction from where I was, something rather unusual, and I had the impression that, similar to Bion's patient (1965, p. 131), she was expelling my words through her eyes. Moreover, I thought that if I had accepted her hypothesis about "remembering my words", I would have initiated a reversible perspective. What is behind this mechanism of reversible perspective is a defence against the pain of growing in relation to the **Oedipus myth** (*ibid.*, p. 63).

Using reversible perspective, a patient can avoid getting into a direct confrontation with the analyst, like experimenting with the **anxiety** of an Oedipus situation; instead he would only go his/her way using a mechanism Bion referred to as "**static splitting**", representing a failure in the capacity to allow the mating of a

pre-conception with a **realization** in order to give place to a **conception**. Sometimes, says Bion, when reversion is not possible, the patient might revert to small distortions of **communication**, in the way of listening to the interpretations, giving some twists or mis-hearings and misunderstanding, or in more serious pathology, making use of **delusions** and **hallucinations** (*ibid.*, p. 60). Although not completely explicit, Bion also associates reversion of perspective with the concept of "**binocular vision**", either as a substitute when reversion does not exist, or as interference if it does exist, something questioned by other analysts (Meltzer, 1978, p. 6). From the point of view of Grid categories, in the reversible perspective, what the analyst might say could correspond to F5, G5 and G6, while what the patient says could be placed on F1, G1 and G2. *See*: **Duality, Point of view, Vertex, Static splitting, Altered focus, Binocular vision.**

Ritual: *see*: **Magic.**

Rivalry, acting (acting-out) of: Considered as a feeling or rather a **constant conjunction** that can dominate during **transformation in hallucinosis** (referring to **psychotic** patients or to the **psychotic part of the personality**), because the patient, enthralled by his feelings of rivalry tries to "occupy" the analyst's place and deprive him of his analytical **vertex**, inducing a sort of dilemma in the analyst, between surrendering his techniques or maintaining the analysis. This condition can sometimes induce in the patient the feeling that the analyst considers himself, as well as his acts and techniques, to be much superior to the patient's **hallucinatory magic**. In such cases rivalry could be **acted out** (1965, p. 136). Bion states that the patient presents himself as "a person anxious to demonstrate his independence of anything other than his own creations", which are the product of his alleged ability to use his senses as organs of **evacuation**. Whatever is projected represents a universe that surrounds the patient in the form of **bizarre objects**. The purpose of this function of the senses and their mental counterpart is to create a "perfect world" (*ibid.*, p. 137), where any sense of imperfection is *ipso facto* experienced as the product of hostile forces intervening from the outside. Thanks to this capacity, the patient is completely independent of the whole world, except from his own products, and therefore he feels beyond any experience of rivalry, **envy**, greed, threats, **love** or **hate**; however, since all defences fail, he is continuously facing the **anxiety** produced by the presence of dependency and imperfection. *See*: **Transformation in hallucinosis, Hallucinations, Magic, Animate-inanimate, Bizarre objects, Envy.**

Roman à clef: French expression used to describe novels written about dramas of real people that were disguised to avoid recognition. Freud (1905) had used the phrase in the introduction to Dora's case, where he criticized the confusion of many medical doctors who were trying to uncover the true identity of Freud's patients for their own lascivious desires. Bion used this concept to illustrate **invariants** present during different forms of **transformation**. For instance, invariants present in photographs are not the same as invariants present in impressionist paintings, and invariants in pornographic literature such as a *roman à clef* (or the capacity to recognize the character in spite of his/her camouflage) are not the same as invariants observed in psychoanalytical treatments. *See*: **Invariants, Transformation, Transformation in rigid movement, Projective transformations.**

Rudimentary conscious: Bion uses this name as well as "rudimentary mental apparatus" to describe the child's undeveloped mind that requires **maternal reverie** in order to elaborate his/her sense impressions into α-**elements**. A rudimentary conscious cannot deal with those tasks that would ordinarily be considered as affairs suitable for an adult's mind, which can contain them. When the relationship between this primitive mind and maternal reverie is broken, such rudimentary conscious cannot deal with the burden that must now support, then giving place to the establishment of an internal object ("projective-identification–rejecting-object means"), which, instead of providing the infant with an understanding, such an object provides a wilful misunderstanding with which the infant is now identified (1967, pp. 116–117). Bion describes four aspects to define the mental structure this rudimentary psyche has: (1) Thinking, associated with modification or evasion (*see*: **frustration, thoughts**); (2) **projective identification**, associated with evasion through **evacuation**, which should not be confused with ordinary projective identification; (3) **Omniscience**; and (4) **Communication.**

This kind of primitive mind can be observed in borderline patients, who often display evasion as a form of deafness or lack of attention. *See*: **Maternal reverie, Alpha-elements, Alpha-function, Projective identification, Frustration, Apparatus of thinking, Thoughts.**

S

Saturated–unsaturated elements: Concept borrowed from chemistry in order to explain when a given situation or state is maintained in maximum impregnation (saturated) of something, or on the contrary, completely free or empty (unsaturated). Bion frequently uses the Greek letter ζ (ksi = x) to depict the presence of a saturated or unsaturated element. For instance, β-elements are described as well categorized objects, equal to things-in-themselves and completely saturated. On the other hand, Bion insists that the mind of the analyst, during the session, should always remain free from any memory or desire, like a blank sheet of paper, in other words be completely unsaturated, just like a pre-conception (1963, p. 70).

Psychotic patients can be afraid of projected elements that show a strong need for saturation, because they often confuse them with their own feelings of greed. For instance, they could experience the analyst's interest in recollecting information as an attempt to rob them of their sanity (1965, p. 122)

Grotstein (1981, p. 14) has argued that the apparent obscurity observed in Bion's form of expression, could be a consequence of the careful selection of words to avoid the penumbra of associations present in some expressions, which might have interfered with the specific meanings he wished to convey. For instance, if we were to say "othered" instead of "altered" (alter = other), etymologically they could both mean the same; however, the latter carries such a penumbra of saturation because it has been used for so many years, that it will not be able to convey the same exact meaning of "being interfered by the other", that the former does. *See*: **Psi, ζ, Pre-conception, β-elements.**

Schism: Bion described it as a form of resistance that can take place in groups that feel forced to "evolve". This form of resistance does not operate in work groups (W) because its "scientific" orientation allows them to face frustration and thus function in a similar way as would a healthy ego. But if this is not possible, the group might then resort either towards **oscillations of the Dependent group (baD)** or towards "schism", meaning a splitting of the group into two sub-groups. (a) One opposed to further advance, maintaining itself dependent to the group's bible or to a pleasing leader who gives in to any demand and is ruled by tradition, like the "word of God"; this kind of leader is made god in order to resist change. Members of this sub-group manipulate the leader to support any new adherence without great demands, making the sub-group very popular. (b) The other sub-group, on the contrary, becomes extremely exacting in their demands, rapidly reducing the number of new recruits, avoiding in this manner the painful confrontation between old sophisticated and new inexperienced members.

> One sub-group has large numbers of primitive unsophisticated individuals who constantly add to their number, but who do not develop; the other sub-group develops, but on such a narrow front and with such few recruits that it also avoids the painful bringing together of the new idea and the primitive state. [1948a p. 128]

Bion concludes:

> I am reminded of allegations that a society breeds copiously from its less cultured or less educated members, while the "best" people remain obstinately sterile. [*ibid.*]

Schizophrenia: According to Bion, schizophrenic pathology originates from disturbances in the integration between environment and personality, although later on he established that it might correspond to a "physical disorder originated in pathological physical states" (1965, p. 144). However, leaving out the importance of the external environment, says Bion, there are some important characteristics found in all schizophrenic personalities: (a) a never-decided conflict between life and death **instincts**; (b) an ascendancy of destructive over life impulses, which could be so destructive that even feelings of love are drowned and changed into sadism; (c) hatred of internal and external realities and of every aspect of the mind (**apparatus of perception**) that might help make it conscious, destroying them with the use of minute splitting and massive **projective identifications**, which result in a mental state that is neither alive nor dead; (d) as a consequence, there is a constant terror of imminent annihilation; (e) a premature and hasty form of object relations of the kind observed in **psychotic transference**, where frailness contrasts with the tenacity that remains, representing in these clinical features a pathognomonic characteristic of schizophrenia (1967, p. 38). Much of what has been said by Bion about psychoses in general, as well as the **psychotic part of the personality**, are in close relationship to schizophrenia.

Asked in 1973 in Rio de Janeiro about the analysis of psychotic patients, Bion answered:

> I have only analysed schizophrenic patients who were able to come to my consulting room. Although I still think the best description of them was "schizophrenic", I do not suggest they were comparable to the kind of patients who have to be hospitalized. I must add that in the psycho-analytic world with which I am familiar "crazes" appear to be frequent. I am amazed how often an analyst seems to think that he can hardly claim his title unless he has treated many schizophrenic patients. I would almost wonder how mental hospitals manage to make a living. From the little I know I find it difficult to believe that so many analysts are treating schizophrenics. Such a claim belongs to the domain not of the science of psychoanalysis but of fashion. As it is sometimes the fashion to wear feathers in hats, so psycho-analysts wear "psychotics in their hair". [1974, pp. 92–94]

Schizophrenic language: Schizophrenic patients use language in three ways: (a) as a form of **action**; (b) as a form of **communication**; (c) as a form of **thought**.

(a) Language can take the place of action, for example the patient who wishes to "take the movement out of the piano" to understand why someone is playing it, or the opposite when the patient tries to use omnipotence of thought to solve the impotence of finding himself in a place when he feels he should be somewhere else.

(b) Language can also be at the service of **projective identification** and used to parasitize an object in order to control it, and avoid the pain of separation anxiety. It can also be used to split the object, like for instance, to split the analyst or his speech.

(c) In view that processes of incorporation are obstructed, due to paranoid **anxieties** from the fear of continuous attacks from his projective identifications on the parasite object, identifications are now experienced as **projective identifications in reverse**, a mechanism Bion has described as responsible for the **agglomeration** and compression of **ideas** that lead in these patients, to "highly compact speech"; a construction more "appropriate to music than the articulation of words as used for non-psychotic communication" (1967, p. 41).

Scientific deductive system (s.d.s. or "system axiomatic deductive"): Throughout most of his work, Bion seriously attempts to provide **psychoanalysis** with the precision of a system based on mathematics and constructs taken from **Euclidian geometry**:

> I wish to introduce as a step towards formulations that are precise, communicable without distortions and more nearly adequate to cover all situations that are basically the same. [1965, p. 125]

Bion attempts to define the substance behind his system, using a quote from Braithwaite (1955):

> . . . consists of a set of **hypotheses** which form a deductive system, that is, which is arranged in such a way that from some of the

hypotheses as premises, all the other hypotheses logically follow. [1992, pp. 2–3]

Concluding that a

... peculiarity of psychoanalysis is that the scientific deductive system is a series of hypotheses about hypotheses about hypotheses ... [*ibid.*, p. 46]

And later on:

[it is] ... any system of hypotheses in which certain hypotheses occupy a high level in the particular system, and are used as premises from which lower-level hypotheses are deduced. [*ibid.*, p. 156]

This particular deductive system must be preceded by the structuring of a set of organized **ideas** accomplished by the use of **symbols**, requiring also the capacity to tolerate **frustration** and depression, similar to Klein's description of the process of "synthesis in the **depressive position**." According to Bion, the problem consists in how a primitive system of ideation reaches the level of sophistication present in a scientific deductive system, related to the formation of permanent knowledge.

From a genetic point of view, or simply from the **vertex** of **psychoanalytic listening**, there would be:

(1) **Awareness** of external **facts**, or "actual **elements**", through the use of sense organs, equivalent to what scientists refer to as "observable facts". Bion gathers them into three groups: (i) touch and smell; (ii) sound and (iii) sight. The first one is non-verbal and related to sex, the second is verbal and musical and the last one, verbal and pictorial.

(2) The possibility of an individual to translate an "actual element" into an idea and then create symbols, would depend on the individual's capacity to tolerate frustration produced by the absence of the object as well as to tolerate the **depression** from the depressive position. This operation is absent in **psychotics**, because for them words are things.

(3) A mental development associated with the "ability to see facts as they really are, [producing] ... internally a sense of

well–being that has an instantaneous and ephemeral effect and a lasting sense of permanently increased mental stability" (*ibid.*, p. 6). In other words, scientific knowledge is the consequence of **growth** of **common sense** knowledge (*ibid.*, p. 26).

Most of these conceptualizations correspond to the role Bion gave to **alpha-function**, as capable of translating sense impressions or **beta-elements** into more sophisticated elements, useful in the process of **thinking**, or creating **alpha-elements**.

The **interpretation** could act as a **selected fact** capable of providing order to the initial chaos of observations (*ibid.*, pp. 6; 7). In order for a scientific deductive system to be achieved, says Bion, it is necessary that selected facts that organize the system, be elaborated by means of a conscious rational process and not by **emotional** experiences; besides, hypotheses in the system should be grouped with the help of logical rules, different from those mechanisms that organize elements following a selected fact (1962, p. 73). A scientific hypothesis should contain three functions: (a) a private event should be made **public** (the interpretation); (b) it should consent to reality testing, be remembered, proved and predicted; and (c) arranged in such a way for it to make sense (1992, p. 14) Let us take for instance the proverb "action without thought is like shooting without aim", which is publicly known, it can predict a fact and organize a sense. "Common sense" is an important aspect in scientific deductive systems; the interpretation, for instance, requires that at least both analyst and patient share a consensus:

> The analyst, however, is also able to claim that his interpretation is based on common sense; but it is common only to some psychoanalysts who may be presumed to witness the same events and make the same deductions. [*ibid.*, p. 10]

In relation to the **Grid**, Bion places the scientific deductive system as part of the **horizontal axis**, or axis of the uses. However, it could also have been located also on the **vertical axis**, because of its tendency towards a successive complexity of thinking, or in row G, or be represented by mathematical **calculus** and correspond to row H.

See: **Symbolic equation, α-function, β-elements, α-elements, Apparatus for thinking, Grid, the, Vertical axis, Horizontal axis.**

Screen of β-elements: It represents a construct in the **phenomenology** of the **apparatus to think thoughts**, structured as an **agglomeration** of **β-elements** placed between the unconscious and **consciousness** within the mind of **psychotic** patients or the **psychotic part of the personality**. It is responsible for a state of confusion similar to **dreams**, as well as the possibility of massive projections of β-elements. These elements might induce **emotional** changes in the analyst that could determine the profile of the **countertransference** and the architecture of the **interpretation**.

Bion explains how the screen of β-elements is created as a consequence of a process he refers to as the "**reversal of α-function**", according to which:

> Instead of sense impressions being changed into **alpha-elements** for use in **dream thoughts** and unconscious waking **thinking**, the development of the **contact-barrier** is replaced by its destruction. This is effected by the reversal of **alpha-function** so that the contact-barrier and the dream thoughts and unconscious waking thinking which are the texture of the contact-barrier are turned into alpha-elements, divested of all characteristics that separate them from beta-elements and are then projected thus forming the beta-screen. [1962, p. 25]

Meltzer (1986) referred to β-screen as a "pseudo communication of non-sense", he also suggested a relationship between the concept of β-screen and "Esther Bick's delineation of the 'gift of the gab' method of 'second skin' formation" (p. 35).

Secondary qualities: *see*: **Qualities, primary and secondary**

Security: Bion refers to **patience** as a feeling that should prevail when analytic listening is dominated by those mechanisms present in the **depressive position**, as described by Klein, different from the emotions that might prevail when a session is dominated by mechanisms present in the **paranoid-schizoid position**. I think Bion is referring to the patience and capacity to tolerate **frustration** with which an analyst must deal when faced with the uncertainties induced in the analysis by object relations of the kind experienced in the paranoid–schizoid position, in contrast to the feeling of certitude stimulated by the security provided by object relations that take place during the depressive position (1970, p. 124).

Segal, Hanna: *see:* **Symbolic equation**

Selected fact: Concept originally used by Henri Poincaré in his book Science and Method (1908) to explain the process of creation of a mathematical formulation. Bion reproduces the text in Learning from Experience.

"If a new result is to have any value, it must unite elements long since known, but till then scattered and seemingly foreign to each other, and suddenly introduce order where the appearance of disorder reigned. Then it enables us to see at a glance each of these elements in the place it occupies in the whole. Not only is the new fact valuable on its own account, but it alone gives a value to the old facts it unites. Our mind is frail as our senses are; it would lose itself in the complexity of the world if that complexity were not harmonious; like the short-sighted, it would only see the details, and would be obliged to forget each of these details before examining the next, because it would be incapable of taking in the whole. The only facts worthy of our attention are those which introduce order into this complexity and so make it accessible to us." [1962, p. 72]

In his "commentaries" about the **"Imaginary twin"**, although by then he had not yet mentioned Poincaré, it is obvious that Bion is referring to the "selected fact", when he said:

[It is] what I now call an **"evolution"**, namely, the coming together, by a sudden precipitating intuition, of a mass of apparently unrelated incoherent **phenomena** which are thereby given coherence and meaning not previously possessed. [1967, p. 127]

And:

From the material the patient produces, there emerges, like the pattern from a kaleidoscope, a configuration which seems to belong not only to the situation unfolding, but to a number of others not previously seen to be connected and which it has not been designed to connect. [*ibid.*]

In **Cogitations**, in an undated note, probably written some time before the previous quotation, Bion correlates selected facts and **common sense**, stating that the former would provide sense to an **idea** which, once proven to be **true** and communicated to others, would integrate, like a selected fact, a great amount of people, societies or groups, according to the sense such an idea has made common to all. At first it would be a private **fact**, and later on, after it is believed to be true because it fits into a **scientific deductive system**, it will become public through **communication** and common sense, and will be able to integrate a large group of minds (1992, p. 193).

A **"cause"** and a selected fact are very much alike, because they can both be associated with an **emotional** experience capable of providing, at a given moment, a sense of synthesis or creative association. At the same time it will also bring knowledge of the existence of discrete, not yet connected objects. A selected fact is associated with the synthesis of objects in a synchronic manner where time is excluded, while cause relates in a diachronic way following time as a **narrative** (*ibid.*, p. 275). For instance, an **interpretation** could act, at a particular instant (timeless), as a selected fact that triggers a series of associations that have unconsciously remained in **constant conjunction**, while leaving out other "discrete" objects not bound to this chain of associations. On the other hand, we know because of the **Oedipus myth** narrative, what exactly—emotionally—follows in time after Oedipus' arrival at the **crossroads**.

Further on Bion explains that the selected fact describes the synthesis processes experienced by the psychoanalyst, similar to the way in which **paranoid–schizoid** objects become coherent and initiate the **depressive positions**, as adumbrated by Klein (1962, pp. 72, 87; 1992, p. 213). The selected fact corresponds to an emotional experience that appears due to feelings of coherence and discovery, which does not necessarily have to be logical, but does require a relaxed attitude on behalf of the analyst in order to provide a matrix of **abstraction** from where the interpretation can spring. If this process is obstructed, on the other hand, it will be accompanied by an emotion similar to the one experienced during a reversible perspective (1962, p. 87).

A young married childless woman stated that not long ago one of her sisters, whom she felt had always been preferred by her father, had moved with her husband back to their parents' house. She complained that her father's preference was terribly unfair and very painful. Her mother, described as "an older sister", she felt might have suffered a lot because of her father's alcohol abuse and unfaithfulness. She cries as she speaks. She refers to having difficulties with her own husband, mostly in relation to sex, for he wants her but she usually refuses to be touched by him, although she might give in and have sex, but does not wish to be caressed. "Perhaps I feel angry because he is too selfish". There is the **countertransference** feeling of two children playing. She recalls seeing a whale at the Miami aquarium, purposely splashing some children that were watching it just beside her, and this made her cry; and as she speaks about it, she cries again. She also recalls when she was a little girl and a whale also splattered her intentionally, and then she also wept.

We could deduce that the "splash from the whale" represented a selected fact, because it clarifies and gives a sense to the whole content of the session. The fact that the whale had deliberately splattered a child, meant that the child was preferred by the whale, and this was what made her cry, then and now, because it reminded her of the times—in contrast to her sister—when she was not chosen. Her parents were not good "splashing whales" for her, and she had chosen to marry a man who was not either; this is the reason for her ambivalence towards him, because she wished that he could have such a fantastic capacity to "splash", in order for her to use him to get revenge on those who, like her sister, have been well "splattered". After this is interpreted, she produces a short dream: *the image of a pregnant woman who walks holding a little girl by the hand.* She said she could be the little girl and that the woman "was really pregnant" because she looked immense. The analyst then asked: "Like a whale?" In tears she smiled. It appears as if there is a narcissistic conglomerate where the patient represents all the characters: "she is pregnant of herself, as a self-splashing whale", representing a manic mechanism to deny the pain of exclusion, for after all, she is continuously "dousing" herself with tears.

Britton and Steiner (1994) emphasized the risk that could be faced when an interpretation is based on an "overvalued idea" instead of a selected fact.

Sense organs: *see:* **Perception, organs of**

Sensuous reality: It corresponds to the reality that can be discerned by means of the sense organs, indispensable to conceive the **phenomenon**, but useless to perceive the ineffable, the **noumenon** or the **thing-in-itself**. Bion states that we are forced to

> . . . talk about things which could be described as phenomenal, while having to use that same language for things which are noumenous. This is a serious problem. If we invent words nobody will understand what those words mean. If we do not, their sensuous history is evoked. As with a "dead" metaphor carelessly used, its ghost begins to walk. Neologisms are the privilege of the mentally ill. They are not available for use by the psychoanalyst. [1974a, p. 34]

And further on:

> . . . we know so little about the mind, or psyche, or spirit—whichever term we borrow to talk about this thing which is not sensuously apprehensible, which does not fall within the spectrum of the sensuous range. [*ibid*., p. 42]

Bion states that the difference can be observed when we listen to someone and we say, "I see what you mean"; in contrast to the analyst who listens to his patient and thinks "I don't know what he is talking about", something that can change during the session and we might then say "now I know what he is talking about". "This", says Bion, ". . . that would be known in the future but is not yet known is the noumena or the thing-in-itself; later on, when it is understood it would change into a phenomena."

> . . . The immediate **interpretation**, now, goes backward and it goes forward. "I think I see what you mean." Or to put it in other terms, "I think I remember something like what you are saying". . . It glances back; it **intuits** "the shape of things to come" . . . A "present" experience is past, is present and is future; it is timeless—unless someone can invent space–time, psychoanalytic **time** and **space**. [*ibid*., p. 36]

See: **O, phenomena, noumena, Thing-in-itself, Truth.**

Sigma (= Σ): Greek letter (= S) used in mathematics to denote a total sum. Bion uses it to represent the totality of the mind, both in a nation as well as in a person. He prefers to use this sign instead of a concept like **noösphere** introduced by Teilhard de Chardin (1947) to describe the collective unconscious. Σ would be equivalent to νουσ (*noos*) of the Greeks (1992, p. 313) (meaning: "intelligence, spirit, mind, **thought, memory**"), and different from small sigma: σ (= s), which Bion uses to represent the soma (*ibid.*, p. 314). He insists on the need to investigate the relationship between Σ and σ, which have been considered equivalent in classical psychoanalysis: "The object of my proposal is to do away with such a limitation and to regard the relationship between body and mind (or personality, or psyche) as one that is subject to investigation" (*ibid.*). Σ and σ should not be confused, notwithstanding the attraction σ could exercise in some individuals: "But psychoanalytic scrutiny convinces one that Σ is the significant fact, and σ important only in so far as it is receptive or emitter[57] of Σ" (*ibid.*, p. 316). In Σ can be found what we call "**psychotic** thinking", an area Bion referred to as of "short wave", that lacks the capacity to discriminate, something musicians refer to as "incapacity to listen". The analyst must adjust his/her aptitude to **listen** in order to penetrate the isolation of the psychotic patient, who will then welcome the **attention** provided by the analyst, feeling that he has finally become comprehensible to somebody. *See:* **Medical model.**

Significant dreams: Bion alludes to several dreams, many in presentations of clinical cases, for example the "imaginary twin" (1967), as well as other **dreams** he uses to explain **theories**, like for instance the dream of the "tiger and the bear" (1965, pp. 15–16), or "the arm that fell off" (1992, p. 231). He refers only once to a dream of his own: "the dream of the Negro" (*ibid.*, pp. 51–52). During the weekend a patient dreams of a tiger and a bear fighting, and wakes up with his own scream, dreadfully frightened, feeling that during their wild tussle they would stumble and kill him. The bear managed to stop the tiger but its nose was bitten off, an image that made the patient shudder when he thought about it (1965, pp. 15–16).

Bion produces no patient history or associations to the dream about "the arm falling off", he only uses it as an example to explain

---

[57] Bion uses the word "emittive" that was changed to "emitter', because it did not appear in the dictionary (Webster Collegiate Dictionary)

that similar to **myths**, dreams can show how α-**elements** are assembled in a **constant conjunction**. He assures us that dreams and myths, although he gives no explanation, can be reduced to an algebraic **calculus** and

> . . . therefore as capable of yielding, after scrutiny, the tools that can interpret, through their suitability to represent a problem, the problem itself, and so open the way to its solution. [1992, p. 230]

In the dream the patient was seated:

> . . . in a railway train and gave the signal usually given to indicate an intention to stop when driving a car, and that his arm fell of, it must be assumed that certain **elements** are conjoined. [*ibid.*, p. 231].

The third one is Bion's dream that took place on the night of the 3–4 of August 1959, after dozing while reading a passage on Quine's *Mathematical Logic* (p. 31) about "dealing with *negative*".

> The dream, I thought as I wakened, was associated with "neg" being both negro and negative. But why did I not write it down then? And now I think of negative and native: "natives" is associated with **memories** of India, my mother, and natives as being coloured people like Indians who were "inferior". Also "dative" as being a present, and dates which I liked. "Ablative", to lift off or take away. Negro, as he appeared in the dream, now seems to me not to be a real person but an **ideogram**. My theory is that this ideogram has enabled me to store all these **ideas**, which I am now producing—maybe because I am a dreamer. Perhaps there is a class of persons, or class of dreamers, to which it might be useful to say some people belong. [*ibid.*, pp. 51–52]

Bléandonu (1994) using Bion's association with the word "date", has the following to say:

> Bion does not consider the overdetermination of "date" through its meaning or "rendezvous": with whom? . . . Unlike a Kleinian or a Freudian, Bion abandons this associative richness to consider the "negro"—not as a real person but as an ideogram . . . What did Bion mean by proposing that the "negro" was not a real person? Simply that it was a person from a dream. He differentiated between the status of a representation during sleep—where the "negro" had appeared to be "real", and had represented an "undigested" fact—

and the status of the "negro" in the **interpretation** given to the reader. By making the "negro" into an ideogram, Bion had partly "digested" the **fact**. The visual image of the "negro" evoked by the writing is part of the process of mental digestion. [pp. 174–175]

Sign Objects: Objects used to represent signs, different from symbols, which make possible **thinking** about objects that are not present. They stand for primitive **forms** of thinking, before proper tools appear. For instance, if someone wished to know how many apples there were if four men carried three each, it would not be necessary to have the four men and apples present in the room, it would be enough to employ mathematical notations to solve the problem "without having to rely on the physical presence of the objects." If objects were present they would be signs and not **abstract** representations or symbols. The "object-sign" corresponds to the **thing-in-itself** or β-**elements** (1963, pp. 38–39).

Silence: Bion referred to silence during psychoanalytic sessions throughout many of his **publications**. As a paradigm of these contributions it would be useful to reproduce a **statement** made by Bion in one of his conferences in 1974 in Rio de Janeiro:

> . . . a patient comes into the consulting room and does not say a word; perhaps he keeps on coming for six days, or six weeks, or six months without saying anything. If one can stand it, then after six months one might begin to think, "I have an idea about the pattern of this silence. I wouldn't like to say at any given moment why his silence today is not the same as his silence on Friday, and it won't be the same tomorrow. But I think that if I can go on listening to him being silent"—in the way that Freud talks about the importance of going on being present in the consulting room with the patient for long enough—"I begin to be aware of a pattern". Although we cannot say whether we have heard anything we could say, "It has an effect upon me—not on my **countertransference**—and I think I have had a respect for the silence of the session". If we cannot respect the silence—"I can't be bothered with this person; I can't come here day after day and have him lying on the couch, saying nothing"—then there is no chance of making any further progress. It is difficult to explain to someone not present why we think that we could hear the difference between one silence and another. The patient, however is present. [1974a, p.94]

Francesca Bion (1995), on the other hand, repeats comments made by Bion about the patient who is silent all the time, as follows:

> ... restricting ourselves to verbal intercourse won't get us far with this kind of patient. What kind of **psychoanalysis** is needed to interpret the silence? The analyst may think there is a pattern to the silence. If they cannot respect the silence, there is no chance of making any further progress. The analyst can be silent and listen—stop talking so that he can have a chance to hear what is going on. [p. 20]

And on another occasion:

> Some silences are nothing, they are 0, zero. But sometimes that silence becomes a pregnant one; it turns into 101—the preceding and succeeding sounds turn it into valuable **communication**, as with rests and pauses in music, holes and gaps in sculpture. [*ibid.*]

Social-ism (Vs narcissism): It seems that Bion, at a given moment, used the **concepts** of **socialism** and narcissism to explain the polarization between both **instincts**, life or sexual and death or ego-instincts, as they were originally explained by Freud (1967, p. 118). It would not be difficult to speculate that such a different **vertex** would be the product of Bion's experience in **group** dynamics. He said:

> This bi-polarity of the instincts refers to their operations as **elements** in the fulfilment of the individual's life as an individual, and as elements in his life as a social or, as Aristotle would describe it, as a "political" animal. [1992, p. 105]

It is preferable, says Bion, to establish a polarization between "group" and "individual" and not between ego and sexuality as Freud did. At some other point, however, he emphasizes the narcissistic **schism** between projected elements and their introjected mirror counterpart.

> These two terms [social-ism and narcissism] might be employed to describe tendencies, one ego-centric and another socio-centric ... They are equal in amount and opposite in sign. Thus, if the **love** impulses are narcissistic at any time, then the **hate** impulses are social-istic, i.e. directed towards the group, and, *vice versa*: if the

hate is directed against an individual as a part of narcissistic tendency, then the group will be loved socialistically. [*ibid.*, p. 122]

The increase of narcissistic intensity would be accompanied by narrowing of the **emotions**, up to the point in which only one emotion, such as **love** or **hate**, can be experienced. Similarly, an increase of social-ism intensity is accompanied by a widening of the emotional spectrum. Bion also admits that the conflict between both extremes, group and individual, should be solved within the ego; but if this fails, that is, when extreme pathologies obstruct such a solution, the conflict might be translated into ego weakness and even its destruction, making it impossible ever to achieve satisfaction. Such a circumstance can determine intense hate towards reality, as is commonly observed in **psychosis** (*ibid.*, p. 106).

Pathology, says Bion, from a psychoanalytical **point of view**, always has an emotional character. Furthermore, this source can be regarded as **lying** in the individual's (a) narcissism and (b) social-ism. Emotions can be understood as a disturbance of ideation, similar to the way in which the reflection on the water surface can be disturbed by the breeze (1965, p. 80). *See*: **Meaning, Turbulence.**
Sophisticated group: *see*: **Work group**

Space: Bion states that the "**no-breast**" is at variance with the breast and it can be represented using geometric similes, like for instance the image of a **point** (.), as something ephemeral resembling a *staccato* mark in a musical score. It could correspond to a breast that has been reduced to a simple position, the place where the breast was; the breast has disappeared consumed by greed or destroyed by **splitting** maintaining only its position. In this sense, and following the analogy of the breast–no-breast, Bion considers space as pure **emotional** violence dominated by greed and by the "no-space", represented by the place where the space was. On the **Grid**, he uses ←↑ as "the ultimate non-existent 'object', the 'space' and '**time**' annihilated object and its all-consuming greed for, and **envy** of, anything that exists . . ." (1965, p. 104).

Frustration tolerance implies awareness of the amount of time there is between the presence and absence of objects, "and of what a developing personality later comes to know as 'time' . . .". In a similar trend, the position where the breast was that now is experienced as the "no-breast", will later on correspond to the notion of "space" (*ibid.*, p. 54). *See*: **no-breast, point, time**.

Splitting in psychosis: Bion discriminates between splitting and **dissociation**. Splitting represents a process that takes place in **psychosis** as well as in the **psychotic part of the personality**, while dissociation is present in more benign pathology, such as neuroses like hysteria. Bion describes splitting as the main mechanism used in massive and sadistic attacks against some aspects of the ego, such as the **apparatus of perception, verbal thinking**, and against the thinking process matrix, which had already been split from the very beginning of the subject's life. An important aspect is the splitting directed towards the **link** that brings together reality sense impressions and their **awareness**, something that makes **symbol** formation impossible. In subsequent stages, splitting also affects word combination, like the use of substantives or verbs, hindering the possibility of articulated language. Splitting is followed by massive **projective identifications** towards internal and external objects, something responsible not only for the creation of **bizarre objects**, but for the impoverishment of the internal world as well.

Splitting, static: *see*: **Static splitting**.

Stammer: Bion describes a patient with a serious form of stammer which brought him to the point where he became completely silent. He tries to understand the dynamic of this patient with the help of the **container–contained** model: "a man speaking of an **emotional** experience in which he was closely involved began to stammer badly as the **memory** became increasingly vivid to him" (1970, pp. 93–94). Bion interprets that this man was attempting to contain his experience within the words of his narrative, like someone who is about to lose control uses language to avoid it; however, the words he uses to contain his feelings are destroyed by them, and therefore such feelings get dispersed "as enemy forces might break through the forces that strove to contain them" (*ibid.*, p. 94). The meaning this man was trying to express itself became denuded, "his attempt to use his tongue for verbal expression failed to 'contain' his wish to use his tongue for masturbatory movement in his mouth" (*ibid.*). From the point of view of a **container–contained** interaction

($♀♂$), this condition represents a **"parasitic"** relationship where on element (emotion = $♀$) depends on another one (word = $♂$) to produce a third one (incoherent **communication**) that will destroy all three of them (*ibid.*, pp. 95–96). *See*: **Parasitic, Commensal, Symbiotic, Palinurus, death of, Container–contained.**

Statements: Bion defined "statements" as synonymous with "formulation" (1997, p. 15). He established that the statement could be,

> . . . anything from an inarticulate grunt to quite elaborate constructions . . . A single word is a statement, a gesture or grimace is a statement; in short it is any event that is part of **communication** between analyst and analysand, or any personality and itself. [*ibid.*, p. 8]

Later on he assures us that all psychoanalytic statements are **transformations** and also **theories** (*ibid.*, p. 15). For instance, a statement that declares that a phobic patient is terrorized by a hidden internal murderer, represents a theory, which also demonstrates in the patient the existence of a **transformation in rigid movement** (meaning that in spite of the changes suffered by the internal object, her criminal part can still be recognized). At a given moment the patient refers to her difficulty travelling by plane, something that might represent a corroboration of the statement-theory, because she might fear that the aeroplane could crash as a retaliation for her criminal part.

Static splitting: Bion considers that the condition he described as **reversible perspective** is ruled by a "passive" form of splitting, different from the more "dynamic" one described by Klein in the paranoid–schizoid position.

> In the situation I describe there appears to be no dynamic splitting. It is as if the splitting was arrested in a static pose action being no more necessary than it is when hallucination is substituted for reality. [1963, p. 58]

When static splitting takes place, the patient would not have to get into a disagreement about **Oedipal** situations within him/herself, or anything like that, which have been considered "dynamic" by

Bion. He just reverses the perspective, that is, changes a dynamic situation into something very "passive" and different from intrusive projective and **introjective identifications** of β-**elements**. In other words, the patient will go "his own way" expecting the analyst to go "his own", but creating the feeling that they are going together.

Subsidiary basic assumption: Other forms of **basic assumptions** (ba), for instance, to consider that the well-being of individuals is secondary to the survival of the **group**. *See*: **Basic assumption, Dependent ba, Fight-flight ba, Pairing ba, Group**

Symbiotic relation: Bion described three different kind of **links** between **container** (♀) **and contained** (♂): **commensal**, symbiotic, and **parasitic**. The symbiotic represents a confrontation where one **element** depends on another for the benefit of both. In this kind of relationship the result can be translated into **growth**, although it might not be easily discerned. In a relationship like the one that takes place between the **establishment** and the **mystic**, for instance, the former can express a sort of benevolent hostility towards the latter, who can in turn be under careful scrutiny; however, "from this scrutiny the **group** grows in stature and the mystic likewise". On the other hand, in the parasitic association even friendliness is deadly (1970, p. 78).

Symbolic equation: Segal (1957) refers to the "equation" between the original object and its symbol in the inner as well as in the outer world, as representing the basis for concrete thinking in **psychotic** patients, where substitutes do not differ from the original objects, and both are treated as if they were one and the same thing. "Symbolic equation", means a lack of differentiation between object and symbol: "penis = violin". Segal says:

> The symbolic equation between the original object and the symbol in the internal and the external world is, I think, the basis of the **schizophrenic's** concrete thinking where substitutes for the original objects, or parts of the self, can be used quite freely, but, as in the . . . examples of schizophrenic patients which I quoted, they are hardly different from the original object: they are felt and treated as though they were identical with it. This non-differentiation between

the thing symbolized and the symbol is part of a disturbance in the relation between the ego and the object. Parts of the ego and internal objects are projected into an object and identified with it. The differentiation between the self and the object is obscured. Then, since a part of the ego is confused with the object, the symbol—which is a creation and a function of the ego—becomes, in turn, confused with the object which is symbolized. [*ibid.*, p. 41]

Bion adds that a difficulty in the treatment of psychotic patients is their impossibility to work without the presence of the real objects the analysis is dealing with. Using his **theory** of **transformations**, Bion states that these patients are unable to transform **O** into **K** (*see* **Symbol formation**).

Symbol formation: For Bion it represents the capacity to place together two objects in such a way that whatever is common between them, makes itself obvious, while their unaltered differences, are avoided (1967, p. 50); for example, the fox and astuteness. The faculty to create symbols depends on: (a) the capacity to conceive whole objects; (b) the ability to overcome the use of **splitting** present in the **paranoid–schizoid position**; and (c) bringing together split parts and initiating the **depressive position** (*ibid.*, p. 26).

Bion published the above comments in 1953; however, 13 years later, he seemed to have disagreed with his previous ideas of the need of a complete prevalence of the depressive position in order for symbolic formations to take place. At that point he questioned Klein's assumption about the fact that disarray of symbol formation could give rise to serious pathologies such as **psychosis**.[58] "The psychotic patient", says Bion, "does not always behave as if he is incapable of symbol formation" (1970, p. 65). The difficulty consists in the privacy of his symbolic formulation, which often cannot be publicly recognized as such, like a "private **communication** made by God (or Devil or Fate)", for instance. He continues:

> The symbol, as it is usually understood, represents a **conjunction**, which is recognized by a **group** to be constant; as encountered in

[58] According to Meltzer (1978), Bion's creativity increased highly after Klein's death in 1960, meaning that perhaps he was submitting his originality to the ideas of his analyst and teacher.

psychosis it represents a conjunction between a patient and his deity which the patient feels to be constant. [*ibid.*]

See: **Symbolic equation.**

Synthesis: In a strict sense it means to produce something out of its own **elements**, like creating water from the union of oxygen and hydrogen; in a wider sense, it signifies the production of something new out of previously existing things, which might also have been produced from a previous synthesis. Kant has distinguished between synthetic and analytic prepositions. The former, different from the latter, can be recognized only through experience; for instance, to say that the "Angel Fall is the tallest fall in the world", would imply having previously measured it. In the analytic preposition, the predicate is part of the subject: "a fat man is a man", "a right–angled triangle is a triangle". Other philosophers deny any difference between them.

T

Thalamic or sub-thalamic terror: Word created by Bion to name the kind of dread that would be experienced if there were no higher mental regulation for such a fear (1987, p. 319). It would be a social and individual fear, to the point that attempts would often be made not to experience this fear but to ignore it: "there are situations in which a patient shows great signs of fear; that patient may also have learnt *not* to show them" (*ibid.*, 253). There are these peculiar zones of the body, which do behave as if they had a brain or mind of their own; ". . . we would have to say, has the parasympathetic got a brain? Does the thalamus do a parasympathetic sort of thinking?" (*ibid.*, pp. 253–254; 1974, p. 99). *See*: **Nameless fear.**

Theorem of Pythagoras: *see*: **Pythagoras, theorem of.**

Theorem of the Bride's Chair: Also known as "theorem of the Bride", because the demonstration of **Pythagoras'** theorem, according to the Arabs, resembles the saddle used by a bride. Apparently the French had confused this **name** with another theorem, that of **Pons Asinorum**, something questioned by Bion who assures us that the latter corresponds to No. 5 of Book No. 1 and it represents an isosceles triangle, while the Bride's Chair represents a right-angled triangle which corresponds to Book 13, No. 47 (1992, p. 207).

Theory of function: *see*: **Function, theory of.**

Theory of observation: *see*: **Psychoanalysis.**

Theory of psychoanalysis: *see*: **Psychoanalysis.**

Theory of thinking: *see*: **Thinking, theory of.**

Thing-in-itself:[59] Term taken by Kant from the Greek *noumenon*, the past participle of νοειν, meaning to think, to conceive; used to describe what the mind conceives beyond the **phenomenon**, but cannot be perceived, that is, the thing in itself, the absolute reality of which there is no **empirical** or sensible knowledge, but can be known through intellectual intuition. Russell (1945) explains the "thing-themselves" as

> ... the causes of our sensations, are unknowable; they are not in space or time, they are not substances, nor can they be described by any of those other general concepts which Kant calls categories. [p. 707]

Bion correlates the thing-in-itself with two completely different aspects: (a) with **O** or the ultimate unthinkable **truth**; (b) with material that cannot be changed into **thoughts** or β-**elements**, and can only be used for evacuation through **projective identifications**. "It is as if in one view man can never know the thing-in-itself, but only **secondary and primary qualities** [he is referring to the analyst **listening** during the analytical session]; whereas in the other view

---

[59] Green (2000) quotes Shakespeare's King Lear, the moment when Edgar, disguised as a madman who has escaped from Bedlam, initiates a conversation between the King, the Fool and Tom. The latter, so much impoverished, is addressed by the King: "... Thou owest the worm no silk, the beast no hide, the sheep no wool, the cat no perfume. Ha! Here's three on's are sophisticated! *Thou are the thing itself*" (King Lear, 3, 4, 106; my italics). Green concludes: "This was long before Kant dreamt of these words" (p. 121).

he can never "know" anything *but* the thing-in-itself [now referring to the **psychotic** patient]" (1965, p. 40).

Bion differentiates between noumena and phenomena:

> When the noumena, the things themselves, push forward so far that they meet an object [a realization] which we can call a human mind, there then comes into being the domain of phenomena. We can guess, therefore, that corresponding to these phenomena, which are something that we know about because they are us, is the thing itself, the noumenon. The religious man would say, "there is, in reality, God". What Freud and psychoanalysis have investigated is phenomena. (1974, p. 41)

The mind, says Bion, is an obstacle to appreciate the unknown, the **noumenon**, which cannot be grasped unless it is exposed. He continues:

> I would not be able to see a stream which was flowing smoothly without any obstacle to disturb it because it could be so transparent. But if I create a **turbulence** by putting in a stick, then I can see a stream which was flowing smoothly without any obstacle to disturb it because it would be so transparent. [*ibid.*]

In 1962, when describing his **theory of thinking**, Bion said that, "What should be a **thought**, a product of the juxtaposition of **preconception** and negative **realization** becomes a bad object, indistinguishable from a thing-in-itself, fit only for evacuation" (1967, p. 112). And later on, in the same article:

> If intolerance of frustration is dominant, steps are taken to evade perception of the realization by destructive attacks. In so far as preconception and realization are mated mathematical conceptions [*see*: **psychic mathematics**] are formed ... as if indistinguishable from things-in-themselves and are evacuated at high speed as missiles to annihilate space. [*ibid.*, p. 113]

In other words, both O as the ineffable, and beta elements as products of sense information, represent things-in-themselves; the difference between them, however, is related to hope and to the outcome that can be expected from each of them, while O can be grasped (O→K) and because of enlightening, β-elements are only good for evacuation through projective identifications. The concept of the thing-in-itself is similar to the Platonic notion of **idea** (*see*: **Platonic forms**). For instance, the idea of a book does not have sensory form, however it is a possibility present in all books, but only one book in particular, let us say book X, can change into a "phenomenon" and be recognized by the senses as book X, which will represent a realization. In the same way, O can be conceived by the senses as a possibility within an individual, but can only be formulated once it is touched by a special event, a realization. *See*: β-**space, noösphere.**

Thinking, apparatus for: Bion considers that thinking depends on the success of two mental developments: the development of **thoughts** and the development of an apparatus he will provisionally call "thinking" which is forced to exist in order to deal with thoughts, and not the other way around. "This" says Bion "differs from any [other] theory of thought" (1967, pp. 110–111). He presents two phases of increasing complexity in the setting up of the apparatus for thinking: in the first part he assures us that thinking is forced into an apparatus, which is not prepared to do this, that develops as a result of external demands and must suffer changes in order to adapt. The situation results in a need to change a non-existing object or "**no-breast**" into a representation. Bion states:

> As a "model" of thought I take a sensation of hunger that is associated with a visual image of a breast that does not satisfy but is of a kind that is needed. This needed object is a bad object. All objects that are needed are bad objects because they tantalize. [1962, pp. 83–84]

If the capacity to tolerate **frustration** is adequate the internal "no-breast" will transform into a thought and an apparatus for thinking will be developed, which will make frustration more bearable. But, if the capacity to deal with frustration is inadequate the internal bad "no-breast" will pressure the mind towards evasion of frustration and, instead of forming a thought, the no-breast will transform into a bad object or a β-**element**, indistinguishable from the **thing-in-itself**, which will serve only to be evacuated. In this case, instead of having an apparatus for thinking, the mind will be dominated by mechanisms of **projective identification**, used to discharge the accumulation of bad objects (1967, pp. 111–112) (or for **acting-out**). According to Bion, the apparatus for thinking and the digestive apparatus have common origins, for it is the same one that has originally dealt with sense impressions related to the alimentary canal: milk and affect or the "good breast" arrive at the same time (1962, p. 57).

The baby is conscious of the existence inside of him of a very bad breast, that is, a non-existent breast which, because it is needed and not present, produces painful feelings dealt with by **evacuation** through the respiratory apparatus or through "swallowing" a satis- fying breast. This breast is then indistinguishable from a "thought" or even better, from a primitive thought or **proto-thoughts** (*ibid.*, p. 84). On the other hand, the "swallowed" thought is independent of the existence of an object that has really been put inside the mouth; in this way, the breast or the "thing-in-itself" is equivalent to the idea in the mind and reciprocally indistinguishable from the "thing-in-itself" in the mouth.

(A) In the second part of the systematization of the apparatus for thinking, Bion adds the concepts of **container ($\female$) and contained ($\male$)** and does so by taking advantage of the **"integrating reticules"**, a notion introduced by Elliot Jaques (1960), understood as a "com- plex mental scheme" that enables the mind to achieve the notion of a total object (1962, pp. 92–93). Bion uses this concept in order to explain the complexity of successive **growth** that takes place between container ($\female$) and contained ($\male$) in the achievement of higher levels of **abstraction** that will allow one to **learn from expe- rience**. This development is typical of what Bion calls a **commensal** relationship between ($\female$) and ($\male$). Theoretically this process will begin at a moment when these elements ($\female\male$) are organized in a **form** previous to what Poincaré (1908) has called the **selected fact**. The containers ($\female$) represent doubts, questions or variables joined by emotional experiences that successively add up inside the con- tents ($\male$) in a continuous series that can be represented as: $\female^n + \male^n$; a process that at the end guarantees the successive growth of the apparatus and the possibility of learning from experience. This learning will depend on the capacity of $\female^n$ to integrate and to keep open at the same time, free of rigidity and ready for further assim- ilations. An individual in whom this mechanism operates will be capable of preserving knowledge and experience, and capable of using his past experiences as well as being receptive to new ones (1962, pp.92–93). Therefore, the level of **K** will depend on this kind of "commensal" relationship, for instance, the successive complexity of new **hypotheses** that will form systems and later on **deductive scientific systems**. Bion also relates the apparatus for thinking to **I** (Idea), assuring us that the material out of which the apparatus is formed and has to deal with is *I* (1963, p.31). *See*: **Thinking, theory of, Thoughts, Verbal thoughts**.

Thinking, theory of: Bion published a paper with this title in 1962, where he depicted a theory about **thinking**, similar, according to him, to a philosophical **theory**, because philosophers are also concerned with the same matters, and yet different in that his theory was created to be used in everyday practice, and its **hypotheses** to be empirically validated by psychoanalysts. However, it can be related to some philosophical theories in the same way that there is a relationship between applied and pure mathematics. He believes his theory has no diagnostic importance, although it can be helpful when some psychological disturbance is suspected (1967, p. 110). Thinking depends on the significant development of two significant constructions: (a) **thoughts**; and (b) an **apparatus for thinking**, absolutely necessary for the development of thoughts. This theory would differ from others, because it defines thinking as a "development forced on the psyche by the pressure of thoughts and not the other way around" (*ibid.*, p. 111). Thought disturbances might be associated with breakdown of thoughts, the apparatus for thinking, or both.

Following Freud (1911), the thoughts originated from ideation and acquired special quality of **action**, something that provided the apparatus for thinking with a capacity to discharge the mind from accretion of stimuli, thorough the use of **projective identifications**. Generally, this theory of thinking introduces the existence of an **omnipotent** phantasy: that it is possible temporarily to **split** undesirable aspects of the personality—sometimes valuable aspects—to place them inside an object and force this object to experience those **emotions** of which they wanted to free themselves. *See*: **Thinking, apparatus for, Thoughts, Verbal thoughts**.

Thoughts: They could be conceived as **space** occupied by **no-things**, marked by signs and words, and used to solve problems in the absence of the object (1965, p. 106). Different from **conceptions**, which result from the mating of **pre-conceptions** with **realizations**, thoughts, on the other hand, also represent the mating of pre-conceptions, but with **frustrations** (1967, p. 111). In other words, the realization of a wish will give place to a conception, but frustration will produce thoughts. The **model** suggested by Bion is based on the baby whose expectation of feeding is confronted with the realization of an absent breast or **no-breast**. The next step will depend on how the baby reacts, either to avoid frustration or to modify it. If frustration tolerance is satisfactory, the internal no-breast will be changed into thoughts, primitive thoughts or **proto-thoughts** (1962, p. 84) and an **apparatus for thinking** that will allow the frustration to be more tolerable. But if the capacity to deal with frustration is insufficient, the internal no-breast will press the mind towards evasion of frustration and instead of a thought being created, the no-breast will become a bad object indistinguishable from a **thing-in-itself**, good only to be **evacuated** by mechanisms of **projective identification**. Thoughts could be classified according to their historical development: (a) pre-conceptions; (b) conceptions; and (c) **concepts** (1967, p. 111). Interchanges between **paranoid–schizoid** and **depressive positions** are also related to the development of thoughts and **thinking**. *See*: **Thinking, apparatus for, Thinking, theory of, Verbal thoughts.**

Thoughts without a thinker: *see*: **wild-thoughts**

Three-kneed thing: Following Plutarch, Bion associates the **Oedipus myth** with a triangle rectangle, where the sides of the right angle represent both parents and the hypotenuse the child. But Bion adds that

> The Greek term [triangle] could be translated as, "a three-kneed thing with equal legs". R. B. Onians [1951] has shown—and he cannot be accused of any tenderness to Freud's theories of sexuality—that the knees, in early Greek literature, are very frequently associated with the genitalia. This has made me look at **Euclid's** Fifth Proposition in a new light. It also makes one inclined to attempt a revaluation of the question traditionally attributed to the Sphinx. [1992, pp. 201–202]

See: **Pythagoras, theorem of, Euclid, geometry of.**

Tiger and the bear, dream of: *see*: **Significant dreams.**

Time: When satisfaction is not possible (**no-breast**), the future will depend on how the ego tolerates **frustration**. According to Bion the ego responds in different ways: (a) it could evade the situation with the use of **evacuatory** thoughts or β**-elements**, which are projected inside internal or, more often, external objects; (b) it could modify the situation; (c) it could establish a **splitting** between **inanimate** (material) and animate (mental) objects; or (d) it could produce a **thought** by mating a **pre-conception** with a negative **realization** of an absent object.

Frustration tolerance implies **consciousness** of the period elapsed between the presence and the absence of objects, that is, what a developing personality would then recognize as "time". It is similar to the place where the object was, experienced as a "**no-breast**" and analogous to the notion of **space**. The factors that reduce the breast to a **point**, said Bion, also reduce time to "now":

> Time is **denuded** of past and future. The "now" is subjected to attacks [extremely **envious**] similar to those delivered against space, or more precisely, the point. [1965, p. 55]

If we say, for instance, "where the past used to be and is now a not-present", or in another form: "where the future used to be there is now a not-present" (*ibid.*, p. 100) we are referring to **transference** and it represents an attack and a splitting of the present reduced to a not-present. The **no-thing** is related to space in the same manner that no-present is related to time. Such incapacity to discriminate past from present and future is responsible for feelings of boredom, of unending tautology or sameness frequently found in borderline pathologies. *See*: **Space, No-breast, Point, No-thing.**

Tolerance or intolerance of frustration: *see*: **Frustration, tolerance and intolerance of.**

Touch: The sense of touch is used as an "antidote" for the confusion that might take place in a **container–contained** interaction, something like to "touch" in order to distinguish, to differentiate between the container and its content (1963, p. 95). Could also be used to calm down, in that the skin can be used as barrier between two objects, something like a "distant closeness" (*see*: **Distance**). It would be different from other **models** using sense organs like sight, hearing or smell, because all these, different from touch, can be experienced from a distance; however, touch produces "the paradoxical effect that the topographically closer relationship implied by tactile contact is *less* intimate, i.e. confused, than the more distant relationship implied by the . . ." other models (*ibid.*, p. 96).

Tower of Babel, myth of the: This is a **myth** that, according to Bion, combines:

> . . . the following components: a universal language; the building by the group of a tower which is felt by the Deity to be a menace to his position; a confounding of the universal language and a scattering abroad of the people on the face of the earth. [1948b, pp. 186–187]

The idea that the tower will reach the sky introduces an **element** of **messianic** hope, present in the "**pairing group**"; however, the possibility that such a hope might become true, violates an important canon of this **basic assumption** (ba): the norm that such a hope could never be achieved; such a possibility, could make "the group dissolve in **schisms**" (*ibid.*, pp. 185–187).

In his autobiography, perhaps imitating Descartes, Bion states:

> I am: therefore I question. It is the answer—the "yes, I know"—that is the disease which kills;[60] it is the Tree of Knowledge which kills. Conversely, it is not the successful building of the Tower of Babel, but the *failure* that gives life, initiates and nourishes the energy to live, to **grow**, to flourish. The song the sirens sing, and always have sung, is that the arrival at the inn—not the journey—is the reward, the prize, the haven, the cure. [1985, p. 52]

The Tower of Babel can also be seen as God's punishment (superego) for men daring to reach his level, his knowledge; in this

---

[60] Possibly Bion is referring to Maurice Blanchot's expression: "*La réponse est le malheur de la question*", something he frequently quoted.

sense Bion considers this myth similar to the Garden of Eden (to eat from the "Tree of Wisdom"), and to the sphinx in **Oedipus** (that destroys the one who knows). This **interpretation,** on the other hand, seems to contradict his statement about Oedipus' epistemophilic instinct, on how Oedipus is dominated by his desire to know the **truth** regardless of its consequences, controlled by strong feelings of omnipotent curiosity and **arrogance**, which change into stupidity and tragedy. The myth in summary represents an attack on the **desire** to reach heaven as a **symbolism** for knowledge, wisdom, α-**function**, **links** and language that makes co-operation possible (1992, p. 241).

Following the **Grid**, it could be understood as follows: a **group** of people express the **definitory hypothesis** of building a tower to reach the sky (C1), looking for knowledge and integration (E3, E4), a message received by a deity who feels threatened (D2) and ends up punishing them all (A6). *See:* **Basic assumption, Pairing group (Pba), Myth, Oedipus myth, Arrogance, curiosity and stupidity.**

Transference: About this concept Bion said:

> The **elements** of the transference are to be found in that aspect of the patient's behaviour that betrays his awareness of the presence of an object that is not himself. No aspect of his behaviour can be disregarded . . . His greeting, or neglect of it, references to couch, or furniture, or weather, all must be seen in that aspect of them that relates to the presence of an object not himself. [1963, p. 69]

Applying **psychic mathematics** Bion represents the mind with the equation $\Psi(\zeta)$, where ζ would indicate the non-**saturated** aspect that must be examined during each session to determine the degree of saturation produced by the transference. From the vertex of **transformation** theory, Bion represents transferential neurosis as: T (patient) β (1965, p. 18):

> This transformation involves little deformation: the term "transference", as Freud used it, implies a model of movement of feelings and **ideas** from one sphere of applicability to another. I propose therefore to describe this set of transformations as **"rigid motions"**. The invariance of rigid motion must be contrasted with invariance peculiar to **projective transformation**. [*ibid.*, p. 19]

Bion states that the presence of the patient in the session shows that he knows about the analyst's existence, but such a fact is used, conformably with column 2 of the **Grid**, to deny the *absence*. "He reacts in the session as if I were absent . . . this behaviour is intended to deny my *presence*":

> The **model** by which I represent *his* "vision" of *me* is that of an absent breast, the place or position, that I, the breast, *ought* to occupy but do not. The "ought" expresses *moral* violence and omnipotence. The visual image of me can be represented by what a geometer might call a **point**, a musician the staccato mark in a musical score. [*ibid.*, p. 53]

Transference has a strong and a weak point, which require distinction in order to avoid confusion. Its strength consists in that "two people have a '**fact**' available to both and therefore open for discussion by both"; the weakness, on the other hand, lies in the fact that the transference "is ineffable and cannot be discussed by anyone else. The failure to recognize this simple fact has led to confusion" (1992, p. 353). *See*: **Transformations, Rigid motion transformations, Projective transformations, Countertransference, No-breast, Point, Line.**

Transference interpretation: Bion explains that during the treatment of patients presenting serious **thought** disorders, "opportunities for orthodox **transference** interpretation occurred and were taken, but the patient often learned nothing from them. The stream of disjointed associations continued" (1962, p. 20). Only after he realised that the patient projected into the analyst his own sanity or the **"non-psychotic part of his personality"** or α-**function**, did the situation change. He states:

> The theory of functions offered a prospect of solving this problem by assuming that I contained unknown functions of his personality and from this to scrutinize the sessional experience for clues of what these might be. I assumed that I was "consciousness". [*ibid.*, p. 21]

Bion concludes that only after he stopped using mechanisms oriented towards the understanding of the transference, did he become aware that the patient was dreaming awake with the immediate events in the session, or in other words, translating sense impressions into α-**elements** but in a wrong way: "I was witnessing an inability to **dream** through lack of alpha-elements and therefore an inability to sleep or wake, to be either **conscious** or unconscious" (*ibid.*). *See*: **Transference, Countertransference, Rigid motion transformations.**

Transformation of the analysis: Bion used this expression to refer to the successive changes of "uses" in the **elements** that set out the **horizontal axis** of the **Grid**. *See*: **Grid, the, Horizontal axis, Transformation, Psychoanalysis.**

Transformations: From a general perspective Bion defines this concept as the series of changes experienced by a **group** of **elements** that vary from a previous to a subsequent stage, where the recognition of the identity of these elements that have changed, would depend on the existing **invariants**. Transformation seems to be related to topology and to the classical concept of "psychoanalytic process."

The total development experienced in any transformation is represented with T, which covers two aspects: (a) the process of transformation = Tα; (b) the final product of the transformation Bion represents as Tβ (1965, p. 10). For instance, the transformation (T) experienced by a landscape (Tα), when it is painted on a canvas (Tβ) by an artist. Another example would be the transformation (T) experienced by a patient's hypochondriacal symptoms (Tα), when they change into violence (Tβ), after the patient has gone through a **psychotic** crisis and the family, which has remained apparently neutral, threatens to prosecute the analyst, who develops, because of the situation, a state of **anxiety**. The whole **catastrophic change**, now experienced by the group, can be equivalent to the hypochondriacal symptoms (invariants) the patient had suffered (Tα) before the crisis. T (patient), in this case, would represent the whole process of changes met by the patient, including T(patient)α and T(patient)β; while the transformation suffered by the analyst can be represented: T(analyst), from T(analyst)α to T(analyst)β (*ibid.*, pp. 7–11). Or: (a) in relation to the patient: T, Tpα and Tpβ; (b) in relation to the analyst: Ta, Taα and Taβ (*ibid.*, p. 24). From the point of view of **O**, Bion states that transformation represents the "**phenomenal** counterpart of O" (1965, p. 40), that allows acting as a **constant conjunction** to recognize a **fact**, an **emotional** state or a representation (*ibid.*, p. 68). The landscape, as well as the patient and the analyst, for instance, represent a transformation that moved from the unknown or the **thing-in-itself** to **K**, or knowledge of O (O → K). O should be available to the analyst (Taα) as well as to the patient (Tpα). All these transformations, depending on the assessment of the associations, can have a place on the **Grid**, for instance A1 or C2 among many others (*ibid.*, p. 13). **Truth** is another important element Bion has considered:

> If truth is not essential to all values of Taβ, Taβ must be regarded as expressed in and by manipulations of the emotions of patient or public and not in or by the **interpretation**; truth is essential for any value of Taβ in art or science. [*ibid.*, p. 37]

Transformations in the patient as well as in the analyst (Tpα and Taα) are influenced by emotional **links** (**L, H** and K), although it is expected that Taα and Taβ should always be free from such influences, at least in an ideal analyst who never acts out his/her **countertransference**. Obviously, the opposite can be expected from the patient.

A model of transformation: In Chapters Ten and Twelve of his book *Transformations* (1965), Bion used the word "cycle" to designate a "**model** of transformation", which appears rather complicated on first reading. He uses a series of trays filled with marbles of assorted sizes and colours to represent different variables. The trays correspond to successive **time-space** lapses of transformations designed as "cycle 1, cycle 2 . . . cycle n"; while the marbles signify dimensions or **elements** experimenting transformations. If we apply this model to a psychoanalytic session, it becomes more comprehensible and easier to follow. In an "ideal" session we will have, in the first place, the patient's free association manifest discourse, and at the same time, the analyst's attentive **listening** without **memory, desire** or understanding (corresponding to the trays in Bion's model). This situation, at the beginning of the session, which undergoes a continuous process of transformation in both minds (corresponding to marbles in Bion's model), would be represented as "cycle 1"; the process of transformation would be characterized as Tα, and the end of the process, as Tβ, or Tpα and Tpβ if effected by the patient, or Taα and Taβ if related to the analyst (*see*: **Transformations**). In the mind of the analyst the transformation is towards emergence of **O**, or "becoming or being O or being 'become' by O" (1965, p. 163). Tpβ would be equal to O (Tpβ = O, cycle 1). **Transformation in O** is followed by **transformation of K** in the analyst's mind, in order to start shaping the **interpretation**: TaO → **K** or TβO = TKα, cycle 2; once the interpretation is formed (TKβ) and phrased, cycle 2 is completed and cycle 3 starts as a transformation taking place in the patient's mind. And so on.

There is a further complication because, at the same time, Bion attempts to place the results of different transformations on the categories of the **Grid**; for instance, the interpretation represented as TKb (cycle 1) could correspond to a **definitory hypothesis** such as B1, or the patient's association to the interpretation might be a denial or resistance that could correspond to "Tpβ (cycle 2) in row A2" of the Grid. *See*: **Projective transformations, Transformations in rigid movement, Invariants, Transformations of K, Transformations of O, Transformations in O, Transformations in hallucinosis, Catastrophic change, Thing-in-itself, O, Grid, the.**

Transformations in hallucinosis: Some **psychotic** patients (or the **psychotic part of the personality** in borderline patients) experience the omnipotence implicit in **hallucinations**—they are able to hallucinate anything they might **desire**—as a method to reach independence, a system they consider superior to **psychoanalysis**. In states of **hallucinosis**, "circularity" and perpetuity is established as a need to compensate for **frustrations**, but since hallucinations are destined to fail, greed increments and the need for further hallucinations increment as well (1970, p. 37). On the other hand, if there is the feeling that the "**magic**" of hallucination is failing, the patient could suspect that the analyst's "**envy**" and "rivalry" are responsible for it. There is the belief that there are "superior" objects related to independence and self-sufficiency, which are more efficient than any other object, and are responsible for all **actions**, possibly occupying the place of the father, mother, analyst, purpose, ambition, **interpretation** or **ideas**. The relationship among these objects is based only on a "superior–inferior" dimension, where it is better to receive than to give. The patient, dominated by important feelings of rivalry, tries to take over "the place" of the analyst and to divert him from his analytical **vertex**, creating a dilemma in the analyst: either to give up his technique, or to maintain the analysis and demonstrate to the patient that he considers his acts and methods superior. Any of these possibilities would probably give place to rivalrous **acting-out** (1965, p. 136). The problem can be summarized as the struggle between the virtues of either a **transformation** by hallucinosis or a transformation by psychoanalysis. When this dilemma is interpreted it can turn into an intrapsychic conflict between different parts of the mind. From the point of view of **container–contained** theory, Bion suggested the existence of a tendency to "exaggerate", that is, a condition characterized by a progressive increment of a need for affection from the contained, and an increment of an evacuatory rejection from the container, a mechanism Bion referred to as "**hyperbole.**"

The patient's attitude would correspond to A6 and the analyst's to F1, F3 or F4, avoiding column 2. The analyst's link with the patient would correspond to **K**, but not to **L** or **H**. From the **point of view** of the patient, the interpretation could be experienced as A6, or elements to be evacuated, representing arguments used by the analyst to prove the superiority of psychoanalysis (*ibid.*, p. 143).

The general picture presented by these patients "is that of a person anxious to demonstrate his independence of anything other than his own creations" (*ibid.*, p. 137), which are a product of their supposed ability to use their senses as **evacuatory** organs to build a background that encircles them. The main purpose of their senses is to construct a perfect world, where any evidence of imperfection is *ipso facto* experienced as a consequence of external hostile forces that require evacuation. Thanks to this capacity, the patient feels completely independent from everything except for his own products, feeling beyond any feelings of rivalry, envy, greed, threat, love or hate; but just as any other psychotic defence, this mechanism fails and threats of imperfection and dependency set in. Rivalry with the analyst is an attempt to prove the superiority of the methods used by the patient for whom the word "**cure**" is an expression of victory (*ibid.*, pp. 137–143).

Bion proposes the possibility of using mathematical elements to represent the conflicts present in hallucinosis and he distinguishes several formulae. In the first place, he tries to represent the normal situation where the absence of the breast and a high frustration tolerance allows **thoughts** or K **links** to take place, an operation that could correspond to **transformation in rigid movement** (*ibid.*, pp. 133–136). He represents this normal condition as follows:

> a^1 The infant feels it is being satisfied by the breast: the breast disappears and the satisfaction with it.
>
> a^2 1 breast + 0 breast = 0 breast
>
> a^3 1 + 0 = 0. [1965, p. 133]

But if frustration cannot be tolerated, as observed in psychotic patients, we have to deal with a situation where absence of the breast is experienced as a presence, the word becomes a thing and the **memory** of satisfaction is used to deny the absence of satisfaction; it corresponds to the mathematics of transformation in hallucinosis:

> (using b instead of a)
>
> b^2 1 breast + 0 breast = 1 breast
>
> b^3 1 + 0 = 1.

Furthermore, says Bion, under the dominion of hallucinosis, the equation $0 - 0 = 1$ is also possible: $0 + 0 = 0^0$, "That is to say that if noughtness is added to noughtness the noughtness is multiplied by itself" (*ibid.*, p. 134).

> The ability of 0 to increase thus by parthenogenesis corresponds to the characteristics of greed which is also able to **grow** and flourish exceedingly by supplying itself with unrestricted supplies of **nothing** . . . In hallucinosis nought denuded of its noughtness is hostile envious and greedy and does not even exist as it is denuded of its existence [*ibid.*]

Previously, Bion had represented this concept using arrows that move in the opposite direction to the axes of the **Grid** and adding a negative sign: $-\leftarrow\uparrow$. *See*: **Transformations, Projective transformations, Transformations in rigid movement, Invariants, Transformations of K, Transformations of O, Transformations in O, Hallucinosis, Conscious awareness.**

Transformations in K are related to "knowing about" something, whereas transformation in O is related to becoming or being O "or to being "become" by O". O evolves in different ways: (a) becoming manifest or knowable; (b) becoming a "remainder" an "incarnation or embodiment or an incorporation" (here Bion is possibly referring to the kind or relationship he described in the "**God-head**"); (c) becoming TbO or, **at-one-ment**, as is expected to take place during analytic listening (1965, p. 163).

There is a great difference between "being" O and having rivalries with O, because this last condition implies the presence of important feelings of **envy**, hate, love, megalomania, and **acting-out**; for instance the case of a thinker who is contained by an **idea**, as observed in religious fanatics or paranoid dictators who become megalomanic. Acting-out should be differentiated from **action**, as considered in the **horizontal axis** of the **Grid**, because action helps being O, but acting-out opposes it.

Although O is related to **growth**, their relationship is different from other **transformations**, such as K, because K induces growth, but O means "knowing about growth". Religious or philosophical transformations are closer to transformations in O than mathematical transformations (*ibid.*, p. 156). There is an important aspect in the relation of O with K, Bion has described as some kind of perverse defence, when a patient induces growth towards K in order to obstruct transformations in O, as a sort of **reversible perspective**. Bion said:

> By agreeing with the **interpretation** it is hoped that the analyst will be inveigled into a collusive relationship to preserve K without being aware that he is doing so. If the manoeuvre is successful transformations in K fulfil an F2 role preventing the inception of $T\alpha$ → $T\beta$ = K → O (1965, p.160).

Transformations of the type TK→ TO, could induce resistances manifested as fear or hatred, because of the emphasis placed on "knowing" something instead of "becoming" something. It can be observed in persons who try to find answers for their suffering in popular self-taught books, or who identify analysis with a university subject, or who idealize transference and expect to be "**cured**" by the analyst (*ibid.*, p. 163). The opposite transformation: TO → TK depends on the capacity of the analyst to listen free from memory and desire (1970, p. 30).

Transformations in O: Because **O** is the unknowable, the ineffable, and is always transcending and becoming, all qualities attributed to O as well as links established with O are really **transformations of O**. **L**, **H** and **K** are links and because of that, they are substitutes for the ultimate relationship with O. They cannot reach O, but they are appropriate for transformation in O; for instance, a feeling experienced in the **countertransference** can help us to know about the patient's O, but such a feeling could also become a "counteracting", a discrimination that according to Bion would demand a good analytical training in the analyst.

Transformations in rigid movements: Concept borrowed from projective geometry and used by Bion to describe a form of **transformations** (T) that show little deformation between the original object or **thing-in-itself** (Tα) and the end product of the transformation (Tβ). **Transference** is a good example of this form of transformation, where the past is transferred to the analyst without any deformation, something that gives this mechanism great credibility as a reliable exponent of the **truth** (1965, p. 19). The rigidity of the **invariants** in this form of transformation, different from **projective transformation**, eases the relationship between **O** and the patient (Op) (ibid., p. 31) and facilitates understanding of the session as well as the creation of the **interpretation**. A good example of this kind of transformation can be seen in Bion's case of the weekend dream of the "**tiger and the bear**" (ibid., pp. 15–16). There are, however, other cases where Op (the patient's O) is so elusive and opaque that the interpretation results are highly speculative, corresponding then to "projective transformations." See: **Transformations, Projective transformations, Transformation in hallucinosis, Invariants, Transformations of K, Transformations of O, Transformations in O, Significant dreams, Transference, O**.

Transformations of K: Taken from the first letter of knowledge, **K** represents one of the links, together with **L** (love) and **H** (hate). Transformation of K is related to **transformations** towards **growth** in the analyst, and eventually, in the patient too. Growth would not correspond to L and H. Bion refers to a form of perverse defence, where the patient might induce transformation towards K in order to avoid **transformation in O**, similar to the concept of rationalization. Transformation from O to K can only be established when the analyst is free from **memory** and **desire**. Bion said:

> By agreeing with the interpretation it is hoped that the analyst will be inveigled into a collusive relationship to preserve K without being aware that he is doing so. If the manoeuvre is successful transformations in K fulfil an F2 role preventing the inception of $T\alpha$ $\rightarrow$ $T\beta = K \rightarrow O$. [1965, p.160]

See: **Transformation, Transformation of O, Transformation in O, Memory, Desire, Links.**

Transformations of O: These describe the series of **transformations** experienced by **O**. Such transformations take place because O is not static, O is a **truth** and is continuously changing or becoming; in other words, O is seriously affected by **time** as well as **space**. What is true for this culture might not be true for a different one, what is true today might not be true tomorrow; O from today's session will never be the same O in tomorrow's session; this is why it is so dangerous to remember. *See*: **O, Transformations, Transformation in O, Transformation of K, Truth, Memory, Desire, Godhead.**

Trays: *see*: **Transformations.**

Tropism: Bion uses the term to describe an inclination towards certain kinds of object relation observed in **psychotic** patients or related to the **psychotic part of the personality**, which makes use of "intrusive" forms of **projective identifications**. It can be associated, although with certain cautiousness, with the classical notion of **instincts**. The concept is portrayed in **Cogitations** (1992, pp. 34–36) and although it is not dated, it probably coincided with Bion's work on "**attack on links**" and "**maternal reverie**", described in relation to his **theory of thinking** and written during the fifties. Bion said:

> Thus, considered individually, the tropisms are seen to issue in seeking (1) an object to murder or be murdered by, (2) a **parasite** or

a host, (3) an object to create or by which to be created. But taken as a whole, and not individually, the **action** appropriate to the tropisms in the patient who comes for treatment is a seeking for an object with which projective identification is possible. [*ibid.*, pp. 34–35]

On the other hand, an object, for example a breast (the mother), can refuse to be used as a depository for a projective identification; something Bion considers to be due to both persecutory **anxiety** and **hate**, or to apathy. These two types of response (opposite to a **reverie** condition) contribute to the environmental components that are responsible for the development of the psychotic part of the personality. The object's refusal to accept projective identifications brings about a re-introjection of these tropisms, now more virulent, together with a primitive form of superego, hostile towards projective identifications, as a form of **communication**. According to Bion, the tropism, not introjected by the refusing breast, or re-introjected by the immature psyche, remains in between, enclosed within the vehicle of communication itself, be that sound, sight or **touch**. "Thus enclosed, the tropism and its envelope become persecuted and persecuting" (*ibid.*, p. 35). *See*: **Linking, attacks on, Maternal reverie, Psychotic and non-psychotic parts of the personality, Projective identification, Communication, Bizarre objects, Hallucinations, Delusions.**

Truth: Bion stated:

> ... healthy mental **growth** seems to depend on truth as the living organism depends on food. If it is lacking or deficient the personality deteriorates. [1965, p. 38]

There is a natural hunger for truth; perhaps because there is the empirical knowledge that **lies** induce suffering (1992 p. 99).[61] Originally Bion defined truth as opposed to falsehood and related to **transformations in K**:

---

[61] In Latin, mind (*mentis*) and lie (*mentior*) have the same root. Perhaps it might be this hunger for truth that motivates patients to attend psychoanalytical treatment for years continuously.

Thus "truth" is the name I give to the quality that I attribute to any statement that is a **hypothesis** relating to **phenomena** with which I have an "I know . . ." relationship. [*ibid.*, p. 270]

Afterwards Bion related truth with **transformations in O**:

> All thinking and all thoughts are true when there is no thinker. In contrast to this, for lies and falsities a thinker is absolutely necessary. In any situation where a thinker is present the **thoughts** when formulated are expressions of falsities and lies. The only true thought is one that has never found an individual to "contain" it. [1970, p. 117]

To say that the "sky is blue", does not need a thinker, although it can be described. On the other hand, **O** represents the absolute truth, which at a given moment is intercepted by a thinker, such as the analyst, a **mystic**, or an artist; although the thinker and O exist independently. The classical resistance of a patient in analysis can be the expression of a thought in search of a thinker; usually this could be his own, although this is not necessarily so. A **transformation of O** in **K** (O → K), for example, when an **interpretation** is formulated, can be **intuited** and translated but not thought, and the capacity to grasp it is achieved by means of an **act of faith**. Following the **container–contained theory**, the relationship between a thought and a thinker who contains it (or *vice versa*) can be **commensal, symbiotic** or **parasitic**. In a commensal relationship all elements involved benefit from each other and grow with the relation, like a thinker who invents something useful. However, in the parasitic relationship, the idea resulting is false and it will proliferate until it becomes a lie.

In schizoid personalities, said Bion, the superego is formed before the ego and it will assume its role generating not only an imperfect development of the **reality principle**, but also an exaltation of morals as well as little respect for the truth. What the analyst expresses should always be structured with truthful **verbal thoughts** belonging to rows E and F, possibly D and G and always within columns 1, 3 and 5 of the **Grid**. What the patient says, on the other hand, can belong to any category because he does not have a compromise with the truth, and can fall anywhere on the Grid.

There is a natural need to be aware of **emotional** experiences, similar to the need to be aware of concrete objects through the use of sense impressions, because absence of such **consciousness** implies a deprivation of truth, which is essential for mental health, "its deprivation is analogous to the effect that physical hunger has on the mind" (1962, p. 56).

The truth, similar to the **Oedipus myth**, has two faces, a private one depending on a **cause–effect** relationship and organized according to a **constant conjunction**, and another one, universal and **narrative** related to **common sense**. *See*: **Lies, O, Transformation of O, Transformation in O, K, Transformation of K, Container–contained, Commensal, Symbiotic** and **Parasitic**.

Two-ness: It refers to the natural presence of pair elements: two eyes, two hands, two ears, etc.; exactly as "decimal" originated from *ten-ness* (Latin *decem*), like ten fingers or ten toes. Bion suggests that the development of mathematical elements, as Aristotle called them, is analogous to the development of **conceptions**, in the sense that they are the result of mating a **pre-conception** (of the breast, for instance) with a **realization** (sucking) for the creation of a conception, or two-ness, like $1+1 = 2$ (1967, p. 113). If a child, for instance, has two marbles and later on finds two more, it will not take long for him to figure out that now he has four. In this sense, says Kant, all pure mathematical propositions exist *a priori*, similar to Bion's conception of the breast, or the statement that "God created natural numbers".

Tustin (1981) has stated that two-ness could represent an important concept related to stages of early separation between the baby and the breast:

> . . . precocious awareness of bodily separateness and "two-ness" brings the knowledge that the nipple is not part of his mouth and that his movements do not always make for completeness and do not produce benign hallucinations. [p. 192]

See: **Intuition, noumenon, phenomenon, pre-conception, realization** and **Psychological turbulence**.

U

Ultimate reality: *see*: **O, phenomena, noumena, Thing-in-itself, Truth**.

Unconscious phantasy: Bion does not speak spontaneously about the classical concept of "unconscious phantasy", neither does he attempt to discriminate, as Klein did, between "fantasy" and "phantasy". During one conference, given in 1973 on his first visit to São Paulo, when asked about including unconscious phantasy on the **Grid**, he answered in a way rather elusive and difficult to grasp:

> Suppose I played a game like "fathers and mothers". That could be described as a "conscious fantasy" at some stage. Then suppose I became so frustrated because I could not be father or mother, that I forgot it. I could say that the fantasy which was once conscious had become unconscious. Today, when I am one of the parents, I may again be unwilling to know anything about this unconscious fantasy, for what is the use of knowing about "fathers and mothers" when I am either too young to be one or too old to be able to do anything about it now. I may say, "I don't want to have anything to do with these psycho-analysts. I do not want to be reminded of these fantasies. The best place for them is the unconscious." The

answer to that might be "I don't object to that, except that that 'unconscious fantasy' of yours, as you call it, is horribly alive; it may be obscured but active and powerful, though beyond the reach of my ability unless psychoanalysis (or something better) can bring it again within my scope." [1974, pp. 55–56]

It seems that Bion disagreed with the concept of an "unconscious phantasy" signifying the existence of a feeling that remains restless and lying in continuous ambush waiting for any opportunity to make itself present. However, unconscious phantasy can also be understood as representing the actual state of the **unconscious** at a given moment, like a cross section of its content, regardless of what it might be, but different from an unconscious phantasy that continuously presses to make itself conscious.

Meltzer (1978) associated the concept of **contact-barrier** with Klein's concept of "**unconscious phantasy**" (pp. 41–42), although the former also resembles the notion of "defence" in classical theory, while unconscious phantasy, on the other hand, can be related to the concept of **O** as introduced by Bion.

Unconscious thoughts: In 1911 Freud established that

> It is probable that **thinking** was originally unconscious, in so far as it went beyond mere ideational presentations and was directed to the relations between impressions of objects, and that it did not acquire further qualities, perceptible to **consciousness**, until it became connected with verbal residues. [p. 221]

Based on such an **hypothesis** Bion established that, at the beginning, there was some kind of thinking, perhaps in the form of visual **ideograms** instead of words or phonemes, which depend at introjection or projection on the object's representations and afterwards became conscious. Bion has referred to the product of these primitive forms of thinking as **proto-thoughts**. This mechanism, present in the **non psychotic part of the personality**, would allow, as Freud stated, that introjected objects could progressively outline unconscious thinking, something that would explain its association with sensory impressions.

Universe of discourse: It refers to a specific entity the dictionary (Webster's New Collegiate) defines as "an inclusive call of entities that is tacitly implied or explicitly delineated as the subject of a statement, discourse, or theory", or—according to The American Heritage, Dictionary of the English Language (Fourth Edition)—"a class containing all the entities referred to in a discourse or an argument." Bion used it in his book **Transformations** when emphasizing the importance of the **Grid** in relation to the **invariants**, variables, and parameters contained within the **concept** of "**psychoanalysis**", or universe of discourse, which, in order to reach meaning, should be defined in such a way that could correspond to a category in the Grid. He said:

> There is opportunity for ambiguity if this is not recognized, the term "variable" may describe something which, in a particular universe of discourse, is given a constant value and so qualifies for description as a parameter (as in a mathematical formulation . . .). [1965, p. 45]

Unsaturated–saturated elements: *see*: **Saturated–unsaturated elements**.

Ur, burial in: Attempting to compare differences between row A of the **Grid** containing β-**elements** and row B corresponding to α-**elements**, Bion uses as a paradigm the history of the death of Ur's king, possibly in the year 3500 BC, as well as his funeral accompanied by all the court including the queen. They were all forced under the effect of *hashish* to be buried alive with the king's body. Bion compares this scene with another one that took place 500 years later, when robbers plunder the tomb. Bion asks if "ignorance", as a "drug" similar to *hashish*, could have dominated the mind of those who accompanied the king to a certain death, contrasting with the feeling that might have dominated the robbers who, fearless of possible revenge from the spirits, were completely subjugated by curiosity and greed. They might have represented the first scientists who set off an investigation encouraged by curiosity; after all, said Bion, archaeologists are also often dominated by cupidity.

> How did the robbers come by the knowledge which enabled them, five hundred years after the event, to sink the shafts into the earth with such accuracy as to find the Queen's Tomb? Was it luck? Should we regard our religious hierarchy as spiritual descendants

of the priests of Ur? Should we erect monuments to the plunderers of the Royal Tombs as Pioneers of Science, as scientific as our scientists? [1977a, p. 10]

While the mind of those who accompanied the king's burial were dominated by β-elements placed in category A6, those who later robbed the Royal Tomb could have represented a C6 category. Bion insists on the systematic attack made on curiosity by many **myths**, like the Garden of Eden, the **Tower of Babel** or the sphinx in **Oedipus**.

Use axis: *see*: **Grid, horizontal axis of the**.

V

Valence: Concept borrowed from chemistry which Bion used to represent the capacity for spontaneous and instinctive emotional combination, between two individuals, or with the total group, depending on the dominant basic assumption (ba) (1948a, pp. 153, 175). It might represent the expression of a "gregarious quality" present in human beings. The capacity for combination could be great or small, to which Bion referred as "high or low valence", respectively. This condition corresponds to the opposite of what Bion has described as "co-operation", present in the work group (W). *See* **Basic assumptions (ba)**, **Work group (W)**, **Pairing group (Pba)**, **Flight–fight group (Fba)**, **Oscillations** and **Groups**.

Verbal thoughts: Much of what will be expressed here has been extracted from Bion's article "Notes on the **Theory** of **Schizophrenia**" (1967, pp. 26–35), which deals with the capacity to **think**, synthesize and articulate sense impressions with words (*ibid.*, p. 60). Since this condition depends on a disposition to integrate, it coincides with the **depressive position** and the appearance of consciousness of inner and outer realities. In 1957 Bion stated that normally, initial structuring of verbal thoughts would be established at very early stages during the **paranoid–schizoid position**; however, **psychotic** patients as well as the **psychotic part of the personality**, would continuously destroy **thoughts** with the use of splitting and mechanisms of **projective identification** (*ibid.*, pp. 48–49, 60). This condition obstructed any possibility of peaceful projections and introjections of sense impressions, necessary to build a strong basis for the configuration of verbal thoughts. In these patients, the depressive position can be experienced as something catastrophic, because painful depressive feelings can induce the patient's mind to defend by increasing **splitting** and projection of verbal thoughts inside the external objects, for example the analyst. Due to retaliatory **anxiety**, introjection (*see* **projective identification in reverse**) and as a consequence, incorporation of the necessary basis to build the good object where verbal thoughts are formed, is also altered. Bion mentioned a psychotic patient who said that "tears were coming out from his ears", something Bion inferred represented an incapacity to associate words properly. Parodying Freud (1915), he interpreted that tears were bad objects that, when coming out from his ears, would be similar to sweat coming out from the holes left by the blackheads pulled out of his skin, or to the urine that came out from the hole left by the penis once it was torn out. When the patient said he couldn't listen very well and afterwards, that he couldn't speak either, Bion interpreted the need to drown his interpretations with bad tears that came out from his ears and that perhaps he had also torn out his tongue. Such **delusional** thought signified an attack on any form of **communication**, because splitting had destroyed his ability to think, something the patient experienced as an expression of insanity (*see* **madness, realization of; perception, apparatus of**). At the end, the dilemma was represented as a trap:

> psychoanalysis was demanding that he should use thinking and a verbal logic, something that terrified him because it was pushing him to a condition of fear, depression and hopelessness, represented by the depressive position, which made the patient experience psychoanalysis as a true "**prison**", as one of his patients expressed it. [*ibid.*, pp. 29–32]

Later on, in his book **Transformations** (1965), Bion said that because psychoanalysts work with sophisticated verbal-thoughts, what they express can be located on the **Grid** on rows E and F, possibly D and G, on columns 1, 2 and 5; while what patients express, since it has no compromise with the **truth**, can fall anywhere on the Grid.

Vertex: From a mathematical perspective, this represents a **point** where one or more **lines**, planes or angles coincide. Bion uses it as a **point of view**, or a projection from a vertex, but with a mathematical association instead of just a simple expression:

> You cannot use terms like "from the point of view of smell" because the patient will say "I don't view things with my nose." It sounds as if the patient was trying to be difficult, but he is in fact being extremely accurate; he cannot understand a phrase which is conversational language. It is, therefore, better to borrow a term from mathematics like "vertex". [1974, pp. 88–89]

Transformations depend on a change of vertex; the vertex held by someone sleeping and **dreaming** is never the same as when awake, or the vertex of the artist will diverge from that of the critic of his work, or the multiple vertexes an analyst could use from one moment to the other during the analytical session. A shift from a vertex of one sense or system to another might prove to be useful in order to improve understanding or explanation of something. A vertex should not be too close or too far, for instance, a man and a woman might not be compatible because they are either too alike or too different: a similar situation could take place between a patient and an analyst (1970, p. 93). In relation to different types of vertexes, Bion suggests that the visual ones are capable of a greater degree of freedom (they could "illuminate"), when compared with others such as "digestive, respiratory, olfactory, auditory, etc. (1965, pp. 90–92). He makes special mention of an "internal vertex" he refers to as the **"inner reproductory system"**, described as a counterpart of the "mental reproductory system", equal to an "inward eye" or mental counterpart of the visual system (*ibid.*, p. 91). This internal vertex might be related to concepts such as **intuition**, the **thing-in-itself**, **O** and an **act of faith**.

An individual makes a trip to city X, for example, as a mechanism to placate an imaginary "castrator" who he thinks had expected him to make such a trip. He could also make the trip of his own accord, without feeling impelled by the need to please the "castrator". The city and the trip might have been the same in both cases, but the "inner" vertexes were different: one vertex authentic, and the other inauthentic. *See*: **Intuition, O, act of faith, Inner reproductory system and Thing-in-itself.**

View-point: *see*: **Vertex.**

Violence: Bion did not try to understand violence from the **vertex** of **instinct theory** or from the relationship with the environment. He considers: (a) in the first place the *dependency* of the **psychic apparatus** on **action** as an important means for discharge; and (b) the inability to discriminate between falsehood and **truth** and between alive and **inanimate** things. It can be summarized in the following expression: "if the tiger were to know about the suffering of the gazelle, it could starve to death". *See*: **Frustration, tolerance or intolerance, Animated and inanimate, Truth** and **Lie.**

W

Wild thoughts: Bion established a difference between "stray thoughts" and "wild thoughts". The stray ones refer to thoughts that can be found by someone who might try to domesticate them if it is found that they have no owner, or that there is an owner but they can be purloined, or could be so old that there is no proprietor. For instance, Bion had said that **truth**, different from a **lie**, does not need a thinker to contain it; however, much earlier than Bion, Latin had provided the same basic root to mind (*mentis*) as well as lying (*mentior*), perhaps meaning that "the mind lies", similar to Bion's expression that "lies need a thinker".

"Wild thoughts", on the other hand, represent thoughts to which "there is no possibility of being able to trace immediately any kind of ownership or even any sort of way of being aware of the genealogy of that particular thought" (1997, p. 27).[62] A good example could be **dream-thoughts**, or "intrauterine thoughts", perhaps linked to the Kantian concept of **the thing-in-itself** or **noumenon**.

---

[62] This note is dated May 28, 1977.

If a thought without a thinker comes along, it may be what is a "stray thought", or it could be a thought with the owner's name and address upon it, or it could be a "wild thought". The problem, should such a thought come along, is what to do with it . . . if it is wild, you might try to domesticate it . . . [*ibid.*]

See: **Truth, Lie, Thing-in-itself, Intrauterine life.**

Wish: *see*: **Desire.**

Without-ness: Bion uses this expression to describe a **container–contained** (♀♂) relationship controlled by **envy**, which as a result would produce **–K**. In such a condition the baby **splits** and projects his fears inside the breast, together with feelings of envy and hatred that preclude a **commensal** relationship. The breast is also felt enviously to remove the good or valuable elements that could be used to neutralize the baby's fear of dying and in its place forces back into the infant worthless residues that will change the fear of dying into a **nameless dread** or terror, which Bion represents as –K. Bion considers this as a very serious condition, because the breast not only does not neutralize the fear of dying, but might also remove the wish to live. This is also represented as –(♀♂), something Bion qualifies as "without-ness", and later on in his book **Transformations** represents as – ←↑, meaning:

> . . . an internal object without an exterior. It is an alimentary canal without a body. It is a super-ego that has hardly any of the characteristics of the super-ego as understood in **psychoanalysis**: it is "super" ego. It is an envious assertion of moral superiority without any morals . . . The process of denudation continues till – ♀ – ♂ represent hardly more than an empty superiority–inferiority that it in turn degenerates to nullity. [1962, p. 97]

See: **Minus K (–K), Container–contained interaction, Commensal, Conscious awareness.**

Work group: Also called "sophisticated group". It represents the moment when a **group** is capable of establishing contact with reality and recognizes the need to evolve, and to work together towards a common aim away from the control of the **basic assumptions**. It is dominated by the tendency to deal with conflicts in a rather "scientific" manner (1948b, p. 99), and it is equivalent to the ego according with Freud's postulates (1911) (*ibid.*, p. 143). Organization, structure, co-operation, and verbal **communication** are its greatest weapons (*ibid.*, p. 185). It represents the direction a group would follow if it were not dominated by a basic assumption; this is why, in order for any group to remain on a sophisticated level (W) it has to deal with the **emotions** of the predominating ba (*ibid.*, p. 135). This group can last hours or months, depending on the capacity of the group to solve the pressure of the emotions from the latent ba that continuously attempts to dominate the group. The leader of this kind of group has access to the external reality of the group, different from the leader of the ba group who only has contact with the internal reality of the specific ba (*ibid.*, pp. 144–145).

Later on, in *Attention and Interpretation* (1970), Bion states that this form of group, under a religious **vertex**, has to discriminate and to maintain such discrimination between God and man, between idealized superego and man himself, similar to the idealization placed on Freud by the psychoanalytic group who followed him, who made any criticism about his work something absolutely unsustainable (p. 75). *See*: **Group, Basic assumption, baD, baP, baF, Valence, Duality.**

X

Xi = ζ: Greek letter which corresponds to "small x". It is used by Bion to represent a "**mathematical object**" (1970, p. 90), equivalent to a non-saturated **element** or **factor**, similar to a **pre-conception** that is open to any realization that comes near and **saturates** it. Bion also used it to symbolize the mathematical aspect of an **emotion**, and also as a factor that is part of a **function**, like: (Ψ)ζ or **K**(ζ).

Z

Zen Buddhism: Concepts such as **O** (Origin), **transformation** in O, **truth, act of faith** and **hallucinosis**, among others, remind us of some Zen conceptions, a Japanese sect of Mahayana Buddhism that aims at enlightenment by direct intuition through meditation. "[Men] is best awakened not by the study of scriptures, the practice of good deeds, rites and ceremonies, or worship of images but by sudden breaking through of the boundaries of common, everyday, logical thought".[63] Although Bion never mentioned any form of Buddhism, we should not forget that he was born, in a British family, in India's Punjab. Referring to O, Bion establishes:

> Some consciously believe the curtain of illusion to be a protection against truth which is essential to the survival of humanity ... Even those who consider such a view mistaken and truth essential consider that the gap cannot be bridged because the nature of the human being precludes knowledge of anything beyond phenomena save conjecture. From this conviction of the inaccessibility of absolute reality the mystics must be exempted ... The belief that

---

[63] *The New Encyclopedia Britannica*, Vol. 12, p. 905.

reality is or could be known is mistaken because reality is not something which lends itself to being known. It is impossible to know reality for the same reason that makes it impossible to sing potatoes; they may be grown, or pulled, or eaten, but not sung. Reality has to be "been": there should be a transitive verb "to be" expressly for use with the term "reality". [1965, pp. 147–148]

According to the Symingtons (1966), many British psychoanalysts considered that Bion had mentally deteriorated after leaving England for Los Angeles, and they believed everything he wrote afterwards, was "to be dismissed as the rambling of a senile man", and that some Kleinians, "were quick to dissociate themselves from his thinking from that time onwards" (p. 10). The Symingtons believed that Bion's concept of O is "essentially a religious and metaphysical concept" (*ibid.*), understanding for religious ". . . a **model** of the human being as a creature with intentionality that transcends immediate physical needs" (*ibid.*, p 10n).

But interpreting O as a religious concept places serious doubt on the understanding of its true nature and about what Bion had attempted to express. I am unable to find any religious position in any of his contributions; his understanding is always above the human **phenomenon**, and even when he seems to defend the position of the **mystic**, he is just appreciating the attitude behind the human act, but not his beliefs. The sudden understanding of the **unconscious phantasy** during the analytical session, or the swift and religious illuminations of **Meister Eckhart** or Saint John of the Cross, have, for Bion, a human correspondence in the act of **at-one-ment** with their particular truth, or with O, as he had decided to name it. Although, in Bion, both situations are the same from the point of view of O, they diverge exactly on the "intentionality of transcending immediate physical needs": it might have been present in Eckhart, but in the analyst, says Bion, if he wants to **"listen"**, **"memory, desire** and understanding," must be avoided.

About Zen, on the other hand, we can read directly from one of its masters:

Every Master who practices an art molded by Zen is like a flash of lightning from the cloud of all-encompassing Truth. This Truth is present in "It," as his own original and nameless essence. He meets this essence over and over again as his own being's utmost possibilities, so that the Truth assumes for him—and for others through him—a thousand shapes and forms . . .[64]

And further on,

> He must dare to leap into the Origin, so as to live by the Truth, like one who has become one with it. He must become a pupil again, a beginner; conquer the last and steepest stretch of the way, undergo new transformations. If he survives its perils, then is his destiny fulfilled; face to face he beholds the unbroken Truth, the Truth beyond all truths, the formless Origin of origins, the Void which is the All; is absorbed into it and from it emerges reborn. [Herrigel 1953, pp. 80–81]

See: **O, Act of faith, At-one-ment, Meister Eckhart, Godhead.**

---

[64] Taken from the *Hagakure*, written circa 1600, and quoted by Herrigel (1953, pp. 80–81).

REFERENCES

Articles by Wilfred Bion:

1940   The war of nerves. In: *The Neurosis in War*. E. Miller & H. Crichton-Miller (Eds.), London: Macmillan.

1943   Intra-group tensions in therapy: their study as the task of the group. *The Lancet*, 27th November.

1946   The leaderless group project. In: *Bulletin of the Menninger Clinic*. May 10, pp. 77–81.

1948a   Psychiatry at a time of crisis. *British Journal of Medical Psychology*, 21, pp. 81–89..

1948b   *Experiences in Groups*. London: Tavistock, 1961.

1950   The imaginary twin. In: *Second Thoughts*. London, Karnac Books, 1993.

1952   Group dynamics: A re-view. In: M. Klein, P. Heimann & R. Money-Kyrle (Eds.), *New Directions in Psycho-Analysis*. London: Karnac Books, 1985.

1953   Notes on the theory of schizophrenia, in *Second Thoughts*. London: Karnac Books, 1993.

1955   Language and the schizophrenic. In: M. Klein, P. Heimann & R. Money-Kyrle (Eds.), *New Directions in Psycho-Analysis*. London: Karnac Books, 1985.

1956   Development of schizophrenic thought. In: *Second Thoughts*. London: Karnac Books, 1993.

1957   Differentiation of the psychotic from the non-psychotic personalities. In: *Second Thoughts*. London: Karnac Books, 1993.

1957a   On arrogance. In: *Second Thoughts*. London: Karnac Books, 1993.

1958   On hallucination. In: *Second Thoughts*. London: Karnac Books, 1993.

1959   Attacks on linking. In: *Second Thoughts*. London: Karnac Books, 1993.

1962   *Learning from Experience*. London: Karnac Books, 1984.

1962a A theory of thinking. In: Second Thoughts. London: Karnac Books, 1993.

1963   *Elements of Psycho-Analysis*. London: Karnac Books, 1984.

1965   *Transformations*. London: Karnac Books, 1984.

1966   Catastrophic change. In: *Attention and Interpretation* (Chapter 12). London: Karnac Books 1970.

1967   *Second Thoughts: Selected Papers on Psycho-Analysis*. London: Karnac Books, 1993.

1967a Notes on memory and desire. In: *Cogitations*. London: Karnac Books, 1992.

1970   *Attention and Interpretation*. London: Karnac Books, 1984.

1974   *Brazilian Lectures*. São Paulo No 1. Río de Janeiro: Imago Editora.

1974a *Brazilian Lectures*. Rio/São Paulo No 2. Río de Janeiro: Imago Editora.

1975   *A Memoir of the Future, Book One: The Dream*. London: Karnac Books, 1990 [reprinted as trilogy, London: Karnac Books, 1991].

1976   Emotional turbulence. In: *Clinical Seminars and Other Works*. London: Karnac Books, 2000.

1976a On a quotation from Freud. In: *Clinical Seminars and Four Papers*. Oxford: Fleetwood Press, 1987.

1976b Interview with Anthony G. Banet. *The International Journal for Group Facilitators: Group and Organization Studies* 1 (3).

1977   *Seven Servants*, New York: Jason Aronson, 1977.

1977a *Two papers: the Grid and Caesura*. London: Karnac Books, 1989.

1977b *A Memoir of the Future, Book Two: The Past Presented*. Rio de Janeiro: Imago Editora [reprinted as trilogy, London: Karnac Books, 1991].

1978   Four discussions with W. R. Bion, *Clinical Seminars and Other Works*. London: Karnac Books, 2000.

1979   *A Memoir of the Future, Book Three: The Dawn of Oblivion*. London: Karnac Books, 1990 [reprinted as a trilogy, London: Karnac Books, 1991].

1979a Making the best of a bad job. In: *Clinical Seminars and Other Works*. London: Karnac Books.

1980   *Bion in New York and São Paulo*. London: Karnac Books.

1981   *A Key to A Memoir of the Future*. [Reprinted in *A Memoir of the Future*, London: Karnac Books, 1990.

1982   *The Long Week-End 1897–1919*. London: Karnac Books, 1991.

1985   *All My Sins Remembered* and *The Other Side Of Genius*. London: Karnac Books, 1991.

1986   *Seminari Italiani*. Rome: Borla [published in Italian only].

1987   *Clinical Seminars and Four Papers*. Oxford: Fleetwood Press.

1990   *Brazilian Lectures*. London: Karnac Books.

1990a   *A Memoir of the Future*. London: Karnac Books.

1992   *Cogitations*. London: Karnac Books.

1994   *Clinical Seminars and Other Works*. London: Karnac Books, 2000.

1997   *Taming Wild Thoughts*. London: Karnac Books.

1997a   *War Memoirs 1917–19*. London: Karnac Books.

Other references

Adrian, E.D. (1947). *The Physical Background of Perception*. Oxford: Clarendon.

Anzieu D. (1986). Beckett et Bion. *Revue de Psychothérapie Psychanalytique de Groupe*, 5–6: 286.

Appleton New Cuyás Dictionary (1972). Englewood Cliffs: Prentice-Hall.

Aray, J. (1992). *Momentos Psicoanalíticos*. Caracas: Monte Avila.

Aray, J. & Bellagamba, H. (1971). Observaciones sobre el fenómeno del doble in la situación analítica de un paciente homosexual. In A. Raskovsky (Ed.), *Niveles Profundos del Psiquismo*. Buenos Aires: Kargieman.

Bahía, A.B. (1977) New theories: their influence and effect on psychoanalytic technique. *International Journal of Psychoanalysis, 58*: 345–364.

Bianchedi, E.T. (1993). Lies and falsities. *Melanie Klein and Object Relations, 11*(2).

Bianchedi, E.T., Bregazzi, C., Crespo, C. *et al.* (2000). The various faces of lies. In: P. Bion Talamo, F. Borgogno & S.A. Merciai (Eds.), *W.R. Bion, Between Past and Future*. London: Karnac Books.

Bick, E. (1968). The experience of the skin in early object-relations. *International Journal of Psycho-Analysis, 49*: 484–486.

Bion, F. (1995). The days of our years. *Melanie Klein and Object Relations, 13*(1).

Bion, F. (2000). Random reflections on Bion: past, present, and future. In: P. Bion Talamo, F. Borgogno & S.A. Merciai (Eds.), *W.R. Bion: Between Past and Future*. London: Karnac Books.

Bion Talamo, P. (1997). The clinical relevance of *A Memoir of the Future*. *The Journal of Melanie Klein and Object Relations, 15*(2) 235–241.

Bion Talamo, P., Borgogno F. & Merciai, S.A., (Eds.) (1998). *Bion's Legacy to Groups*. London: Karnac Books.

Bion Talamo, P., Borgogno, F. & Merciai, S.A. (Eds.) (2000). *W.R. Bion: Between Past and Future*. London: Karnac Books.

Bléandonu, G. (1994). *Wilfred Bion. His Life and Works 1897–1979*. London: Free Associations.

Borgogno F. & Merciai S.A. (2000). Searching for Bion: Cogitations, a new "Clinical Diary"?. In: P. Bion Talamo et al. (Eds.) *W.R. Bion: Between Past and Future*. London: Karnac Books.

Braithwaite, R.B. (1955). *Scientific Explanation*. Cambridge: Cambridge University Press.

Britton, R. & Steiner, J. (1994). Interpretation: selected fact or over-valued idea? *International Journal of Psycho-Analysis, 75*: 1069–1078.

Brown, D.G. (1985). Bion and Foulkes: basic assumptions and beyond. In: M. Pines (Ed.) *Bion and Group Psychotherapy* (pp. 192–219). London: Routledge and Kegan Paul.

Clapham, C. (1990). *Concise Dictionary of Mathematics*. New York: Oxford University Press.

Descartes, R. (1641) Meditations. In: *The Philosophical Works of Descartes* (pp. 133–199). E.S. Haldane & G.R.T. Ross (Eds.), Boston: Cambridge Univ. Press, 1973.

Eigen, M. (1995). On Bion's No-thing. *Melanie Klein and Object Relations, 13*(1).

Eizing P. (1949). *Primitive Money*. London: Eyre & Spottiswoode.

Fairbairn, W.R.D. (1952). *Psychoanalytic Studies of the Personality*. London: Tavistock.

Ferreira, R. B. (2000). The fundamental role of the Grid in Bion's work. In: *W.R. Bion, Between Past and Future*. London: Karnac Books.

Foulquié, P. (1967). *Diccionario del Lenguaje Filosófico*, Madrid: Editorial Labor S.A.

Freud, S. (1886). Project for a Scientific Psychology, *SE 1*. London: Hogarth Press, p. 281.

Freud, S, (1900). The Interpretation of Dreams, *SE 5*. London: Hogarth Press, p. 339.

Freud, S. (1901). On Dreams, *SE 5*. London: Hogarth Press, p. 629.

Freud, S. (1905). Fragment of an Analysis of a Case of Hysteria SE 7, London: Hogarth Press, p. 1.

Freud, S. (1911). Formulations on Two Principles of Mental Functioning, *SE 12*, London: Hogarth Press, p. 213.

Freud, S. (1915). The Unconscious, *SE 14*. London: Hogarth Press, p. 159.

Freud, S. (1917). Introductory Lectures on Psycho-Analysis. *SE 15, 16*. London: Hogarth Press pp. 13, 241.

Freud, S. (1919). The "Uncanny" *SE 17*. London: Hogarth Press, p. 217.

Freud, S. (1924). Neurosis and Psychosis. *SE 19*. London: Hogarth Press p. 149.

Freud, S. (1926). Inhibitions, Symptoms and Anxiety, *SE 20*. London: Hogarth Press, p. 75.

Gitelson, M. (1952). The emotional position of the analyst in the psycho-analytic situation. *International Journal of Psycho-Analysis, 33*: 1–10.

Gooch, J.A. (1993). An elementary description of Bion's Grid with clinical exemplification. *Melanie Klein and Object Relations, 11*(2).

Green, A. (1992). Book Review: *"Cogitations"*, International Journal of Psycho-Analysis, 73: 585–589.

Green, A. (2000). The primordial mind and the work of the negative. In: P. Bion Talamo, F. Borgogno & S.A. Merciai (Eds.), *W.R. Bion, Between Past and Future*. London: Karnac Books.

Grinberg, L. (1957). Perturbaciones en la interpretación motivadas por la contra-identificación proyectiva, *Revista de Psicoanálisis*, 14: 1–12.

Grinberg, L. (1962). On a specific aspect of countertransference due to the patient's projective identification, *International Journal of Psycho-Analysis*, 43: 436–440.

Grinberg, L. (2000). Foreword, In P. Bion Talamo et al. (Eds.) *W.R. Bion, Between Past and Future*. London: Karnac Books.

Grinberg, L., Sor, D. & Bianchedi, E. (1972). *Introducción a las Teorías de Bion*. Buenos Aires: Ediciones Nueva Visión.

Grotstein, J. (1981). Who is the dreamer who dreams the dream and who is the dreamer who understands it. In: *Do I Dare Disturb the Universe?* J. Grotstein (Ed.), London: Karnac Books, (pp. 357–416).

Grotstein, J. (1981). Wilfred Bion: the man, the psychoanalyst, the mystic. A perspective on his life and work. In : *Do I Dare Disturb the Universe?* J. Grotstein (Ed.), London: Karnac Books, p. 7.

Grotstein, J. (1993). Towards the concept of the transcendent position: reflections on some of "The Unborn" in Bion *"Cogitations"*, *The Journal of Melanie Klein and Object Relations*, 11(2): 57.

Grotstein, J. (1996). Bion's transformation in O, the "thing-in-itself" and the "real": toward the concept of the "transcendent position." *The Journal of Melanie Klein and Object Relations*, 14(2): 142.

Heimann, P. (1950). On counter-transference, *International Journal of Psycho-Analysis*, 31: 81–84.

Heisenberg, W. (1958). *Physics and Philosophy.* London: G. Allen & Unwin.

Herrigel, E. (1953). *Zen in the Art of Archery.* Toronto: Vintage.

Hinshelwood, R.D. (1989). *A Dictionary of Kleinian Thought*, New York: Jason Aronson.

Hume, D. (1960). In: N. Kemp Smith, *The Philosophy of David Hume.* New York: Macmillan.

Jaques, E. (1960). Disturbance in the capacity to work, *International Journal of Psycho-Analysis*, 41: 357–367.

Joseph, B. (1981). Toward the experiencing of psychic pain. In: J. Grotstein (Ed.), *Do I Dare Disturb the Universe.* London: Karnac Books. (pp. 93–102).

Keats, J. (1958). *Letters of John Keats.* Hyder Edward Rollins (Ed.), Cambridge: Harvard University Press.

Kierkegaard, S. (1941). *Fear and Trembling and the Sickness unto Death.* New York: Doubleday Anchor Books.

Klein, M. (1928). Early stages of the Oedipus Complex. In: *Contributions to Psycho-Analysis, 1921–1945.* London: Hogarth Press, 1948.

Klein, M. (1929). Personification in the play of children. *International Journal of Psycho-Analysis*, 10: 193–204.

Klein, M. (1931). A contribution to the theory of intellectual development. *International Journal of Psycho-Analysis*, 12: 206–218.

Klein, M. (1946). Notes on some schizoid mechanisms. In: *Envy and Gratitude.* London: Hogarth Press, 1975.

Klein, M. (1938). La importancia de la formación de símbolos in el desarrollo del yo. In: *Contribuciones al Psicoanálisis*. Buenos Aires: Hormé, 1964.

Lacán, J. (1947). La Psychiatrie Anglaise et la guerre, *L' Evolution Psychiatrique*, quoted by Bléandonu G., in *Wilfred Bion. His Life and Works*. London: Free Association Books, 1994.

Lawrence, W.G., Bain, A. & Gould, L. (1996). The fifth basic assumption. *Free Associations*, 6 (1) 37: 28–55.

Le Bon, G. (1896). *The Crowd: a Study of the Popular Mind*. London: Benn, 1947.

Lipgar, R.M. (1998). Beyond Bion's *Experiences in Groups*: group relations research and learning. In: *Bion's Legacy to Groups*. London: Karnac Books.

López-Corvo, R.E. (1973). *El niño y su inteligencia*. Caracas: Monte Avila.

López-Corvo, R.E. (1980). *Símbolo y Mutación*. Caracas: Monte Avila.

López-Corvo, R.E. (1987). Transitional dreams: a Kleinian approach. *Journal of the Melanie Klein Society*, 5(2).

López-Corvo, R.E. (1990). *Adictos y Adicciones*. Caracas: Monte Avila Editors.

López-Corvo, R.E. (1992). About interpretation of self-envy, *International Journal Psycho-Analysis*, 73: 719–728.

López-Corvo, R.E. (1993). *La Maldición Eterna*. Caracas: Monte Avila Editors.

López-Corvo, R.E. (1994). *Self-envy, Therapy and the Divided Inner World*. New York: Jason Aronson.

López-Corvo, R.E. (1997). Self-envy and intrapsychic interpretation. *Psychoanalytic Quarterly*, 68: 209–219.

López-Corvo, R.E. (2000). Comentarios a la conferencia de J. McDougall "Violencia somática". El viaje psicoanalítico de una paciente con cáncer del seno. *Revista Trópicos, 8*.

Meltzer, D. (1973). *Sexual States of the Mind*, Perthshire, Scotland: Clunie Press.

Meltzer, D. (1978). The Kleinian development Part III, *The Clinical Significance of the Work of Bion*, Perthshire, Scotland: Clunie Press.

Meltzer, D. (1986). *Studies in Extended Metapsychology, Clinical Applications of Bion's Ideas*. Perthshire, Scotland: Clunie Press.

Meotti, A. (2000). A dreamlike vision. In: P. Bion Talamo, F. Borgogno & S.A. Merciai (Eds.), *W.R. Bion, Between Past and Future*. London: Karnac Books.

Milton, J. (1674). *Paradise Lost* [reprinted Merritt Y. Hughes, New York: Odyssey Press].

Nebbiosi, G. & Petrini, R. (2000). The theoretical and clinical significance of the concept of "common sense" in Bion's work. In: P. Bion Talamo, F. Borgogno & S.A. Merciai (Eds.), *W.R. Bion, Between Past and Future*. London: Karnac Books, pp. 164–177.

Onians, R.B. (1951). *Origins of European Thought*. Cambridge: Cambridge University Press.

Philips, F. (1983). A personal reminiscence. Bion, Evidence of the man. In: *Do I dare Disturb the Universe*, J. Grotstein (Ed.), London: Karnac Books.

Piaget, J. (1952). *The Origins of Intelligence in Children*. New York: W.W. Norton.

Piaget, J. (1971). *Biology and Knowledge*. Chicago: University of Chicago Press.

Pines, M. (1985) (Ed.) *Bion and Group Psychotherapy*. London: Routledge & Kegan Paul.

Poincaré, H. (1908). *Science et Méthode* (pp. 43–63). Paris: Flamarion.

Polito, P. (2001). Gemelos, niños, muertos, amantes y otras personificaciones. Read at the Venezuelan Psychoanalytical Association, November 17th 2001.

Quine, W. van Orman (1955). *Mathematical Logic*. Cambridge, MA: Harvard University Press.

Racker, H. (1953). Contribution to the problem of countertransference. *International Journal of Psycho-Analysis, 38*: 4–10.

Rank, O. (1914). Der Doppelgänger., *Imago 3*, 97–164.

Raskovsky, A. (1958). *El Psiquismo Fetal*. Buenos Aires: Paidos.

Richard, P.A. (1993). Bion on groups. *Melanie Klein and Object Relations, 11*(2).

Rosenfeld, H. (1971). A clinical approach to the psychoanalytic theory of life and death instincts, *International Journal of Psycho-Analysis, 52*: 169–178.

Russell, B. (1945). *A History of Western Philosophy*, New York: Simon and Schuster.

Sartre, J.P. (1956). *Being and Nothingness, an Essay on Phenomenological Ontology*, New York: Philosophical Library.